Praise for *Creating Compassionate Change in School Communities*

"Education has changed drastically in the past five years. This book humanizes the difficulty of the changes and provides tangible steps educators can take to support their students and the people many often overlook—themselves."

—**Autumn Rivera,** 2022 Colorado Teacher of the Year and 2022 National Teacher of the Year Finalist

"This exceptionally written book reminds us to engage our work in education with our heads *and our hearts*. A much-needed text during these times of intensified stress, anxiety, self-doubt, and blame, these authors shepherd readers through strategies and tools to help us heal individually as we renew and reset our commitments to practices of listening, compassion, empathy, and understanding, in service with and to others. An accessibly written book, grounded in transformative and rigorous research, this book should be read by any of us determined to keep pressing and fighting for education for all."

—**H. Richard Milner IV**, Professor, Vanderbilt University, and author *of The Race Card*

"What a timely gift of a book! Filled with gratitude and hands-on support for healing spaces of learning, *Creating Compassionate Change in School Communities* is a text that is poised to (gently) transform the lives of students and teachers."

—**Antero Garcia,** Associate Professor, Stanford University

Creating Compassionate Change in School Communities

Creating Compassionate Change in School Communities

Leading Together to Address Everyday Suffering in Schools

Ashley Seidel Potvin

William R. Penuel

Sona Dimidjian

Thupten Jinpa

JB JOSSEY-BASS™

A Wiley Brand

Published by John Wiley & Sons, Inc., Hoboken, New Jersey.
Published simultaneously in Canada.

ISBNs: 9781394265220 (Paperback), 9781394265244 (ePDF), 9781394265237 (ePub)

For general information on our other products and services or for technical support, please contact our Customer Care Department within the United States at (800) 762-2974, outside the United States at (317) 572-3993 or fax (317) 572-4002.

Wiley also publishes its books in a variety of electronic formats. Some content that appears in print may not be available in electronic formats. For more information about Wiley products, visit our website at www.wiley.com.

Library of Congress Control Number: 2025008658 (print)

Cover Design: Paul McCarthy
Cover Art: © Getty Images | Marco Bottigelli

SKY10100149_031325

We dedicate this book to you, dear educator, and to all those reading this book who care for and tend to the hearts and minds of young people. It is our genuine wish that whatever benefit this book brings to you ripples out to benefit the communities of which you are a part, to help bring about a more just and compassionate world.

May you be happy.

May you be well.

May you know peace and dignity.

May you lead with curiosity, courage, and compassion.

Acknowledgments

We are deeply grateful to the educators who joined us in collaborative design to develop the arc of the digital compassion and dignity certificate: Adrienne, Ambika, Amy, Cindi, Dana, Halie, John, Karen, Katie, Lindsey, Loren, Naomi, Nikki, Max, Michelle, Stacy, and Taylor. Your thoughtfulness, commitment, and care for one another, your students, and the future educators in the digital certificate during a particularly challenging year continues to motivate and inspire us.

We wish to thank all of the educators who found their way to our compassion and dignity community, who enrolled in our programs, and who supported our efforts through showing up, providing feedback, and spreading the word. In particular, we want to thank those educators who gave voice to many of the ideas within this book, and who so often said it better than we ever could: Adam, Adrienne, Ben, Brittany, Colleen, Crystal, Emma, Fabi, Gricel, Kaelyn, Karen, Kendra, Madison, Maggie, Meaghan, NB, Raquel, Samila, Sara, Sarah, Stephanie D., Stephanie P., Taryn, Tina, and Vincent. You are the heartbeat of this book!

Thank you to our district partners, especially Anna and Lora, for their commitment to the well-being of educators and students and for their ongoing support of compassion in their schools.

We wish to express our gratitude to our community at the Renée Crown Wellness Institute for showing us what a compassionate community looks and feels like. Thank you to Julia Zigarelli, Leah Peña Teeters, Michele Simpson, Donna Mejia, Michelle Reininger for their enthusiasm, friendship, and support. We would also like to thank our incredible Compassion & Dignity for Educators team who were involved in various stages of envisioning, designing, revising, and teaching the digital certificate: Michelle Shedro, Caitlin McKimmy, Erica Van Steenis, Jovita Schiffer, Irfanul Alam, and Marisa Mendoza-Mauer.

We also wish to thank Caroline Pfohl and the Hemera Foundation for their generous and abiding commitment to contemplative practices that promote compassion and dignity in the world broadly and among educators specifically. Our partnership has helped to grow healthy, nurturing, and creative environments for educators and young people to thrive. Thank you, also, to the team of compassion and dignity meditation coaches who facilitated coaching and practice sessions with such care for educators enrolled in the certificate: Carla Burns, Sumi Kim, Amy Kisei Costenbader, Jeremy Lowry, Charlotte Rotterdam, Jogen Salzberg, and Claire Villarreal.

Thank you to the CU Boulder Teacher Leadership Program team for their ongoing support and encouragement of the compassion and dignity certificate: Kathy Schultz, Emily Gleason, Paula Battistelli, and Tyler Caldwell.

Thank you also to early advisors to this work, Kimberley Schonert-Reichl and Rob Roeser, and for championing the wellness of teachers through their work and service in the world.

Ashley: Thank you to Tom for his generosity, patience, steadiness, support, and compassion and to our girls for teaching me to find joy in life's smallest moments. I am also so grateful to my parents, Mary and Fred, who were my first teachers and the first people who loved me into being.

Bill: Thank you to Edie for her incredible support in always inviting me to pursue work that reflects who I am and want to become and to my spiritual teachers who have provided guidance and wisdom to help me cultivate an open mind and heart, especially the Ven. Dhyani Ywahoo, Gil Fronsdal, and Peter Williams.

Sona: I express my deepest gratitude to my friends and colleagues in the Crown Institute and all the young people, families, and teachers with whom we have the honor to work. I thank all the teachers who have supported and guided my learning and my crescent family for holding compassion, dignity, and love at our core.

Jinpa: First and foremost, I would like to express my deep gratitude to His Holiness the Dalai Lama to whom I owe much of what I know of compassion. I thank my co-authors for inviting me to be part of the team, my colleagues at the Compassion Institute, and, last but not least, my wife Sophie for sharing insights gained from her years of offering workshops on Social Emotional Learning to teachers.

Collectively, and finally, we express our deepest gratitude to Dr. PC Crown for her visionary commitment to the wellness of educators, kids, and families and the reminder to lead and teach always with heart.

About the Authors

Ashley Seidel Potvin, Ph.D., is a Research Associate in the Renée Crown Wellness Institute at the University of Colorado Boulder. She works in partnership with PK-12 educators to bring compassion and dignity to school communities. Ashley designs, studies, and teaches programs focused on supporting educators to cultivate compassion and dignity for themselves and others, to deepen their leadership capacities, and to envision and work toward just and compassionate schools. Through qualitative methods she examines educator learning and wellness, teacher–student relationships, and the development of caring, inclusive, and humanizing classroom and research environments. Her research has been published in journals such as *Journal of the Learning Sciences*, *Mindfulness*, *Teaching and Teacher Education*, *Education Sciences*, *Learning Environments Research*, and *Professional Development in Education*. This is her first book.

Ashley earned a B.A. from the College of the Holy Cross, an M.Ed. in Secondary Education from Providence College, and her Ph.D. in Curriculum and Instruction with a focus on teaching and teacher education from the University of Colorado Boulder. She is a former middle and high school teacher and has experience supporting teachers in various roles as curriculum leader, coach, mentor, and university instructor.

William R. Penuel, Ph.D., is Distinguished Professor of Learning Sciences and Human Development in the Institute of Cognitive Science and School of Education at the University of Colorado Boulder. He is also a Faculty Fellow at the Renée Crown Wellness Institute. He designs and studies curriculum materials, assessments, and professional learning experiences for teachers in STEM education. He also studies how contemplative practices and critical inquiry can support educators in cultivating more compassionate schools. A third line of his research focuses on how long-term research–practice partnerships can be organized to address systemic inequities in education. He is a co-developer of an approach to partnership research called Design-Based Implementation Research (DBIR).

He is the author of two books in education, *Creating Research-Practice Partnerships in Education* (with Dan Gallagher, Harvard Education Press, 2017) and *The Connected School* (with Barbara Means and Christine Padilla, Jossey-Bass, 2001). In addition, he has co-edited two volumes on collaborative education research: *Connecting Research and Practice for Educational Improvement: Ethical and Equitable Approaches* (with Bronwyn Bevan, Routledge, 2018), and *The Foundational Handbook on Improvement Research in Education* (with Donald Peurach, Jennifer Russell, and Laura Cohen-Vogel, Rowman & Littlefield, 2022). He earned a B.A. in Psychology from Clark University, an Ed.M. in Counseling Processes from the Harvard Graduate School of Education, and a Ph.D. in Developmental Psychology from Clark University. He is an elected member of the National Academy of Education and a Fellow of the American Educational Research Association, the International Society of the Learning Sciences, and the International Society for Design and Development in Education. In addition, for six years, he served on the Board of Science Education at the National Academies of Sciences, Engineering, and Medicine.

Sona Dimidjian, Ph.D., is Director of the Renée Crown Wellness Institute and Professor in the Department of Psychology and Neuroscience at the University of Colorado Boulder. She also holds the Sapp Family Endowed Chancellor's Chair for Research Excellence. Her research focuses on cultivating mental health and wellness among women, children, and families by engaging people's capacities for learning to care for themselves and their communities. She develops and studies programs and practices in education and healthcare settings, with an emphasis on navigating key developmental transitions, such as the perinatal period, early childhood, and adolescence. She also has a longstanding interest in expanding access, scaling, and sustaining effective programs, using both digital technology and community-based partnerships. Her current research projects focus on preventing depression and supporting wellness among new and expectant mothers, promoting healthy body image and leadership among young women, and enhancing mindfulness and compassion among youth, families, and educators.

She is the co-author with Sherryl Goodman, Ph.D., of a book for new and expectant mothers, *Expecting Mindfully: Nourish Your Emotional Well-Being and Prevent Depression During Pregnancy and Postpartum*. She is also the co-author of *Behavioral Activation for Depression* and *Behavioral Activation with Adolescents* and the editor of *Evidence-Based Practice in Action: Bridging Clinical Science and Intervention*. She is the recipient of numerous awards acknowledging her teaching and clinical research, including the Dorothy Martin Women's Faculty Award, the Outstanding Graduate Mentor Award, and the Robert L. Stearns Award at the University of Colorado Boulder along with the Susan Hickman Award from Postpartum Support International and the Women and Psychotherapy Award from Division 35 of the American Psychological Association. She received her B.A. in Psychology from the University of Chicago and her Ph.D. in Clinical Psychology from the University of Washington.

Thupten Jinpa, Ph.D., is the Founder and Chairman of Compassion Institute, and the principal author of Compassion Cultivation Training™ (CCT©), the Institute's flagship compassion education offering, developed while Jinpa was at Stanford University. Jinpa also serves as an adjunct professor at the Faculty of Religious Studies at McGill University, Montreal, and is the founder and president of the Institute of Tibetan Classics. He has been a core member of the Mind and Life Institute and its Chairman of the Board since January 2012.

Jinpa trained as a monk at the Shartse College of Ganden Monastic University, South India, where he received the Geshe Lharam degree. Jinpa also holds a B.A. in Philosophy and a Ph.D. in Religious Studies, both from Cambridge University. Jinpa has been the principal English translator to H.H. the Dalai Lama since 1985, and has translated and collaborated on numerous books by the Dalai Lama including the *New York Times* bestsellers *Ethics for the New Millennium* and *The Art of Happiness*, as well as *Beyond Religion: Ethics for a Whole World*. His own publications include *A Fearless Heart: How the Courage to be Compassionate Can Transform Our Lives* and translations of major Tibetan works featured in The Library of Tibetan Classics series.

Contents

Creating Compassionate Change in School Communities

Introduction

I hope that everyone feels seen and heard. And that they have people there who are supporting them and people who love them. And that every kid and every staff member has someone whom they trust. And hopefully more than just one person, someone whom they can go to and know that they're there for them. And I would just hope that all the families too feel like we're really there for them to support them and to help them in any way. And that there's no division, and everyone just feels together and welcome.

—Taryn, First Grade Teacher

I hope that school's a place that people want to be, that they feel safer there than anywhere else or as safe as they do anywhere else. And that is created by a staff that is patient with each other and themselves and the kids and understands that big picture of common humanity and common suffering. I think that for my school, we feel it. There are some days that it feels like that, where it just feels like love and support all day, and you don't hear any enraged comments. In a great world, it would just be that warm, positive, supportive environment. We're going to acknowledge the difficulty and we're still going to try to be positive and supportive.

—Adam, High School English Teacher

Our schools today need to become spaces of healing, like the schools envisioned by these educators. Spaces of healing for young people from marginalized and minoritized communities, who are often asked to prove their humanity and worth just to gain access to a meaningful education. Spaces of healing for parents and families, who had to carry heavy burdens of teaching and caring for their children during the pandemic and who may be still carrying grief and wounds from that time. Spaces of healing for educators who have been asked to transform their teaching to meet the twin realities of the pandemic and racial reckoning and then have been criticized for teaching truths about our nation's injustices. Healing cannot come soon enough, and a key premise of this book is that you are the leaders who can help bring it about.

The healing we need requires courageous attention and care for ourselves and others to address everyday suffering in schools. As leaders, we need to address the manifestations of suffering that are in our own hearts and minds: the fatigue we feel from the empathy we hold for our students' suffering, the distress we feel from not being able to do what is right by our students or protect them from harmful systems, and the agitation and resentment we feel from difficult interactions with students, colleagues, administrators, and parents. We also need to address manifestations and the root causes of suffering that are present in our schools, by introducing new policies, practices, and routines that center caring relationships and that honor the dignity of each person who walks through the doors of our schools every day. We need especially to address policies and practices that cause harm to those students who are most vulnerable in our schools and in our society, including newcomer students impacted by immigration policies that threaten to separate their families or LGBTQIA2S+ (lesbian, gay, bisexual, transgender, queer or questioning, intersex, asexual or agender, and two-spirit) students and many others whose very identities are made invisible in our curriculum. And we need to maintain hope that this kind of healing is possible, that it's possible to create compassionate and dignity-affirming schools where children, families, educators, and communities feel seen, heard, and valued.

For this difficult work, we all need support to move past our own fatigue and overwhelm and resource ourselves for the long haul, and we need tools for transforming schools to eliminate everyday suffering in schools. To that end, this book presents a set of foundational ideas, practices, and educator experiences that can help prepare you to work with others in your school to create more compassionate, dignity-affirming schools. Our book is different from most books on self-care for educators and books on leadership. While other books focus on the power of contemplative practice for helping individual educators become more skilled at caring for themselves and others, our book is unique in its focus also on transforming schools into compassionate organizations. It takes up opportunities both within and beyond the classroom to promote compassion by changing policies and practices within schools that can be sites of suffering. Our aim in this book is to inspire educators like you to take up compassion as a focal point for collective leadership, to provide hope for compassion's power to rejuvenate educators as professionals in a time of difficulty, and to offer a pathway toward healing in schools through creating compassionate change.

We wrote this book for people in and around schools who are especially concerned with addressing the everyday suffering in schools that are experienced inequitably. That includes teachers in schools and other educational settings at all grade levels and content areas, school leaders, counselors, mental health professionals, social workers, librarians, and student support staff. This also includes teacher educators, preparing the next generation of teachers and current teachers for the classrooms of today and tomorrow. In many ways, we wrote this book as an act of love for educators—including you—who do such important and difficult work every day.

Origins of This Book

The book's content draws on a coherently crafted integration of contemplative practices, psychology and the science of compassion, theories of learning and organizational change, and experiences of educators, an integration that is reflected in a course of study we co-designed with educators to prepare educators to be changemakers in their schools. That course of study exists as an online master's certificate, *Cultivating Compassion & Dignity in Ourselves and Our Schools*, developed by the Renée Crown Wellness Institute in partnership with educators and the Compassion Institute and offered through the University of Colorado Boulder. It is a four-course certificate that begins with three asynchronous courses and concludes with a synchronous capstone course. In this book, we offer a synthesis of the ideas and practices of the program, along with educators' experiences and insights from the course, with the aim of making its lessons accessible to a broad audience.

During the 2019–2020 school year, we collaboratively designed (co-designed) with a group of educators—including teachers, counselors, administrators, librarians—the arc of the year-long digital compassion and dignity certificate for education leaders. Little did we know when we began this work that a pandemic would sweep the globe in the middle of the school year, soon to be followed by racial uprisings in the wake of the murders of George Floyd and others. The need for compassion, care, and connection was acutely felt both within our team and around the world as many suffered from illness, isolation, grief, confusion, and loneliness, as well as anger and frustration.

We began the co-design process by completing Compassion Cultivation Training© (CCT™) together to ground our work in a shared experience, to develop common language, and to be inspired. CCT is an 8-week evidence-based training program developed by Jinpa, in collaboration with Founding Faculty from the Compassion Institute. CCT integrates the science of compassion with secular approaches for cultivating compassion adapted from Tibetan Buddhist practices (Goldin & Jazaieri, 2017). Now taught around the world by certified teachers, CCT offers tools and resources for relating to oneself and others with empathy, compassion, and kindness. Following the 8-week compassion training, our co-design team met weekly to adapt, extend, and apply core content from CCT to design a digital certificate for educators. Educators drew on their experiences, including their joys and struggles, to contribute to the design of the compassion certificate to benefit other educators and ultimately their schools.

We are filled with gratitude for these educators who dedicated nearly 60 hours of their time during an extremely challenging school year to help create the compassion and dignity certificate with us, signaling to us the urgent need for compassion in schools. We know that as we struggled together to make sense of and make do with the challenges presented by the pandemic, we and our educator partners were transformed through the co-design process. One of the co-design teachers, Karen, reflected on her experience:

> This process has been life-changing in that it has brought consistent mindful practices into a space that is usually so full and stressful. This process has transformed me, bringing self-compassion into a place that is often full of self-criticism. All of this allows me to step into my role as educator with more awareness and the ability to have compassion for others. I hope that this [certificate] brings such insights, awareness and consistent practices fully alive for educators in a profound and powerful way. Just maybe, we can make the world a kinder, more responsive place for everyone.

Another educator shared their wish with the group:

> It will help [educators] to take a step back from things that have become routine and expected, and to look at their students with fresh eyes, to identify our intentions in the thousands of difficult decisions and interactions we have each day, and I think this will go very far to bring more compassion into the world.

Since launching our compassion and dignity programs for educators in 2020, we have engaged nearly 550 educators in our courses, training sessions, and workshops. The educators teach and lead at all levels from PK-20 and represent all content areas. The educators are classroom teachers, principals, superintendents, district leaders, librarians, counselors, school-based mental health professionals, social workers, interventionists, paraprofessionals, researchers, and university instructors. While many participants in our programs live and work in Colorado, through our virtual programs and courses we also engage educators living across the United States and internationally. Our hope is through this book we can reach thousands more educators, providing them with ideas, practices, and tools to create more compassionate schools.

We are also educators and scholars who bring our own experiences, perspectives, and investigations to bear on the content of the book. Ashley is a researcher in the Renée Crown Wellness Institute at the University of Colorado Boulder, where she works in partnership with educators and co-teaches our certificate program with Bill. She is a former middle and high school teacher, curriculum leader, and instructional coach who has been dedicated to creating caring and inclusive classrooms and schools and supporting the well-being of educators. She brings the perspective of both a scholar and educator-leader to this book.

In addition to co-teaching the certificate program, Bill is a faculty member at CU Boulder in the learning sciences. He has devoted many years to building and studying how educators and researchers can work together to design curricula and programs like ours. In addition, he is a long-term practitioner of meditation, and he has engaged for many years with the practices included in this book.

Sona is Director of the Crown Institute and Professor in the Department of Psychology and Neuroscience. Her research focuses on cultivating mental health and wellness among women, children, and families by engaging people's capacities for learning to care for themselves and their communities. Her career has been dedicated to the science of contemplative practices like compassion and mindfulness among youth, families, and educators and to teaching these practices as an educator and clinical psychologist (and in her own life).

Jinpa is the Founder and Chairman of Compassion Institute, and the principal author of CCT, the Compassion Institute's flagship compassion education offering, developed while Jinpa was at Stanford University. He is also an adjunct professor at the Faculty of Religious Studies at McGill University and is the founder and president of the Institute of Tibetan Classics. Jinpa trained as a monk at the Shartse College of Ganden Monastic University, South India, where he received the Geshe Lharam degree. Jinpa has been the principal English translator to H.H. the Dalai Lama since 1985 and has translated and collaborated on numerous books by the Dalai Lama. Jinpa and Sona began working together as Board members at the Mind and Life Institute, a beautiful and rich context for a long-term collaboration dedicated to the wellness of educators and our world at large.

What We Know About the Power of Compassion

As this book is centered on compassion, we start with a definition that can provide a common starting point for exploring how to cultivate compassion in ourselves, our relationships, and our schools. We know there are lots of ways that we talk about compassion in everyday conversation. But as the research base for compassion has expanded over the last two decades, some general agreement on a useful definition has emerged (Mascaro et al., 2020). Drawing from scientific and contemplative approaches, we define *compassion* as having four basic components: (1) an awareness of suffering; (2) a feeling of concern and connection to one who is suffering (empathy); (3) a desire to relieve that suffering (motivation); (4) a willingness to respond or act to relieve suffering (Gilbert,

2017; Goetz & Simon-Thomas, 2017; Jinpa, 2015). As the definition implies, compassion involves empathy but it is more than that—it pushes us to move from concern to intention and action in the world.

Compassion is a basic instinct—something that humans evolved to naturally feel (Gilbert, 2017; Goetz et al., 2010). Consider, for a moment, someone who is close to you—a family member, a friend, or even a pet. When they are sick or hurting, you naturally feel concern for them and you want to do something to help them to feel better. This instinctual aspect means compassion is always available to us.

Compassion is also something that we can purposefully grow or train ourselves in, much as we train our bodies for exercise (Condon et al., 2013; Kirby, 2017). The good news is that it doesn't take years of training to receive the benefits from cultivating compassion (Hutcherson et al., 2008; Jazaieri et al., 2017), and you can begin today. Throughout this book, we'll offer guidance, meditation practices, reflections, and other exercises to help you deepen and grow your compassion.

Cultivating compassion and generosity not only brings benefit to others, but it also can benefit you. Researchers have been studying compassion to understand the benefits of compassion. Compassion has been shown to contribute to physical health as well as emotional well-being. Compassion can serve as a buffer against stress (Breines et al., 2014), increase resilience in times of challenge (Presnell, 2018), and protect against loneliness (Ramahlo et al., 2021). When leaders express compassion and act compassionately, others feel a sense of support (Cosley et al., 2010) and can even act with more creativity (Peng et al., 2017).

We have been among those scholars contributing to this growing body of research on compassion. Several years ago, I (Sona) conducted a study with my colleagues Tor Wager, Yoni Ashar, and Jessica Andrews-Hanna to examine the impact of brief compassion meditation on people's cognitive, affective, and behavioral responses to the suffering of others and on changes in their neural processing of images and stories of suffering others (see Ashar et al., 2016). We wanted to know how to cultivate more compassionate responding in our world and we wondered: What is the impact of compassion meditation on responses to the stories and images of suffering others?

We decided to ask participants at the start and end of the study to come into the lab to view photos and hear stories of suffering others, and to answer questions about their feelings about the suffering others, the attributions they made about them, and how similar they thought they were to them. We also gave each participant $100, with instructions that they could keep the money for themselves or donate to groups that helped the suffering individuals.

We divided participants into three groups. The first group was asked to listen to guided secular compassion meditation practices that Roshi Joan Halifax from Upaya Zen Center recorded. The second group was asked to use a nasal spray daily, which we told them was oxytocin and would help them to become more compassionate, although it was actually a saline placebo. The third group, the repeated exposure group, was asked to view the same photos and hear stories each day but they were not asked to take any other particular action.

Our findings provided support for the benefits of compassion practice at the behavioral and brain levels. For example, our data showed that with respect to donations, there was no significant change in compassion meditation participants, and in contrast, a significant decrease in donation among participants in the repeated exposure condition, with the placebo group falling right in the middle. One of the potential effects of compassion meditation in this trial may have been in buffering against the decreased response to suffering observed in the repeated exposure condition. This may be consistent with the notion that repeated exposure to the suffering of others, in the absence of having tools or a framework to guide one's response, leads to a kind of empathy fatigue in which ultimately people are at risk of being numb or blunted in their responses to such suffering. This study tells us both about the potential benefits of very brief compassion meditation practice and perhaps equally importantly about the risks of failing to provide people with tools when they are repeatedly exposed to suffering.

When I (Sona) shared this study with educators, they told me how powerfully they related to the study participants who were asked to see images and hear stories of suffering people without being given any tools to respond. They shared that their jobs are like the people in the repeated exposure condition. Educators shared that it can be deeply challenging to sustain compassion when exposed repeatedly to suffering experienced by students in their classes, their families, and members of their school community. Educators wanted to know: What can we do to ensure that we don't become numb or disengaged over time? What can we do to sustain our love of teaching, our original intentions that led us to this profession, instead of feeling burned out over time? Their questions spurred us to undertake the research and curriculum design work that led to this book.

The great news about our research and the ideas presented in this book is that we *can* do something to counter the burnout or fatigue that can come from repeated exposure to suffering. Even brief compassion practice, like the practices we share in this book, can bring you a lot of personal benefits and can support you in meeting the suffering of students, their families, and others in your school community with an open heart and with steadiness. You also learn how to bring this same compassion for others, right back to care for yourself during tough times too!

Affirming Dignity

Recognizing the dignity of oneself and others is an essential component of cultivating compassion. We draw on a definition of dignity from Espinoza et al. (2020), who define dignity as "the multifaceted sense of a person's value generated via substantive intra- and interpersonal learning experiences that recognize and cultivate one's mind, humanity, and potential" (p. 326). Their definition highlights the fact that dignity is inherent to all human beings by virtue of our common humanity, but we can also do things that either affirm or deny others' dignity, by how we treat people. A dignity-affirming school environment is one where each person can find meaning and purpose in what they do, and where people feel seen and heard (Espinoza et al., 2020). When we see the dignity in ourselves and others, we see all as worthy of our care and attention and as deserving of compassion.

In schools and classrooms, dignity is always on the line, shaped by policies, practices, and daily interactions. These can either support or undermine the dignity of students and staff. Dignity is more than just a right—it's also a responsibility. It involves recognizing each person's value through meaningful learning experiences that honor their mind, humanity, and potential.

As educators, we play a crucial role in recognizing students' inherent worth and creating environments that affirm their dignity. This happens when we design learning experiences where students see themselves reflected in the curriculum and are given meaningful opportunities to participate. Affirming dignity means allowing students to share in decision-making and ensuring they are seen and heard by those in positions of power. It also involves being mindful of the often invisible struggles and identities students hold who are part of our schools.

Compassion Organizing and Leadership

Our approach to supporting the well-being of educators and schools is unique in that in addition to a focus on cultivating compassion and dignity for oneself and others, we also focus on developing capacities for creating change at the systems level. We draw on a framework for *compassion organizing* to help leaders put compassion and dignity into action to transform the policies, routines, and practices of their schools. The compassion organizing framework, developed initially in organizational studies (Dutton et al., 2006; Worline & Dutton, 2017), emphasizes the need for leaders to gather resources and support that allows for a timely response to suffering in the organization, as well as customizing responses to meet the needs of those who are suffering and for creating dignity-affirming environments. In education, compassion organizing involves attuning to the causes of social suffering that are experienced inequitably—that is, the policies and practices that cause harm to those most marginalized in our society (Penuel et al., 2024).

Organizing for compassionate change and addressing suffering in your school requires leading with others. Collective leadership makes it possible to create and sustain compassionate change in ways that contribute positively to the well-being of your school community, even when the suffering feels intense. Collective leadership, coupled with the cultivation of compassion and the affirmation of dignity, allows you to persist in the face of suffering, and to do so skillfully. Working with others, you can create healing spaces by cultivating conditions in schools where everyone can grow and know that someone cares for them and sees them as a human being worthy of their respect.

As we use this term throughout the book, "leaders" are not just people with titles and formal responsibilities for administering schools, because you are a leader if you are a teacher, librarian, counselor, resource specialist, or custodial staff member who is working alongside others to create conditions for compassion and dignity in your school. You are a leader if you use your knowledge of students, your connections with others, and resources to organize responses to sources of suffering in schools that perpetuate inequities, such as discipline policies, grading practices, and exclusion of groups of students from the curriculum.

Organization of the Book

This book is organized into four sections that follow the sequence of our program at the Renée Crown Wellness Institute for supporting educators' growth in compassion and for helping them organize their schools to become more compassionate places for them and their colleagues, their students, and their families and communities.

In the opening section of the book, *Cultivating Awareness and Setting Intentions*, we introduce you to foundational aspects of cultivating compassion that can support wellness: developing awareness and setting intentions. Grounded in the realities of the current system of schooling and educators' lived experiences, these chapters explore what it means to recognize and get close to pain and suffering in today's educational contexts, to reconnect with the joys of teaching, and to set intentions to act with compassion.

The second section of the book, *Embracing Self-Compassion and Affirming Dignity*, focuses on what it means to offer compassion to yourself when faced with your own suffering. For many educators we've worked with, the idea of self-compassion, of bringing attention to your own care and needs, is one of the most impactful concepts in our program and it's also often the most challenging. Many people in the helping professions, such as education, find it much easier to extend compassion to others than to themselves.

The third section of the book, *Widening the Circle of Compassion*, focuses on cultivating compassion for others to prepare for action to cultivate more compassionate schools. We share practices for cultivating awareness of common humanity in the world in our everyday interactions with those with whom we have weaker or even challenging relationships.

The final section of the book, *Creating Compassionate Schools*, guides you through a process for developing your school as a compassionate and humanizing system. We invite you to deepen your leadership capacities for collective organizing. We offer tools and practices for attuning to the forms of social suffering that impact groups inequitably, building a shared commitment to compassionate action, seeing your school as a system, and implementing compassionate change to alleviate a form of social suffering in your school community.

Each chapter includes an introduction to key concepts and research, educator stories and examples of compassion in action, meditation practices, on-the-spot practices, journal reflection prompts, and activities. If compassion can be cultivated and dignity can be affirmed, leaders need skillful means—that is, the ability to use tools and practices to develop their own compassion and see their own dignity and that of others. This book introduces you to a sequence of contemplative practices and guided inquiry, including structured reflection activities, to help develop those skillful means. Both are necessary, in that contemplative practices can help stabilize awareness and prepare you for meeting suffering with an open heart, while inquiry can help you see more clearly your values, biases, and the impacts of your actions on others (Potvin et al., 2023).

At the heart of our work are educators' own journeys of coming to develop their understanding and skills for showing compassion and creating dignity-affirming school environments. We foreground the voices of educators from our workshops and certificate program, to highlight both their successes and challenges and to ground these ideas in the real and messy work of people in schools. Their voices appear in every chapter, and they have been our partners in design since we began developing our certificate program (Potvin et al., 2023).

Practical Activities to Support Your Growth and Work

Throughout this book, we invite you to attune to the experiences of your own mind, heart, and body in meditation practice, in interactions with others, and even as you engage with research-based ideas we introduce. We offer different kinds of activities that are aimed at helping you learn and grow and at working with others to develop plans for a more compassionate school. There are four kinds of activities:

Meditation practices: In the first three sections of the book, we'll introduce you to contemplative practices to strengthen your capacity for mindfulness and compassion. You are invited and encouraged to establish a daily, consistent practice. Educators we've worked with have found these practices to be crucial resources throughout their journeys as compassionate educators. We recommend trying out the practices introduced in each chapter every day for at least a week. You can always revisit the practices as you continue through the book.

On-the-spot practices: On-the-spot practices are intended to help you try out the skills you gain from meditation practice and apply compassion in your day-to-day interactions. The on-the-spot practices offer a way to practice compassion even within the busy-ness and hectic pace of your workday. These practices are quick and concrete ways to integrate mindfulness and compassion into your day-to-day life.

Journal reflections: Many of the chapters also include journal prompts and we encourage you to pause and reflect on the experiences of your heart and mind. Choose a journal format that works best for you: a document on your computer, a notebook, or audio recordings.

Activities: We have included some written and dialogue activities throughout the book as well. These activities are designed to further your inquiry into key topics. In the final section of the book, we provide templates and guidance to help you, along with a team, develop action plans for bringing more compassion and dignity to school policies and practices. These templates and guidelines are grounded in the compassion organizing framework and allow for integration of insights drawn from contemplation and inquiry into your day-to-day work.

Orienting to Meditation Practice: Practice Makes Practice

We encourage you to try out and discuss the practical activities—including the meditation practices—with your colleagues and to think of your meditation practice as a gift to yourself. While you might share the practices with colleagues, it's beyond the scope of this book to provide instruction to you on how to teach meditation to others, whether that be to other educators in your building or to students in your class. For now, we invite you to find a rhythm to your own practice and to notice with curiosity how engaging with practices impacts your capacity for creating and sustaining your own efforts to create compassionate change in your school.

As you try out the meditation practices in this book, remember that there is no such thing as a "perfect" practice. Practice doesn't make perfect; practice makes practice. It may be difficult to get used to this idea, but practice does not have to look or feel a certain way to benefit you and others. There isn't a "right" way to practice, and practice won't always feel calm and peaceful.

Sometimes, practice makes you aware of your own level of tiredness, distraction, and anxiety. In these moments, you are encouraged to invite whatever arises to be part of your practice. At times during your practice, your mind will certainly wander, and you may experience boredom or discomfort. This is not a problem; it's part of the process. Challenge, distraction, and discomfort present valuable opportunities to cultivate awareness and compassion for yourself. If you find a specific practice challenging, be gentle with yourself. The recognition that practice is hard can actually be an opening to self-compassion. We can say,

(continued)

(continued)

"Oh, this is hard" and soften our hearts. When you notice that you are distracted, we invite you to gently guide your focus back to the breath as an act of self-compassion, without judgment.

In the same way, when you forget to do the practice or run out of time, bring compassion to yourself. Notice the forgetting as part of your practice and gently return to your intention(s) for your practice. And, if you feel like a specific practice is not for you on a given day for any reason, you always have an option to take a break, return to your breath, or engage in a different practice. Remember, you have choices related to when and how you engage with the practices. Adapting to who you are and what you are experiencing in any moment is critical.

If you are new to daily practice, look to establish a set time in your day to do the formal practice. You will likely find that the best times for formal meditation practice are before or after school. When you are starting out, it can be helpful to tie it to another routine in your day, such as while you are waiting for your morning coffee to brew. It can also be helpful to add your practice as an event in your daily calendar. Think of it as an experiment within the laboratory of your life. Make a commitment to develop a daily habit, while also giving yourself the flexibility to learn from what doesn't work.

If you already have a consistent, daily practice we recommend that you try the compassion practices introduced in this book 2–3 times a week and continue with your other practices on the remaining days. We encourage you to maintain the practice that you've worked hard to cultivate and to allow yourself to grow through the compassion practices.

You may find the following tips helpful as you develop or deepen a daily habit of practice. Some of the tips will work better for you than others; experiment and see what's most helpful to you.

- **Set up an easy place to practice each day:** You could decide to practice in a quiet room in your home or a calm corner of your classroom before school begins.
- **Schedule practice:** Some educators find it helpful to schedule practice into their daily calendars as an event or set an alarm.
- **Write a reminder:** For other educators, scheduling in the practice makes it feel like another "to-do" or "chore." Instead, you might find it more helpful to jot a reminder to yourself on a sticky note and put it in a high visibility place, such as near your computer screen, in your plan book, on your bathroom mirror, or on your refrigerator.

- **Find a "practice buddy":** If you are reading this book as part of a book study with colleagues, consider supporting one another as "practice buddies." If you are reading this book on your own, consider reaching out to someone in your life who already has a regular meditation practice. Set up quick, regular check-ins with your practice buddy so that you can talk about how it's going and hold each other accountable. You could check-in through email, text, or brief meetings.
- **Find a community:** It can also be very helpful to find a group of people who are committed to contemplative practice and who meet regularly to practice in community. There may be local groups or organizations in your own town or city, or you might find a virtual community to join.
- **Pair the practice with a routine you already have:** You might also try pairing practice with another activity, such as sitting down to practice while you wait for your coffee to brew or meditating in the evening just after you brush your teeth.
- **Set or reset intentions:** Sometimes it can feel overwhelming to start practicing after missing several sessions. Try to be gentle with yourself. Remember, it's never too late to set (or reset) your intentions for practice and to begin again.
- **Try practicing without the script:** After you've practiced any given meditation with the script a few times, you may wish to practice in silence by recalling the guided practice on your own.

Guidance on Using This Book

A key premise of this book is that creating and sustaining compassionate change in your school community requires coordinated, collective action and leadership. We have observed the power of bringing educators together to discuss the forms of suffering they, their students, students' families, and colleagues experience in schools. When teams come together to face this suffering, they can see they are not alone in noticing and wanting to respond to suffering and they can collectively reimagine their schools as healing and dignity-affirming spaces. Thus, we recommend that you read this book with colleagues. You might consider organizing a book group, pausing to talk about the key concepts in each chapter, sharing reflections, and then planning together for compassionate change using the guidance and templates provided.

You can also read this book on your own. If you are reading this book alone, we encourage you to find a trusted colleague or thought partner at your school who you can share ideas with as you read. This person might even become an important ally as you plan to bring compassion into your school community.

We suggest reading the chapters of this book in order because they follow an intentional sequence that mirrors what educators in our certificate program experience. You may also find it helpful to return to certain sections or chapters, or to revisit meditation practices or written reflections. We encourage you to take your time to digest the content and to engage in the practices and activities. Don't just gloss over them. Annotate, highlight, or jot reflections within the pages of the book.

Whether you are reading this book alone or together with others, it is our sincere wish that whatever benefit comes from reading it and engaging with its ideas and practices may support your actions toward creating more compassionate schools. We also hope that you reconnect with your purpose for educating and leading in schools and find moments of joy within your daily interactions. Know that you are joining a larger community of educators who have committed to bringing compassion into the policies and practices of their schools and into their everyday relationships. Welcome to this journey and to this community.

Part 1

Cultivating Awareness and Setting Intentions

Chapter 1
Pausing to Attune to Our Own Experience

Instructions for living a life:
Pay attention.
Be astonished.
Tell about it.

—Mary Oliver, "Sometimes," in Red Bird

The first invitation for creating more compassionate schools is to pay attention. When you start your journey to school every day, what feelings arise? What do you think about? When you enter the building, what do you notice? When you walk into your classroom, the staffroom, or office, what is happening? Who is there, and how does it feel when you picture them, right now as you sit reading this book? How does your heart respond, right here and now, when you imagine yourself encountering different students as you walk down a hallway—a student you know well and with whom you have a positive relationship? A student who has given other students trouble? A student who is standing alone at a locker, appearing sad or lonely? Perhaps see yourself as you were in school. What details call your attention? What feelings arise? Just take a moment, breathe, and pay attention.

When we stop to pay attention, the poet Mary Oliver (2009) invites us to be astonished; astonished at the beauty of the world. The instructions for life come in the middle of "Sometimes," a poem that is a meditation on the beauty of nature, on love, and the mysteries of life itself. It might be easy to be astonished if we are in the middle of a field of flowers. But if we return to what we notice when we picture ourselves in the middle of our school, we might wonder how we could be astonished by the routines we follow, the intense emotions of colleagues and students we encounter and have to reckon with, the burnout we might feel from time to time. And how could talking about what we see, notice, and feel not just lead to a better life for ourselves, but to more compassionate schools?

Mary Oliver's invitation here is to pay attention to what is before us in a way that we don't typically pay attention. She's inviting us to slow down and to see things from a fresh perspective. To pay attention to something we see every day, but with fresh eyes. That's how we become astonished, and it's through paying attention to what is before us that can awaken and open our hearts. Before we can take up the rest of her instructions, though, we need to understand more about attention, specifically in ways that relate to what happens daily in the life of schools.

The Power of Attention

We know that attention is important to what we do as educators, because we are so often trying to engage and maintain our students' attention. Without attending to a text, to a problem, or to a teacher's guidance or a peer's ideas, individual learning is impossible. In collaborative learning, paying joint attention to what we are doing together is critical for people to be able to pitch in and contribute to group problem solving. Attention, in a very real sense, is one of the most important resources for learning.

Our attention is also an important gateway to compassion. Suffering is all around us, in our schools and in the wider world. To do something about the suffering we encounter in the world, we have to notice it. And we need to balance our attention both inward and outward to be able to really notice the full range of suffering that might be present. If our attention is inward, only on how we are impacted by some turn of events or a situation that's bothering us, we might not even notice that others are suffering, too. And if our attention is outward, only geared toward responding to a crisis external to us, we might not notice how we are reacting to it, perhaps with anxiety, sadness, or anger. It can be hard to keep our attention present to another's suffering and to our own in a way that doesn't cause us to get overwhelmed or even to shut down, and yet the heart of compassion is learning how to show up for ourselves and others in those moments. It's about intentionally directing and sustaining attention to what's arising in the moment.

Of course, like other resources, our attention is limited. Many of us have an intuitive sense of just how limited it is, because our ability to keep focus and attention declines over the course of the day. When we focus our attention on something, our brain cells become active, and there's more flow of carbon dioxide in the brain, but as we try to sustain attention, we can't maintain that flow at the same rate, suggesting that limited resources are getting used up in the process (Warm & Parasuraman, 2007). The only way to build back up our reserves of attention is to stop giving our attention and effort to what we are focusing on that's draining us.

But just switching to another task has costs as well. And being in a school provides far fewer opportunities to focus on a single task; instead, it demands ongoing attention to a wide range of demands, often many at the same time. In her study of principals during the pandemic, educational researcher Angel Xiao Bohannon (2023) found that principals experience a near-constant barrage of what she calls "attentional dilemmas," that is, "situations where school leaders—due to multiple demands competing for their limited attention—experienced messy choices between paying attention to multiple, highly desired values or goals, all of which could not be fully satisfied" (p. 2). Notably, even though the intensity of demands on principals' attention was experienced as more intense during the pandemic, these principals said they had *always* experienced attentional dilemmas. They were no strangers to situations where their attention was pulled this way or that and where they rarely felt that they could meet the demands that were placed upon them. They described feeling less personally and professionally satisfied that they were doing the best they could to meet the needs of everyone in the school community. The only partial relief available to them was to take time away from their roles as principals to care for themselves and to practice delegating responsibility to other school leaders for specific issues. These experiences are not unique to principals in schools. In fact, we could probably all use strategies that refresh our attention.

Where Our Attention Goes on Its Own Versus with Cultivation

Our attentional resources can be replenished by good sleep, healthy eating, exercise, taking a walk outside, and resting. They are supported by external conditions, too, like healthy air and safe neighborhoods. A good place to start with thinking about attention is to take an inventory of the kinds of things we do and conditions in our lives that deplete our attentional resources, and those that nourish them.

Writing Activity: Inventory of Attention-Depleting and Attention-Nourishing Activities

In this activity, adapted from cognitive psychologist, Zindel Segal et al. (2002), we invite you to take an inventory of attention-depleting and attention-nourishing activities you engage in throughout the week. Take a moment to write down the activities you do on a typical weekday, as well as those you do on a typical

(continued)

(continued)

weekend day. For each of those activities, write down one or two things or people that you attend to, when engaging in those activities. Then, write down a "D" for depleting beside those activities that use up your reserves of attention, and an "N" for nourishing beside those that replenish them. Take a moment to review the activities you labeled as attention-depleting and those you labeled as attention-nourishing.

- What patterns do you notice?
- Where and when might you more intentionally cultivate attention?
- Do you have some initial ideas about how you might cultivate attention in these moments?

With this inventory in hand, ask yourself: Where and how might I be more intentional about cultivating my attention?

These activities of replenishment on a personal level are a good start, but they aren't enough on their own. Just as the skilled principals in Angel Xiao Bohannon's study could never manage their attentional dilemmas in a way that felt satisfying, people need to work together to change the conditions in the school that lead to a constant array of demands on attention being placed on everyone. We'll come back to this idea again and again in the book—that we need to both take care of ourselves and create structures for care that make it easier for people to care for themselves and others.

Paying attention also requires that we take breaks from regular activity to quiet the mind. A break here means interrupting our constant doing and planning for what's next, our worrying about the future, and ruminating about the past. When we first try to take a break, to quiet our thoughts, we may notice that our minds are all over the place. Our thoughts don't just stop, and we tend to follow them wherever they take us. We might even be operating on autopilot, for instance, not even tasting the coffee we are sipping. We may have set a beautiful intention to pause and rest, but it's hard for us. There is all this forward momentum, and the emotions that come up with our thoughts can take us away from just resting. We may remember something we need to do, we may feel anxious, and we feel our muscles tighten. There's a difficult meeting we think about, and dread arises. It's easy when these kinds of things happen to get up from our seat and get on with our day. After all, we didn't have time for this break, did we?

The first thing to know about stopping to pay attention is that science tells us that attention to whatever is arising in the moment often drifts away from the present.

Psychologists use the term "mind-wandering" to refer to the thoughts that we have unrelated to what we are doing, whether that's creating a lesson plan, talking to a student, or meditating. Sometimes our mind-wandering is pleasant, as in daydreaming. Other times, though, our mind-wandering involves thoughts of fear, anxiety, and guilt. And sometimes, our mind-wandering just feels like a fog. The kinds of thoughts that arise in mind-wandering are generated internally, not in relation to the world outside us. Our minds are like "thought machines," capable of generating thoughts all on their own, and they do so all the time.

Amishi Jha is a neuroscientist who has spent decades studying attention. What she and her colleagues have found is that we only pay attention to 50% of what's happening in the present moment. Jha and her team conducted a series of studies, searching for situations where people could pay attention 100% of the time and they found none. In her book, *Peak Mind*, Jha (2021) notes that people couldn't pay attention if they were told to pay attention, paid to do so, when the stakes were high, or even when very motivated to pay attention. Moreover, stress and the continuous demands of preparing for important situations left the people in her studies feeling depleted, making it even harder to pay attention.

Mind-wandering is present across cultures, and it may be tempting to think that the presence of cell phones, email, or television in our lives causes mind-wandering, but philosophers, poets, and other keen observers of the human condition have been describing the phenomenon for millennia. It is little wonder, then, that when we sit down with the intention to pay attention, one of the first things we may notice is how hard it is to sustain our attention on an object like the breath.

All this mind-wandering has a cost, in terms of our attention. On the one hand, our mind-wandering tendencies are helpful in planning, in creating space for new ideas to emerge for solving a problem, and for just taking a break from the demands of the world. But studies show that mind-wandering negatively affects our ability to pay attention when reading or listening to others, impacting our comprehension of text (e.g., Schooler et al., 2004) and lectures (Farley et al., 2013). It can also negatively impact performance on tests (Mrazek et al., 2012). The unpleasant thoughts that arise more naturally draw our attention than do positive or neutral thoughts (Fiske, 1980). When we generate images that cause us guilt, fear, or anxiety, it causes us stress that diminishes the power of our attention.

The Power of Cultivating Mindfulness

The good news is that it is possible to strengthen our capacity to pay attention to present moment experiences. And in fact, Jha (2021) found that the only brain-training tool to be effective for strengthening attention was mindfulness. Mindfulness has two components, one about *where* we place our attention, and a second about *how* we relate to the objects of our attention (Bishop et al., 2004). When we are mindful, our attention is on our present moment experience; that is, we take notice of whatever arises in our experience, without elaborating on it or making stories up about it (Kabat-Zinn, 1990). Our attention can be on anything that arises in our experience—the breath, the cup we are holding, a sensation in the body, or it can be on our thoughts and feelings in the present moment. When we are mindful, we relate to the objects of our attention with curiosity, openness, and acceptance. Here, "acceptance" doesn't mean that we necessarily like what is arising, but we accept that it is here in front of us, like it or not. In fact, what shows up when we try to cultivate mindfulness is that we come to notice that our orientation to what arises in awareness can be unpleasant, pleasant, or neutral.

In meditation, we actively cultivate mindfulness. We start with something simple, like paying attention to our breath. [See "Formal Practice: Settling the Mind with Awareness of Breath" later in this chapter.] We start simple because we're engaged in a path to train our attention. Just as with exercise, we don't start our training by running a marathon, but if we are starting from scratch, we begin with a short walk or jog, and we build up our strength slowly over time. The instructions are simple: pay attention to the breath, and when your mind wanders, come back to it gently and appreciate the moment you return—you're here again! We're training the mind in sustaining attention on an object and in flexibly turning the attention from one object (whatever is distracting us) to another (back to the breath). When we meditate, we are "cultivating" mindfulness by directing our attention this way, with kindness and gentleness. Mindfulness isn't something we make happen, it emerges from us creating the kinds of conditions—both in meditation practice and in everyday life—for it to arise. Throughout this book, we'll describe ways to sustain and deepen the practice of mindful awareness, adding practices to cultivate other states of mind, like loving-kindness, compassion, and joy.

There is strong evidence that mindfulness practice can benefit educators. One of the longest-running programs for educators is the Cultivating Awareness and Resilience in Education (CARE) program, developed by Patricia Jennings and colleagues at the Garrison Institute in New York. One of the goals of CARE is to support educators in becoming more aware of and regulating their own emotions, particularly emotions that arise in classroom interactions, since how teachers show up in their interactions with students matters for student outcomes (Jennings & Greenberg, 2009). In CARE, teachers are introduced to brief meditation practices, and they also explore how to bring mindfulness to difficult interactions in schools. Experimental studies of the CARE program show that it contributed to multiple aspects of teacher well-being, including reducing their psychological and physical distress, building mindfulness, regulation of emotion, and emotional support that they were able to provide for students (Jennings et al., 2017, 2019).

Being Mindful of Intentions for Cultivating Mindfulness

Today, appeals for educators and education leaders to "become more mindful" are couched in a variety of messages, some of which can be problematic for addressing the suffering that is present in our schools today. A common idea people bring to mindfulness is the idea that we are learning how to control our minds; we may even find it appealing to bring mindfulness to students, because we think it will help them with self-control. There may indeed be changes we can observe from mindfulness that are beneficial to us and to others, but these don't come from us becoming better at controlling our minds. The very practice of mindfulness is one of letting go and accepting as real whatever is in front of us right now—an angry colleague, a grieving parent, a physically active child who is moving around the room.

It's just as problematic to use mindfulness as a method for numbing ourselves out to inner experience, interactions, and circumstances that need to change. Mindfulness does not require us to say "yes" to schedules and obligations that leave us perpetually stressed and burned out. It does not require us to say "yes" to harmful interactions between students that we see, or when others harm us in some way, whether physically or psychologically. And it doesn't require us to say "yes" to policies and practices that put us continually in a bind, when it comes to doing what will benefit the students we serve. The goal is not to use mindfulness to accept suffering that could be addressed through setting different intentions, coming to agreement about how we want to treat each other as members of the school community, and identifying and changing policies that repeatedly cause suffering.

A different "why" for mindfulness that we offer in this book is that we cultivate mindfulness for the benefit of cultivating mindfulness for *all of us*—ourselves, the people who are kind to us, the people we barely know, the people who push our buttons, animals, birds, fish, all living beings—because we appreciate how we are fundamentally all connected to one another, a topic we take up more in Chapters 7 and 9. We cultivate our own minds, because we recognize and clearly see the impacts that our words and deeds have on others, words and deeds that have their origin in our thoughts—as impulses we feel, intentions we set, as feelings about what's happening right now. By taking care of our minds, pausing to become aware of what is arising, we can become less reactive and respond to others and to situations in a way that allows us to remember our wish to benefit others.

Another way of thinking of why we cultivate mindfulness is that we do it so that we can be safe people for others to turn to. We might think of mindfulness as somehow selfish because we are turning inward. But if we pay attention with curiosity and kindness to what is happening inside us, we actually become less preoccupied with ourselves and less lost in our thoughts and worries. When we cultivate mindfulness, we grow in our confidence that we can be present to others who are in pain, in anger, in fear, or who need something that they cannot quite articulate (Fronsdal, 2020). As adrienne maree brown (2019) writes, cultivating awareness can open up space within us that is "as vast as the ocean" and give us the resources we need to feel all of our feelings, to be in our dignity, to make mistakes, and still be connected to others (p. 158). Our ability to be calm and present to others is something that grows with mindfulness, and it becomes a gift to others. When we are mindful, others don't need to be afraid of how we will react to them, and that is what makes us safe for others.

Another motivation for mindfulness can be gratitude. We cultivate our own minds, because we are grateful for the very fact that this planet and people around us have created conditions for us to be alive, here, and now. As Robin Wall Kimmerer (Potawatomi, 2015) writes in *Braiding Sweetgrass*, "The land is the real teacher. All we need as students is mindfulness. Paying attention is a form of reciprocity with the living world, receiving the gifts with open eyes and open heart" (p. 213). With gratitude as our "why" for mindfulness, we can see how this idea of taking responsibility for our thoughts, words, and actions is already a response to the ways the world—in all its complexity—is making it possible for us to live, even when we ourselves might be struggling.

Paying Attention "Right on the Spot"

Mindfulness on the surface may sound simple—it's about paying attention to what you are experiencing in the moment. But *actually* being mindful, *really* paying attention to and staying with our thoughts, feelings, and experiences, can be tricky and it takes quite a bit of practice to train our minds. It's different from the way we typically pay attention throughout the day in the form of quick scans to gather information and to adjust our approach or instruction on the spot. We can practice mindfulness and get better at paying attention, just as you might help a student practice their writing to get better at articulating their thoughts. We can cultivate mindfulness by paying attention to where joy and suffering are present in our everyday lives. We can experiment with and practice mindfulness within the laboratories of our own lives. We don't have to do anything elaborate, and it doesn't always have to take a lot of time. We can practice bringing attention to the full range of our experiences, right on the spot.

Mindful attention can be cultivated within everyday activities, so we can see each moment unfolding and be present to it within our lives. When we pay attention in our everyday lives, we can make room for joy, appreciation of beauty, and as Mary Oliver has instructed us, being astonished. As Thich Nhat Hanh, Vietnamese Buddhist monk and peace activist, explained in his book, *Happy teachers change the world: A guide for cultivating mindfulness in education*:

> The first step to come back to yourself—the way out is in. Come back to yourself to be able to take care of yourself: learn how to generate a feeling of happiness; learn how to how to handle a painful feeling or emotion; listen to your own suffering, so that understanding and compassion can be born and you will suffer less. This is the first step, and as a teacher, you have to be able to do this. (Hanh & Weare, 2017, p. xviii)

When we practice mindfulness throughout our day—while we eat our lunch or during our third period class or as we watch students on the playground—we can notice with curiosity and appreciation small moments that we might have otherwise missed. We might even realize that our days hold potential for a number of these small moments that offer us glimpses of joy and beauty, perhaps even more glimpses than we were initially aware. It's easy to go home at the end of a hectic and full day and recall the challenging and difficult moments, the experiences that brought us pain. But by practicing mindfulness on the spot, we can grow in our ability to pay attention to a fuller range of experiences. We might even be astonished when we do!

Paying Attention for Equity

As educators, we face many competing demands for our attention throughout the day. Learning to pay attention mindfully can help us to bring awareness to patterns in what we tend to notice, what we overlook, and what is invisible to us. This is an important part of equity work. What we notice (or don't) as teachers is often informed by our prior experiences in teaching (Erickson, 2011), as well as by other life experiences, our identities, histories, and community memberships. From this perspective, being skillful at paying attention mindfully means we simultaneously acknowledge our noticing is always partial and limited, while striving to see different perspectives. Paying attention mindfully can help us to notice when interactions are equitable or inequitable. For instance, we might notice that we provide more support to some students than others or we are more patient with certain students than others, and that our own attention depends on a student's gender identity or their race. In fact, recent studies point to the potential of mindfulness practice for helping us reduce implicit racial bias (Hirshberg et al., 2022). This kind of noticing might also help us to see patterns that show up across the school community. We might begin to notice, for instance, that students of color are more frequently sent to the office (Skiba et al., 2002) or are underrepresented in advanced courses (Solórzano & Ornelas, 2002).

When noticing inequities or injustices you might also become aware of your own experiences. You might notice that you feel distress, anger, sadness, or even a strong pull to do something. When you notice your experience and name it for yourself, it can be a powerful motivator in learning to act with compassion. As Rhonda Magee (2019) tells us, "Justice begins with our awareness of the present moment, extends through caring for ourselves, and shows up in the love we bring to our interactions with others and our responses to the social challenges of our time" (p. 7). In the next chapter we'll consider what it means to get close to suffering, and how the suffering we experience reflects in part our identities, lived experiences, histories, and community memberships and in Chapter 8 we'll focus on self-compassion resources as preparation for action toward justice.

Developing a Daily Practice for Paying Attention

By now, you may be realizing that it takes practice to pay attention. We invite you to heed Mary Oliver's call for paying attention through trying out the meditation practices and the on-the-spot practice at the end of this chapter. The practices in this book begin with paying attention mindfully through developing awareness of the breath and build to cultivating active compassion. Notice your experiences with the practices, especially as you get more familiar with each practice, and notice if and how you grow in your ability to pay attention to a fuller range of experiences within your days.

Formal Practice: Settling the Mind with Awareness of Breath

To practice paying attention mindfully, we invite you to practice Settling the Mind with Awareness of Breath. This practice can help you calm and focus your mind so that you can begin to cultivate awareness and compassion. You might liken this process to a student who is agitated or who is having a hard time listening—it's important to first help the student settle down so that they can learn. If you encounter challenges with this practice (like your mind doesn't settle so easily), please know that this is common and expected. You may find that some days it is easier to focus than others. The benefit of this practice comes from returning your attention gently to your breath, over and over again. Trust that as long as you are gently returning back to the breath, you are cultivating awareness, mindfulness, focus, and self-compassion.

Begin by finding a comfortable position that allows you to feel a sense of alertness. You can sit in a chair, on a cushion, on the floor, or lie down.

Take a few deep breaths; inhale through the nose and exhale through the mouth. As you inhale through your nose, draw the breath all the way down, letting your belly expand. As you exhale through your mouth, release the breath fully. As you exhale, imagine releasing all the tensions in your body, clearing your mind of any worries or anxieties. Take a few more breaths in this way.

Now let your breath settle into its own natural pace, inhaling and exhaling through your nose.

We provide instructions for several techniques to focus on the breath.

The first involves labeling the breath. As you inhale, silently say to yourself, "Inhale." As you exhale, silently say to yourself, "Exhale." Try that for a few breaths.

The second technique involves focusing on the sensations of breathing. Notice the flow of your breath in and out of your nostrils. Feel the breath at the upper lip and nostrils, flowing in and out of your nose. Feel your belly expand as you breathe in, and release when you breathe out.

The third involves counting the breath cycles. Each time you exhale, count in your mind, "one," "two," and so on until you reach "ten." Then begin again at "one." If your mind wanders and you lose your count, simply begin again at "one."

Choose the technique that makes sense for you and continue focusing on the breath.

Your mind will wander. That's not a problem, that's part of the process. When you notice your mind wandering, let it point you back to the breath. Each time you notice the mind daydreaming or planning or worrying or whatever the mind does, this is an opportunity to bring your awareness gently back to the present-moment experience of breathing in and breathing out.

As best you can, bring a spirit of kindness and compassion to yourself when you notice your mind has wandered. Notice if you are judging yourself or getting pulled by the thoughts. These are simply habits of the mind. Again and again, return your focus to breathing.

Now drop the focus on your breath, and rest in a state of awareness. Notice any effects this practice has had on your mind or your body. See if you can be like a child, when seeing something new and interesting, viewing it with wonder and without judgment.

Formal Practice: Settling the Mind with Awareness of Sound

As in the previous practice, you'll work on paying attention mindfully—this time to sound. You can focus your attention on a consistent sound in your environment such as the gentle whirring of a fan or the low hum of a projector. You may find that one anchor (the breath or sound) works better for you than the other. Bring curiosity to your experiences of both practices.

Invite your attention to focus on the experience of hearing. Open to sounds as they arise, wherever they arise.

Now invite your attention to focus on the sounds in your environment. As best you can, simply open your awareness so that it is receptive to the sounds arising and falling away, waves of sound rising and falling. Noticing sound and also the space between sounds, aware of silence. Aware of sounds simply as sensations.

(continued)

(continued)

As you focus on the sensations of hearing, perhaps also imagine allowing any tension or tightness in the body to wash away as the sound fades in your awareness. Releasing tensions in the body and clearing the mind of any worries with the sounds in your environment.

Whenever your attention wanders, escort it gently back to the sensations of hearing, maintaining your awareness simply on the waves of sound and silence, perhaps noticing pitch, loudness, and duration. Focusing on hearing, as sounds arise and pass from one moment to the next.

Invite the mind to settle through this practice of focusing on the sounds in your environment.

Now let go of the focus on the sounds in your environment, and just relax in the open space of mind.

On-the-Spot Practice: Cultivating Awareness in Everyday Activities

On-the-spot practices are brief contemplative practices intended to help you practice mindfulness and compassion in the moment, even in the middle of a busy day. In this on-the-spot practice, we invite you to choose one activity that you engage in every day at school or work where you would like to bring greater awareness. It does not have to be a big event, and in fact the practice works best if you choose a very small moment in your day to pay attention to. An everyday activity could include walking into the door of your school or classroom, greeting a student, eating your lunch, giving feedback to a student, or checking email. If you'd like, you can also try this practice outside of school. For instance, you might bring awareness as you brush your teeth or cook dinner.

Each time you enter into the activity, pause for a few seconds to notice your breathing. Notice any thoughts or feelings that might be arising at this moment.

Pay careful attention while you do the activity. Notice any sensations that are present. For example, as you walk into the school building each morning, pay attention to the movement of your hand as you push the door open, the air temperature on your skin, the way the ground feels beneath you, the subtle smells that arise, or the sound of a colleague's greeting.

You may notice that your awareness wanders elsewhere during the activity. You might think about the past or the future. Gently come back to the experience of the activity.

Repeat this practice each day, bringing awareness to the same everyday activity.

Sarah, an elementary world language teacher in a rural district, shared her experience of this practice noting, "When I was approaching the activity as something that needed to be done, to be checked off my to-do list, it brought me anxiety and frustration. When bringing presence and focus, I noticed it was more meaningful and enjoyable." Fabi, an elementary teacher in a large urban district, chose to bring awareness when talking with students who did not appear to be engaged in her class. When she first began, it was difficult to stay mindful and present. She worried about the other students in her class who she felt were also waiting for her attention. Fabi noted that as she became more consistent with her formal practice of Settling the Mind, her everyday awareness practice became easier and she "started feeling more relaxed and aware of my own feelings and thoughts and was more patient with myself. I also noticed I was enjoying my days at school and being with my students a little more." As you bring awareness to everyday activities, see if you can approach the practice with presence and focus, and perhaps you may even find yourself "astonished."

Journal Reflection: Planning for Daily Practice

In your journal, make a plan for daily practice that works for your life right now. Be realistic. Then, share your plan with someone else to help hold you accountable.

Key Ideas from the Chapter

- Our minds wander, but with practice we can cultivate mindful attention to the present moment.
- Practicing mindfulness can be for the benefit of others and arise from an awareness of how our thoughts, words, and actions impact others.
- We can pay attention to equity, applying mindfulness to suffering that impacts students and colleagues from marginalized and minoritized communities more than others.
- We can cultivate awareness through formal meditation and through attention we give to everyday practices.

Chapter 2
Getting Close to Suffering in Our Schools

When it comes to systems of oppression, we have many students who, unfortunately, coming out of poverty or marginalized communities, continue to face systems of oppression that are built-in by our schools themselves. For example, one student, because of having multiple behavior issues in the beginning of the year, the opportunity to learn with his classmates has been taken away through the rest of the year. How we contribute to systems of oppression that create and continue to create barriers for our students and continue to further marginalize them, it's hard to see or to notice sometimes, but this one's kind of blatant. Instead of setting them up for success, a family that is already struggling in life, it is just continuing to create those barriers to education, even social and emotional learning and development for a student like that.

—Raquel, K-8 School Social Worker

It was my (Ashley's) first week teaching in a new school, but I was not a new teacher. One of my strengths was the ability to forge strong and positive relationships with my students and foster a sense of belonging in my classroom. So, it took me by surprise when two students began physically fighting in the back of the classroom as I was dismissing the class. Concerned for their safety and the other students' safety, I stepped into the middle of the altercation and stopped the fighting. Another teacher, who was alerted to the struggle, appeared, scolding me for intervening. The teacher then told me, "Next time, just let them fight. It's the fastest way to get students kicked out of your classroom and put into in-school suspension." Stunned and heartbroken, I wondered how I could possibly teach students who weren't in my classroom. I knew my students had been suffering, even before they began fighting (and maybe that's what led to the fighting). I also knew that my colleague and many other teachers in my school were exhausted, stressed, and overwhelmed, and they needed resources to support themselves and their students. The accepted practice at the school was to allow fights to continue, so that the policy of issuing punishment in the form of in-school suspension could be enacted. As a school, we added to students' suffering, further isolating them, when in fact they needed connection and someone to help them develop more peaceful ways to navigate conflicts with peers. The school also ignored teachers' suffering, which in this case, further compounded students' suffering. It was clear to me that our school was in desperate need of healing. Unfortunately, scenes like the one I describe and the example from Raquel at the start of this chapter are far too common in many schools. We need to work toward healing in our schools.

Suffering in Schools

While schools can be vibrant places of learning and joy, the reality is that they can also be places of suffering for students, their families, and educators (Dumas, 2014; Garcia, 2019). The policies, systems, and structures within schools can lead to or increase the pain and suffering felt by students, their families, and educators, especially those from marginalized and minoritized communities. The lived experience of suffering depends on students' social locations—that is, their race, ethnicity, gender, sexual identity, disability status, class, language, and more (James et al., 1998). Many children sit at multiple social locations where they suffer from policies that cause harm, such as Black girls who face consequences from disciplinary policies that impact Black students disproportionately and label Black girls as dangerous (Annamma et al., 2019). Researchers have documented many different forms of suffering that can arise in schools, such as feeling isolated, unseen, and left out when people who look like them aren't shown in the books or curricula they use in schools (Teeters et al., 2022). Researchers have also shown that students suffer when they are excluded from participating in school sports or accessing appropriate restroom facilities because of their gender identity, or made to feel invisible when documents don't reflect their self-determined gender (Meyer et al., 2022). Families of students suffer when they perceive that their children are stigmatized or othered in schools and when they experience challenges in navigating systems in schools that are intended to help them but don't (Lalvani, 2015). And teachers suffer when they feel there is no place to address their own stress, overwhelm, grief, or loss (Garcia, 2019). These examples speak to the urgent need for compassion in schools.

Compassion invites us to see suffering, to turn toward it, and even to get close to it, just as Raquel, the educator quoted at the beginning of the chapter did. As you read this chapter, you might see your students' or your own experiences reflected. The chapter may inspire you to think in new ways about how you respond to suffering. You might also consider the ways in which policies, practices, and routines—especially those that we take for granted or view as common sense (Kumashiro, 2015)—contribute to suffering in schools. It takes courage to look at suffering in schools in this way, because it means that we are willing to not only get close to suffering but to recognize our part in upholding practices that cause it.

Getting and staying close to suffering may bring up a lot. It might initially feel sad or heavy to recognize suffering. You might notice a tendency to turn away from your students' suffering or even your own. Raquel could have turned away from looking at the suffering caused by a student being excluded from activities because of their behavior, instead choosing to focus on the breach of a rule and their need to be held accountable for it. It's hard to hold both these things together—the need for compassion and for responsibility.

This is where the practices and tools in this book can help—by building our capacity to stay with suffering and get close to it, without getting stuck in it. Getting close to suffering isn't an end point, but it's an important part of the path toward healing in our school communities. Because true compassion doesn't stop with seeing pain. We have an enormous capacity to act, to do something. Compassion invites us to find ways to act to alleviate suffering, and this includes the suffering caused by systems and structures within our schools, as well as how we interact with one another in schools. As one educator told us, "Until we and the school system see it as a community of people that interact and engage, then we're never going to make a difference."

Pain and Suffering

All of us experience distress—physically, mentally, and emotionally—and for some of us, that distress is chronic. Pain refers to a sensory experience we have that is unpleasant and associated with potential or actual damage to the body (Raja et al., 2020). When we experience pain, our minds can react as if this distress presents a threat to our basic well-being—and we recoil. While pain is experienced individually, it's shaped by expectations developed through past experiences and beliefs (Atlas & Wager, 2012) and by social factors (Williams & Craig, 2016). While we may have different experiences of and sensitivities to pain, pain is part of our common humanity.

Suffering is related to pain, but it is useful to distinguish it from pain for purposes of understanding compassion. When we layer on top of the direct experience of pain our fears, our anger, our stories, we call that suffering. It's rare for us to experience the unpleasantness of pain without wishing it to go away, without reacting to it in some way. It's hard to let our own pain just be, as a raw sensation in the body. Suffering is that something that the mind adds to the experience of pain—that leads to a different quality of anguish, bound up in our thoughts, feelings, and stories.

The Buddha recounts a story that is helpful for building an understanding of the distinction between pain as a universal experience and suffering. In the *Arrow Sallattha Sutta,* the Buddha's followers ask him to explain how it is that both wise people and unwise people experience feelings of pleasure, pain, and things that are neither pleasurable nor painful. The Buddha's response is to give an analogy, saying that the unwise person is like a person who is shot by two arrows in succession. The first arrow, he explains, inflicts pain. The second, the one that follows, brings about sorrow, lamenting (telling stories about our pain), and a feeling of being distraught. The unwise person resists and recoils from the experience of pain. The wise person, by contrast, has a different relationship to the pain caused by the first arrow. The wise person does not resist, make up stories, get angry, doesn't identify with it in any way, the Buddha explains. The wise person has a relationship of ease and openness to the experience of pain.

Most of us react like the unwise person to pain. The promise of compassion practice is that we build our capacity to relate to pain in new ways, ones that are less reactive, less angry and fearful, and more open to the experience of pain in ourselves and others. Through compassion practice, we don't end pain, but we can come to a more open relationship not just to physical pain, but also to emotional pain in ourselves and others. This is not about becoming stoic or numb: the cultivation of compassion prepares us to stay and be with pain that we might have been afraid to allow ourselves to fully experience. To develop this different relationship to physical and emotional pain, we need to recognize and stay with our own pain.

The Role of Discernment in Skillful Action to Relieve Suffering

There is a role for thinking about pain and suffering in learning how to help relieve it in ourselves and others. Cultivating compassion requires both courage and dedication to understand the causes, prevention, and alleviation of suffering (Gilbert, 2017). One aspect of discernment we need is about the forms and origins of our own and others' suffering.

Understanding our own suffering requires us to understand our own emotional responses to events and their origins. We can ask ourselves and begin to notice: What happens when I experience pain? What happens when I see pain in others? Most of us instinctively react to pain in ourselves and others with fear, anxiety, or anger. These emotions can make it hard for us to stay with pain, unless we grow familiar with them and learn to notice the situations in which they arise. We can also reflect on where we learned about emotions and how to relate to them. While all humans feel and have common basic needs, we also all learn about emotions in the crucible of family life from our caregivers and siblings at home, through observing their reactions to us and through the stories they tell about us (Eisenberg et al., 1998; Miller et al., 1990). We also learn about emotions from our teachers, specifically what emotions they show and how they model how to manage emotions; some of us who experienced social–emotional learning got explicit instruction in how to relate to our emotions (Meyer, 2016). All this "training" in emotions we get from participating in the different cultural contexts in which we live is deep and includes how to code certain sensations as particular feelings and emotions, how to tell stories about our feelings, and what kinds of feelings are acceptable for different kinds of people through interaction (Miller et al., 1997).

Our own internal suffering has an interpersonal dimension that shows up in our everyday interactions, interactions that are in turn shaped by community dimensions as well, namely the cultural values, beliefs, and practices to which we are exposed in our families, our schools, and other settings. To develop discernment about the interpersonal and community dimensions of suffering that we encounter in ourselves and others benefits from bringing multiple lenses to bear on suffering. A significant amount of suffering originates in different forms of oppression. These include violence, exploitation of people's labor, exclusion and marginalization, domination through the exercise of power over people to limit their autonomy, and taking a dominant group's cultural values and ways of being as the expected norm for everyone (Young, 1990). These causes of suffering influence interactions that take place in school communities, and we can get a sense of how by reflecting on how adults exercise authority over students, which students are more subject to harsh punishment than others, the status hierarchies that emerge within student peer groups, and whose faces, ideas, and histories are represented in the curriculum, celebrated at school events, and displayed in hallways. The systemic roots of these practices are important to discern—if we are to identify and transform problematic practices that cause suffering in our schools. Similarly, it's helpful to ask ourselves: "What systems might we create, if compassion were our conscious intention for being the basis of organizing our society" (Jinpa, 2015, p. 232)?

Oftentimes, as educators we *do* see how these causes of suffering are operating, but our schools are not set up to respond to them. This is not uncommon in organizations, where unskilled or insufficient responses to the inevitable challenges can make things worse for people (Frost, 2003). But some of these causes of suffering are a byproduct of our systems and processes, and we can prevent suffering (Kanov, 2021) by changing those systems and processes. This is the kind of suffering we'll return to in the book's last section, as we share tools and resources for diagnosing causes of suffering in school policies and practices and addressing them through collective action.

There are other causes of suffering that show up in our schools, as well, that relate to the life experiences of people in our school communities. Some people have experienced trauma. Some have become separated from people and places or lands they love, whether through death, family conflict, moving, or immigration, both forced and voluntary. Students may be facing food or health insecurity, which can contribute to a range of emotional, behavioral, and academic problems for them (Shankar et al., 2017). Others may be unsheltered or experiencing housing insecurity. Whether or not we are aware of the causes of suffering for the children, families, and colleagues in our building depends partly on our own experience and biases, and partly on whether people have the kinds of relationships to one another in the community that creates the sense of safety required for sharing one's experiences of suffering. These causes of suffering also can be addressed through policies developed and enacted by people working together, sometimes in partnerships with external organizations that can help address the needs that arise from these kinds of experiences.

Beginning with Cultivating Awareness of Our Response to Pain and Suffering

In the midst of such complexity, it can be hard to know where to start to make changes in our lives and our schools. Fortunately, the first step toward compassionate action is clear: awareness. We first need awareness of the ways we relate to our own reactions to the pain we experience and see in the world, that is, to suffering. It helps to start in the body, with how it feels there, when we are in pain and when we are reacting to it. We can notice where our thoughts go, and the stories we tell ourselves when we are in pain or in the presence of another's pain.

Becoming aware also involves becoming more conscious of how our own experiences can lead us to close off empathizing with others and acting compassionately. We can also reflect in writing or with trusted friends to gain some perspective on how our experiences bias us toward some ways of relating to our emotions or appraising situations where there is suffering. We also need to become aware of the views we hold that make it difficult to turn and face suffering and respond to it with an open heart. An obvious obstacle to compassion is if we feel a strong dislike or even hatred toward someone. Not only does hatred cloud our ability to discern suffering in others, but it also makes it more likely that our response to suffering will perpetuate suffering or even make it worse. As Martin Luther King, Jr. (2010) wrote, "Hate cannot drive out hate, only love can do that" (p. 47).

Other obstacles to compassion are more subtle, and perhaps difficult to see. Pity is such an obstacle, that is, when we see the suffering of another and compare ourselves to the other. Feeling sorry for someone is grounded in a view of others as less-than-us, and it makes it difficult for us to appreciate that we, too, could experience suffering like this, and to open our hearts in a way that greets another as a whole human being who is suffering now, rather than as someone who is defined by their suffering. Seeing someone as less than can involve holding *deficit* views of another person, tied to their racial or ethnic identity, their gender or sexual identity, or their family or community (Valencia, 2010). In educational contexts, deficit views might take the form of believing some students—by virtue of a social identity they hold—are "less prepared for learning" when they arrive at school, less able to participate because of their "lack of parental support," or less motivated because of their "disinterest in school." Such views are often hard to see and change, because we may have experiences with students whom we can't seem to reach or impact that we think these beliefs help us explain. Our schools and societies are structured to make it hard to see deficit beliefs because power systems benefit from individualizing these challenges rather than seeing them as systemic and interdependent. Searching for explanations, we often turn to personal characteristics, forgetting the systemic and interpersonal dynamics that may help explain our own difficulties. Addressing these problematic views requires both a change in perspective—toward becoming curious about how the world looks from this other person's point of view—and also a turn to face our own reactivity and emotions about not being able to reach a student.

Even if we work through beliefs and views that inhibit our wishes for others to be free of suffering, we may still doubt what we can do about suffering. It might put us at risk to show compassion for someone whom others do not believe deserves it. We ask, "What will happen to me? What will others think?" We might also feel hopeless or despair that anything can be done about the suffering. We may think there's simply no escape and adopt an attitude of stoicism or resignation. These views get in the way of compassionate action, and we need to discern when they are present either alongside other problematic views or even alongside a wish to make a difference in eliminating suffering.

Learning to Get Close to Suffering

It's not always easy to get close to suffering. We can't simply will ourselves into this kind of awareness. But we can strengthen our capacities to be aware of pain and discomfort through contemplative practice, reflection, and inquiry into our own and others' experiences of pain and suffering. This includes investigating and acknowledging our own biases. One important step toward attuning to suffering in our school communities is by understanding who we are and how who we are is shaped by our contexts, relationships, and communities we are a part of. We can then begin to recognize and acknowledge the ways in which who we are makes visible or obscures pain experienced by those around us. We can work to become aware of our own gaps in understanding. Being aware of and addressing our unconscious bias is essential as we engage in compassionate action, so that we can take action that is skillful. It's important to note that we need to build up our skill over time, starting where we can and where it feels possible to generate a feeling of awareness and concern for someone who is in pain. Practicing loving-kindness and compassion for a loved one is a helpful place to start the path to engaging with pain and suffering.

Formal Practice: Loving-Kindness and Compassion for a Loved One

To build the foundation of noticing and responding to suffering you can begin by cultivating loving-kindness and compassion for a loved one. This practice helps you to realize your natural capacity to attune to another's suffering and to care about them. Loving-kindness is a genuine wish to see another be happy, joyful, and safe.

In this practice, adapted from Jinpa (2015) and Compassion Cultivation Training© (CCT™), you may select someone who is dear to you at school, such as a student or colleague, or you may select someone in your personal life, such as a family member or friend or even a pet. As you begin the practice, we recommend starting with someone who is uncomplicated for you. Whom you choose is not as important as your intention to cultivate loving kindness and compassion within yourself.

In this meditation, you'll think of a time when your loved one was in pain or suffering. This is the first time that you will turn toward pain and suffering in meditation in an exercise within this book. You are invited to notice how you relate to the pain as you begin to notice the emotions and thoughts that accompany it, as well as what's going on in your body. This meditation can evoke strong feelings, but it is also okay if specific emotions and feelings do not arise during the meditation. If the feelings arise, allow yourself to experience them. If not, continue to focus your attention on the words, images, and ideas during this practice. Directing your mind in this way allows your mind and heart to align with the qualities of loving kindness and compassion.

Begin by picturing someone for whom you feel a great amount of love. It might be someone who is dear to you at school, such as a student or colleague, or you may wish to select someone in your personal life, such as a family member or friend or even a pet. Notice any sensations you feel around your heart as you picture your loved one. As you breathe out, imagine that you extend a warm golden light from the center of your heart that carries all your feelings of love. Imagine that this light touches your loved one, bringing them peace and happiness.
Silently repeat these phrases in your mind, for your loved one:

> *"May you be happy.*
> *May you find peace and joy."*

Now think of a time when this loved one was going through a hard time. Notice how you feel when you think of them suffering. Perhaps you feel tenderness, concern, or even a desire to help your loved one.
Silently recite these phrases:

> *"May you be free from suffering.*
> *May you be free from fear and anxiety.*
> *May you find safety and peace."*

Notice the sensations you feel around your heart as you imagine your loved one suffering. As you breathe out, imagine that you extend a warm golden light from the center of your heart that touches your loved one. As it does so, imagine that this eases their suffering, bringing peace and tranquility.
Then, with a strong heartfelt wish that your loved one be free of their suffering, silently repeat these phrases:

> *"May you be free from suffering.*
> *May you be free from fear and anxiety.*
> *May you find safety and peace."*

Notice and welcome any feelings of tenderness and open-heartedness that arose from cultivating loving-kindness and compassion for a loved one.

Journal Reflection: Our Identities and Our Experiences of Pain and Suffering

One way we can organize our reflection is through journaling about pain and suffering. It's important to note that there may also be pain that we are not aware of. As we observe a setting, we might begin to notice people's facial expressions or body language are not all the same, although they are engaging in the same activity. We might notice that our reactions are different from other people's reactions to something and feel surprised by that. Just a moment of engaging with the topic we can see how it affects us in our body, our thoughts, maybe it even calls us to action. Writing about this can help us develop a new relationship to these

(continued)

(continued)

identities—one that is more flexible and allows us to see clearly the strengths and limitations of where we sit in the world for helping us to notice and respond to suffering.

Begin by considering and writing about the social contexts you are in—think about where you have traveled, your family and background, where you live and work, your social circles. Think about your multiple identities and roles, including those that have changed for you over time. These could be identities related to your age, your race, your ethnicity, your gender, your sexual identity, your class, your mental and physical capabilities and challenges, the languages you speak, your immigration status, your religion, where you live, or any practices that make up an important part of who you are. Roles you might consider are teacher, student, child, parent, sibling, or ones that cut across activities and that your friends might describe you as taking on, such as "organizer," "comforter," or "peacemaker."

- What aspects of your identity influence what you notice? What aspects affect what pain you see in yourself and others, and how you respond to it?
- What perspectives do you have special insight into because of where you sit within the world?
- What perspectives might you not see because of where you sit within the world?
- How might the aspects of your identity influence the suffering that you notice or that you don't?

We aren't alone in our suffering, and we can use the suffering we've experienced to connect to others. Let's return to Raquel, the educator whose words about student suffering in schools began this chapter. As a school social worker, Raquel draws upon her multiple identities as a parent, a child, an educator, an advocate, a Latina, and an ally to students of color and LGBTQIA2S+ students to consistently bring awareness to her own emotional experiences and to attune to the suffering of parents and students with whom she works. Raquel shared about a meeting request she received from a student, Max, who was experiencing challenges with their family. Max's parents wanted them to play a school sport. Max identified as transgender and shared that they did not want to play sports because they would not feel comfortable playing on the team the school assigned. As she listened intently to Max talk about their struggles and dilemmas, Raquel noticed her body tense. Bringing awareness to her own physical reaction allowed her to attune to Max's suffering.

Raquel then acknowledged and validated Max's feelings, extending kindness and compassion so that they "felt heard sharing with me." She considered ways to extend compassion and connection to Max and their family. She told Max the ways in which they "make our school special by being at it." Raquel set an intention to "use my voice" to work toward creating "an inclusive school environment for students, normalizing stories of people who are trans or non-binary." Raquel was able to connect with Max because of her own lived experiences of pain and suffering as a child, a parent, and someone who has experienced the impacts of marginalization. Cultivating awareness, recognizing suffering, and considering the perspectives of those suffering—practices she learned in our compassion courses—allowed Raquel to extend kindness and compassion to both Max and their parents.

Perspectives and Activities to Transform Our View

Reflection through journaling isn't the only tool for helping us open our hearts and get close to suffering. We can also actively try on new perspectives about suffering and learn about different ways that people can express compassion, expanding our own repertoire for caring for others in our school.

One perspective we can try is the idea that all people are deserving of compassion. That means that students don't need to earn our compassion, they deserve our compassion simply because they have inherent worth. This is a radically different way to think about our students—the culture of our schools tells us that students need to work hard and follow the explicit and implicit rules of school to prove themselves worthy. We consistently reward students whom we deem as worthy, focusing our attention on this select group. When students don't meet these criteria for worth, we often overlook them or blame them or their families, reifying deficit views.

Let's return to the story at the start of this chapter about Ashley's first week teaching in a new school. If the school and adults in it had viewed students as worthy of care and attention and had discerned about the possible causes of students' suffering, the response to students fighting would not have been to remove them from the rest of the student body, but rather to find ways to acknowledge their suffering, repair relationships, and strengthen connection and a sense of belonging. Compassion asks us to reexamine the ways that we ascribe worth and value in schools, disrupting traditional models of who receives our attention, our patience, and our care.

Seeing all students and their families as deserving of compassion, regardless of the situation, may be counter-cultural in your school. Because of this, we have to consistently challenge ourselves and those around us, especially those who hold power, to truly see the dignity of students and their families. One helpful strategy for doing so is to remember that every student is someone's child, and they are deeply loved by someone. Calling this to mind when interacting with students, invoking rules and consequences, or revising a school policy can help us to see the dignity within our students. We can also practice this strategy when working with colleagues who challenge us—we can recall that the person in front of us was once a child and is someone precious to another.

We can also expose ourselves to different ways people show care in the face of suffering in different cultural communities. What might be considered respect for privacy in one community might be seen as indifference in another. What is required for us to develop skill in compassion is gaining insight into others' suffering and taking an interest in learning about their needs (Gilbert, 2017). It means becoming a person that people can turn to with their stories and becoming curious about how they might want to be responded to, when they are suffering.

Last, we can consciously call to mind people who have mattered to us and shown compassion to us in ways that helped us to grow and become who we are. By reflecting on them, we can consider both what it is they did that showed compassion for us, but also how the ways that they related to us mattered for our own well-being. The activity below is one we include in our course to help educators recall who loved them into being.

Journal Reflection: Who Loved You into Being?

In his 1997 Emmy Lifetime Achievement Award acceptance speech, Fred Rogers invited the audience to reflect upon the people who loved them into being: "All of us have special ones who have loved us into being. Would you just take, along with me, 10 seconds to think of the people who have helped you become who you are, those who have cared about you and wanted what's best for you in life?"

- Who loved you into being and how? If this person is still in your life, the next time you interact with this person, see if you can remember that this person has been loved into being by others. If you wish, write them a letter to share what they meant to you. Or if this person is no longer in your life, share a story with a friend or family member, a memory of this person, and describe what they meant to you.
- Now call to mind someone who is challenging for you, someone who pushes your buttons in some way—perhaps it's a student or colleague, perhaps it's a family member. Who are the people who have loved that person into being?

Remembering that We Do Not Suffer Alone

When we meet our students, or colleagues, or families in ways that value them and honor their inherent dignity, we can shift our response from pity (*I feel bad for you*) to compassion (*I am moved by your pain and wish to see it alleviated*). When we see all people as deserving of our compassion, we no longer see ourselves as better (or worse) than anyone else. Rather, we realize that pain and suffering are part of our shared human experience (Jinpa, 2015). In a *New York Times* essay, Rabbi Sharon Brous recounts a story from the Mishnah, a Jewish legal text from the third century. The passage describes a pilgrimage by thousands of Jews to Jerusalem, where travelers would enter the plaza, turn right, and walk together counterclockwise. Those among them who were mourning or broken-hearted would turn left and walk against the crowd. As those journeying counterclockwise were met with someone walking in the opposite direction who was suffering, they would pause and ask, "Why does your heart ache?" After listening to the response, the traveler would offer a blessing and say, "You are not alone."

This story reminds us that we are not alone and that we can be present for one another in ways that matter. It calls us to show up for members of our school community in ways that signal to them they are not alone. We can also begin to recognize that next time we may be the ones who need comforting. Rabbi Sharon Brous (2024) writes, "This year you walk the path of the anguished. Perhaps next year, it will be me. I hold your broken heart knowing that one day you will hold mine ... We cannot magically fix one another's broken hearts. But we can find each other in our most vulnerable moments and wrap each other up in a circle of care."

Getting close to suffering in this way, we can make a remarkable discovery, that we have enormous capacity to respond to it. Compassion invites us to call upon our agency and think creatively about how we as individuals and we as a community respond when faced with pain. Compassion invites us, as Raquel talked about in the opening quote of this chapter, to find ways to remove barriers rather than "create barriers ... to further marginalize" students, so that schools can be sites of healing. And the compassion practices we share within the pages of this book can help you to grow that capacity and resilience to be with suffering and to respond with care and skill. A key premise of this book is that it's not just individuals who have capacity to respond to suffering, but we can shift, disrupt, and even harness the power embedded within our schools to organize collective responses to social suffering experienced by groups of students. And, we don't have to wait for laws to change or policies to be updated (although these are important actions too)—there are things we can do within our schools today and tomorrow that can make a difference.

On-the-Spot Practice: Seeing Students

This on-the-spot practice invites you to establish a routine with your class or a group of students you work with focused on building relationships with students and recognizing their dignity (Potvin, 2021). We suggest that you try this 5-minute routine at the start of your class period or session at least once a week. This activity should be fun and engaging for students and should not be graded. Set up structures to support students in feeling safe to share in small groups. Encourage students to share with one another, but don't require it.

- Provide a prompt for students to reflect upon and then share with a small group. The prompt should be an invitation for students to share something about themselves, such as aspects of their culture, background, interests, home, family, friends (e.g., *Think of a place where you feel comfortable to be yourself. What's the place and what about the place makes you feel that way? What is one thing about you that you would not change and why?*). When possible, try to connect the prompt to the lesson for the day. After you model a couple of prompts over several days, invite students to create prompts for the class.
- Give students time to reflect and then share in small groups.
- Select a student who you don't know well and join this student's group during the sharing time. This might be a student who you struggle to engage in the curriculum, a student you don't often give much attention to during class, a student who you sometimes view in a negative light, or a student who you cross paths with frequently but about whom you know very little. Listen intently to student sharing, and also participate in the sharing yourself.
- After trying this activity several times, reflect. What was your experience of listening to the student? What was your experience of sharing something about yourself with the student? What new insights do you have about the student?

Key Ideas from the Chapter

- Schools are sites of suffering for students, educators, and families.
- Pain and suffering are different. Suffering involves reactivity to pain in ourselves and others.
- To address suffering, we need to learn how to get close to and stay with pain.
- Responding more skillfully in the presence of pain requires awareness that we can cultivate through meditation perspectives.
- Responding skillfully requires a shift in our perspective, such as embracing the idea that everyone is deserving of suffering.
- We can learn about and reflect on how others show care and compassion, to help extend our repertoire of ways of responding to pain we encounter.

Chapter 3
Curiosity and Friendliness as Resources

may there be a listening
rather than a making

curiosity over expectation,

lightness and ease,
no straining
toward some glut of air.
　　　　　—Andrea Potos, "When Beginning the Poem," in Marrow of Summer

Breakfast is an energetic time in my (Ashley's) home. My 5- and 8-year-old children bound out of bed each day with such gusto, their wonder, zeal, and curiosity for the world bursting forth. They are often so full of stories, questions, and wonderings that they forget to eat. They might wonder about how hot the sun is, how black holes are created, or what koalas eat in a day. Perhaps some of your students are like this too!

Teacher, educator, and psychologist Eleanor Duckworth (2006) writes about the "having of wonderful ideas," capturing the curiosity that children have to spark big ideas. In the moments when I pause and really listen to my daughters' breakfast time stories and questions, I realize that they are inviting me to see the world anew, to experience these wonderful ideas from their fresh perspective. Suddenly we are together in their world, thinking about space or animals or anything else that piques their curiosities that day. It's also easy to miss these moments. Some mornings, I find myself glancing at the clock, wondering if they will be ready for school on time, and then nudging them to finish eating so they can move on to the next part of the morning routine. Other mornings, I think to myself, *"I'm not awake yet, it's too early for such lively conversation!"* It strikes me that within the routine and rhythm of my life, it's easy to overlook these precious opportunities to open to what's unfolding before me. But these breakfast musings serve as a reminder of the power curiosity holds, and of the ways that curiosity can be a resource for staying present with awareness, for considering a fresh perspective, and for recognizing the complexities that these moments offer. It's in reflecting on these moments, too, that I can be aware of my children's curiosity for the world and the way they invite me, with open hearts, to join them.

Curiosity isn't just for children. As educators, curiosity can be an especially useful resource within the context of our busy school days. We often feel pressure to know the answer, to be ready with on-the-spot responses, or to offer immediate and effective solutions. Approaching challenging situations from a place of curiosity can relieve us of the burden to know it all or have the perfect solution in the moment. Strengthening our capacities for curiosity can help us to stay in the present moment and open to whatever arises—joy, suffering, and anything in between—which can in turn help us to consider other perspectives and possibilities. Thus, curiosity is an important inner resource that we can nurture to help us to care for ourselves and others.

In this chapter we'll discuss what we mean by curiosity, and we'll also talk about another resource that can accompany curiosity—approaching what arises with *friendliness*—and we'll share tools and resources for practicing curiosity and friendliness for our own and others' experiences.

Curiosity Helps Us to Be Open

Curiosity supports us in taking an inquiry stance to investigate our own experiences, including our interactions with others. Curiosity is about approaching the present moment with an open heart and an open mind, allowing us to see different perspectives as they emerge from interacting with the world and from others' stories. When we are curious, we gather information about ourselves and the world around us, much as Ashley's children do each morning. Curiosity in this sense requires that we attune to what is arising in the moment, that we approach the moment with "curiosity over expectation" (Potos, 2021). We focus on the details of what's happening in the moment, rather than jumping to conclusions or making predictions about the future or comparing it to the past. Curiosity involves staying open to what's happening by refraining from judgment or criticism.

This kind of inquiry stance helps us to see what we are thinking and feeling. It also helps to distinguish what is skillful and unskillful in our thoughts and actions.

When thoughts and actions are skillful, they are constructive, bring benefit to ourselves and others, and create conditions for compassion to develop more widely and deeply in our school communities (Potvin et al., 2023). Curiosity can help us to investigate our thoughts and actions and can enable us to see when our actions are caring or when they cause hurt to others.

When we take an inquiry stance, we can't always know what awaits us. As we open to the present moment with curiosity, we may find joy as well as suffering. We may discover aspects of ourselves or others that make us feel uncomfortable (Hanson, 2011). Thus, being truly curious, without judgment and criticism, also means being vulnerable and brave. Being curious often means moving outside of our comfort zone and being willing to meet pain or difficulty (Brown, 2018).

Nurturing Curiosity

If that childlike sense of curiosity that occurs at Ashley's breakfast table each morning doesn't always come easily, the good news is that curiosity can be nurtured. We can provide opportunities for wonderful ideas to arise for our students and foster curiosity, and we can do this for ourselves through practice. We may find that our curiosity needs encouragement and nurturing (Engel, 2013), perhaps because we have gained knowledge and experience and the world around us doesn't seem so new.

There's a helpful concept in Zen Buddhism, *shoshin*, the beginner's mind. Beginner's mind is about experiencing something as if for the first time, even when we already have advanced knowledge or experience of it. Embracing beginner's mind is about letting go of expectations or preconceived notions and experiencing the moment with openness and curiosity. As educators we often feel pressure to know the answer and be ready with quick and effective on-the-spot solutions. But beginner's mind, the sense of not-knowing, is a strength rather than a weakness. Beginner's mind is something that awaits us whenever we tap into it. One meaning of beginner's mind is that we can always "begin again," no matter how far we feel we have strayed from the present moment, no matter how far our hearts and minds feel from being at peace.

Beginner's mind provides a different stance for approaching and responding to a parent's question, a challenging interaction with a student, or a conflict at a faculty meeting. It gives us permission to first be present and curious about the challenge before us, taking pressure off ourselves from the need to give a ready answer or response. It also allows us to lighten up, knowing we can always begin again if it turns out our initial response isn't a beneficial one. Each time you try a practice offered in this book, we invite you to bring a beginner's mind, to experience the practice as if for the first time and to see what happens when you nurture your curiosity.

Formal Practice: Nurturing Curiosity— Mindfulness of Feeling-Tone

Curiosity requires a willingness to be open and to investigate, knowing that what you discover could be pleasant or joyful, or it could also be neutral or unpleasant. One tool for staying in a curious place about what arises for us is to cultivate something called mindfulness of feeling-tone. Feeling-tone doesn't mean emotions, but rather a basic reaction our minds have to the things that come into our minds or that we see, hear, touch, taste, or smell. If we pay close attention, each of these things gives rise to one of three types of feeling-tones: pleasant, unpleasant, and neutral. Those feeling-tones themselves are not in any way problematic, but we can build up stories and react in unskillful ways when we grasp onto what is pleasant, push away what is unpleasant, or ignore what is neutral.

In this practice, you'll foster curiosity by focusing on your present experience and noticing the feeling-tone of your experience as positive, negative, or neutral. You might notice the feeling-tone can be connected with a sensation in the body, a perception of something in the world, or a thought or emotion. Importantly, this practice isn't about getting rid of unpleasant experiences, but rather learning to approach unpleasant and neutral experiences with a sense of curiosity, rather than pushing them away or avoiding or ignoring them. With neutral sensations, there can be a tendency to overlook or ignore them. Lots of sensations in our body are neutral. They don't grab our attention one way or another. Equally so, when pleasant sensations arise, the invitation is to notice them. The practice instructions for whatever feeling-tone arises are simple—just notice with curiosity. We don't need to analyze, diagnose, judge, or compare. Different people can and do experience different feeling-tones when we come into contact with the same object. And feeling-tone can change. A food, for example, that we once experienced as unpleasant becomes pleasant, or vice versa. This practice is one that helps us learn to stay with unpleasant emotions and thoughts that often arise, by getting beneath them, to the raw qualities or sensations in the body that we experience as pleasant, unpleasant, or neutral.

We invite you to bring an open heart and an open mind to this practice. In this practice, you will notice whether sensations in the body are pleasant, neutral, or unpleasant.

Take a few deep cleansing breaths. As you do, notice your body relax. Let go of thoughts that may arise, let them float by.

Now turn your awareness to where your body is making contact with the seat beneath you. What does it feel like for the body to be sitting? Feel the sensations of the body, where it touches the chair or whatever you are sitting on. What are those sensations? Bring curiosity to them. If another part of your body has a particularly strong sensation, it's okay to let your attention go there.

Wherever you focus your attention, just see if you can stay with the sensation. Does it stay the same? Does it shift at all?

Now turn your attention to hearing, perhaps to a sound, loud or faint, and bring it to awareness. Notice whether it is pleasant, unpleasant, or neutral for you.

Maybe there's a wish it wasn't there at all, that there be complete silence. Allow yourself to just pay attention to a sound that calls your attention for the next minute or so. Is it pleasant, unpleasant, or neutral?

Come back to the body, turn your attention to some sensation in your body. Again, just notice: Is it pleasant, unpleasant, or neutral? Notice if there are any thoughts that come up when you become aware of whether the sensation feels pleasant, unpleasant, or neutral.

There's no need to pursue those thoughts, just notice the thoughts that come.

And as a final part to this practice, turn your attention to your hands. What are the sensations there? And with those sensations, notice whether they are pleasant, unpleasant, or neutral.

When you are ready, you can wiggle your toes and fingers, stretch, and raise your gaze or open your eyes.

Curiosity About Our Own Experiences

It can be uncomfortable, uncertain, or vulnerable to investigate our own experiences, tendencies, and habits, especially those we don't feel proud of. We might avoid doing so, judge ourselves harshly, or even blame ourselves or others. One of the educators in our program, Stephanie, wrote about a difficult interaction with a colleague that brought her some pain. Stephanie's colleague approached her in front of their vice principal, pointed out a mistake Stephanie made, and then offered to take over the project Stephanie had been leading. Stephanie ruminated over this interaction for days afterward, feeling "attacked" and "embarrassed." Eventually, she was able to bring curiosity to her experience of the conversation. She realized that she had "felt a sickness in my stomach and started to feel as though I failed at my job" and she recognized that she had been "putting myself down for not doing well on this project, comparing myself to others." Once Stephanie was able to investigate her own experiences, she began to let go of the self-blame and to talk to herself as she would a friend. (We will return to the concept of treating yourself as a friend in Chapter 6.) Stephanie recognized that she made a mistake, just like everyone makes mistakes. She was also able to try on a new perspective, that her colleague was "most likely not judging me at all," but simply offering to help.

Stephanie grew from investigating her own experience, noting that she learned to "move on to make things better rather than worrying about it" and setting an intention in future interactions to be "more compassionate and help [the person who made a mistake] understand that everyone makes mistakes." Bringing curiosity to her experience, although uncomfortable and vulnerable, allowed Stephanie to "feel and see conflict as an opportunity to change and remember that my past does not define my future."

As Stephanie's case teaches us, curiosity becomes a useful inner resource, one where we can stay with our own suffering and even avoid adding to our own or others' suffering. We can be accountable for our actions, habits, tendencies, without seeing an unskillful action as defining us. We don't have to beat ourselves up over something we said or did or should have done differently, but rather we can investigate it to determine how to best move forward with care for ourselves and others. Curiosity can help us to stay open to reflection and to set intentions that align our actions with our values moving forward.

Curiosity for Those in Our School Communities

Curiosity can also help us to be better educators. Just as we can bring non-judgmental curiosity to our own experiences, we can bring this same spirit of curiosity to others' experiences. Being curious about our students and their lives can help us to build stronger relationships and connections with students (Neto et al., 2022). Approaching interactions with students with curiosity in the moment helps us to respond compassionately and skillfully rather than react. Adam, a high school teacher at an alternative school, explained that he took away from the compassion certificate the understanding that often students'

> behavior toward me is not about me at all, and that is really helpful because it allows you to be less affected by people's different behavior, but it also allows you to be curious about it. *What's going on with this person?* Wonder why they're acting so swiftly to this one little request I made or this news that's happening. And so that curiosity is a safe harbor instead of reacting, taking things personally, and getting reactive yourself.

When we find ourselves in the midst of an interaction with a student who is pushing our buttons, we can stay open and curious about their experience, perspective, or behavior, rather than jumping to conclusions and consequences. Staying curious can be a "safe harbor" as Adam noted, to help us realize new or different responses to such a difficult interaction.

Noticing what our students are going through and bringing non-judgmental curiosity to their experiences and to our interactions also provides an important foundation for seeing our students in new ways. We may begin to notice, for instance, that the student we thought "didn't care" about our class, actually cares a lot but that the assignment is challenging, or they feel that they can't do it. Rather than blowing off the assignment because they don't care, the student avoids it because they aren't sure where to begin or they lack confidence in their own abilities. Bringing curiosity to why a student appears disengaged in the material can allow us to see new ways of supporting that student and inviting them into class activities. And this kind of curiosity for our students can provide us with important clues about how we might skillfully meet a student's suffering with compassion. One thing that can help with bringing curiosity is for us to notice our own feeling-tones when we perceive a student doing something, alongside the judgments that may arise when we are not paying attention to these feeling-tones.

Thus, practicing curiosity within the context of compassion can also help us to see our students from an asset-based perspective. Professor, author, and activist Shawn Ginwright (2018) invites us to ask, "What's right with you?," approaching students from a place of compassion, healing, and hope. This kind of curiosity builds connection and belonging by "acknowledge[ing] that young people are much more than the worst thing that happened to them, and builds upon their experiences, knowledge, skills and curiosity as positive traits to be enhanced" (Ginwright, 2018). When we are curious about the brilliance of the young people before us, we powerfully recognize their humanity and open to possibilities for skillful and creative responses.

We can apply this same asset-based curiosity to the experiences of staff, colleagues, parents, and families. Our colleagues and students' parents are much more than their problems or the trauma they may have experienced. Like us, they experience joy observing the success of children, and celebrate birthdays, rites of passage, and other milestones where their growth is recognized by others. And like us, they suffer and respond to their own suffering in ways that may benefit from our curious attention.

When another member of our school community does something that provokes an unpleasant response in us, it may be helpful to remember that people may not always reveal what's going on in their lives, but their actions may signal that they are hurting. Once we've attuned to the suffering, we can open to their experience, which can inform a skillful response. We can realize that their experience may not be the same as ours. When we start investigating, we start to notice things we didn't notice before or we see them in a new way. To witness their pain and offer compassion requires "developing both a comfort and a vocabulary to ask humble, gentle, and kind questions about someone's experience" (Worline & Dutton, 2017, p. 35).

On-the-Spot Practice: Responding with Curiosity

The next time you interact with a student or colleague who challenges you, try this on-the-spot practice for responding with curiosity. Listen carefully to what the person is saying, as if with a beginner's mind. Notice any hurt that the person may be revealing to you through their words, actions, and/or body language. Before you respond, take a few deep breaths. Ask yourself, *What's right with this student (or colleague)?* Ask a question aloud about what the person is experiencing in the moment, without judgment and from a place of asset-based curiosity. Notice how it feels to respond with curiosity rather than react, and notice how the rest of your interaction unfolds.

Unconditional Friendliness

We need not only curiosity but also friendliness when faced with suffering. Naomi Shihab Nye (1995) wrote in her poem, "Kindness": "Before you know kindness as the deepest thing inside, you must know sorrow as the other deepest thing." Experiencing sorrow, distress, or pain can teach us to develop kindness; they can become a kind of fertilizer for kindness to grow. We can turn toward these experiences and allow them, knowing that they are necessary for strengthening our kindness. This kindness becomes a power we can share with others and with ourselves.

Taryn, an elementary teacher we worked with, found herself in conflict with a colleague, Cassie, a special education teacher who supported many of Taryn's students. Taryn revealed that she had "many preconceived thoughts" and feelings about Cassie, noting that she was "frustrated with not having support in my classroom, angry that students were not getting the support and help that they deserved." Taryn requested a meeting with Cassie to discuss the situation. Despite her preconceived thoughts about the consequences of Cassie's actions, Taryn stayed open and curious during the meeting, in a way that allowed her to "tear back previous thoughts and just listen to her struggles and pain. I was able to stay present and not be distracted by other things going on." As Cassie shared her professional and personal struggles, Taryn "listened with my heart."

Taryn responded to Cassie's pain by asking, "How can we [the teacher team] help you? What do you need from us that could make things better for you?" Taryn later reflected that staying curious in this interaction allowed her to see Cassie's actions as part of a "larger puzzle." She recognized Cassie's humanity and offered her friendliness and kindness, reflecting, "This conversation was a reminder to go back into 'being'. We are all 'human beings'. As teachers we are asked to be so many things and I can forget to be me."

Taryn paired her curiosity with friendliness, setting an intention to "connect more deeply with my colleagues, so I am aware of situations like this before they become as big," following up with Cassie to check in on her well-being, and practicing "loving-kindness meditations for Cassie in hopes to relieve her pain and suffering."

Recall that in the previous chapter we introduced you to the practice of loving-kindness for a loved one. Loving-kindness is unconditional friendliness. It's wishing someone, including ourselves, joy, well-being, and safety. It has the characteristics of open-heartedness, optimism, and tenderness. Loving-kindness is boundless and boundary-less, there are no limits to true and unconditional friendliness. Pema Chödrön, an American Buddhist Nun, identifies three components of unconditional friendliness. First, it begins with extending friendliness to ourselves and trusting ourselves, "trusting that we have what it takes to know ourselves thoroughly … without turning against ourselves because of what we see" (Chödrön, 2009). Accepting ourselves unconditionally, as we are, supports us in accepting others unconditionally. Second, it requires keeping our heart open so that we can engage in communication from the heart. And third, unconditional friendliness is altruistic and generous. It involves helping others without expecting anything in return. Thus, unconditional friendliness for someone honors their dignity and accepts them for who they are, without imposing our own judgments upon them.

There's a similar concept from the ancient Celts, *anam cara*, popularized by the Irish author, John O'Donohue. *Anam cara* is a Gaelic term that translates as "soul friend," and refers to the kind of friendship that knows no barriers and defies categories. This kind of friendship involves seeing what's good in another person, bringing out their best, and feeling "like you are home" (O'Donohue, 1997, p. 12) in one another's presence. Thus, *anam cara* is also about connection and belonging. Whether we call it unconditional friendliness, kindness, or *anam cara*, this kind of friendship unites us with others, creates belonging, and affirms our dignity. And it's an invaluable resource when we are faced with suffering—whether it be our own or another's.

Journal Reflection: Receiving Unconditional Friendliness

Generate a list of people in your life who have shown you unconditional friendliness, including people in your school community. Think of a specific time when you received this kind of friendship from someone on your list.

- How did they demonstrate unconditional friendliness to you? What did they say or do?
- What does it feel like in your heart, in your body, and in your mind when you think about receiving unconditional friendliness from this person?

Friendliness vs Niceness

It's important to distinguish this kind of unconditional friendliness from "niceness." Unconditional friendliness is honest, even in the face of conflict. The kind of unconditional friendliness and kindness we describe is about accepting people for who they are and as they are and truly wishing them well. It's about honoring and recognizing the humanity of each person. This means that unconditional friendliness may require advocacy, allyship, and difficult conversations when the humanity of another or a group of people is threatened or undermined. Sociologist, professor, and author C.J. Pascoe (2023) warns that "when kindness is not paired with understandings of justice and equality, then it not only does not reduce inequality, but it also obfuscates the fact that inequality is being reproduced rather than reduced" (p. xviii). Therefore, unconditional friendliness cannot be separated from equity and justice work.

In contrast to unconditional friendliness, the goal of niceness is to preserve the status quo, to keep the peace, and to avoid conflict. Being "nice" may mean being silent or turning away when we become aware that others in our school community are suffering, and that some groups are suffering inequitably. Unconditional friendliness compels us to speak up and out, to act, and when necessary to disrupt. Niceness often operates within a school culture to ensure that people in power remain comfortable and in control. Niceness undermines and obstructs compassionate change when it operates as a cultural norm in the school, keeping the peace and maintaining silence in the face of suffering (Gardiner et al., 2023).

If we are working toward compassion in schools, we need to do more than be nice. We need to recognize the humanity of each person within the school community and how suffering is caused not just through individual actions but through collective ones as well. When we get close to suffering, when we are curious about pain and its causes, we embrace people for who they are, we wish to see them happy, and we acknowledge that alleviating suffering can be messy, complicated, uncomfortable. This is especially true as we come to see how school routines or policies contribute to suffering, and as we bring curiosity to our role in upholding these structures. Here is where curiosity and friendliness demand courage—to act with compassion means that we sometimes have to do hard or uncomfortable things so that our students, their families, our colleagues, and all those in our school communities feel valued, cared for, and that they belong.

Nurturing Unconditional Friendliness

It's easy to see how unconditional friendliness contributes to others' well-being. When we offer unconditional friendliness to others, when we wish them safety and health, and when we do so through a lens of equity and justice, these are important forms of showing up for others. Offering unconditional friendliness to others also brings benefits to us. When we are kind, we feel happy. In a study on the impact of kindness, researchers asked participants to keep track of every act of kindness they performed and then count up their kindnesses at the end of each day (Otake et al., 2006). Participants tracked their kind acts each day for a week. And what the researchers found was pretty amazing. Participants who counted their kindnesses reported significantly higher levels of happiness than participants in a control group who did not count their daily kindnesses. The study showed that simply bringing awareness to the kindnesses that people offered during the day helped them to feel happier.

One way to nurture unconditional friendliness is through loving-kindness meditation. Barbara Fredrickson, professor of psychology, has spent decades studying the impacts of loving-kindness meditation. Through her research, she has found that loving-kindness meditation leads to increases in positive emotions such as love, joy, gratitude, hope, and contentment, which in turn leads to strengthening personal resources such as mindfulness, life purpose, positive relationships, and physical health (Fredrickson et al., 2008). Fredrickson concluded that practicing loving-kindness can enhance one's well-being and leads to greater life satisfaction.

Formal Practice: Nurturing Unconditional Friendliness for Someone at School

If unconditional friendliness sounds like a tall order, it's important to know that it can be nurtured with practice. We can cultivate unconditional friendliness toward ourselves and to others, so that this way of relating to others eventually becomes a habit in our daily lives. Imagine for a moment that everyone in your school community—staff, students, parents, volunteers—treated one another as friends. This way of being and relating can begin with you and ripple out others, just as it did for Taryn and the way she related to her colleague, Cassie.

We invite you to return to the loving-kindness meditation we introduced in the previous chapter. This time, call to mind someone whom you don't know well at school. As you practice, bring curiosity and unconditional friendliness to yourself, especially when the practice feels challenging. When you experience resistance to doing the practice or when you notice your mind is wandering, be gentle with yourself and investigate your experience.

Remember that curiosity and friendliness are important inner resources that we can nurture and that in doing so we can bring benefit to ourselves and to those around us. We can call upon these inner resources when faced with challenge and difficulty, including when we are working to repair harm and move toward healing in our schools. We'll return to the concept of unconditional friendship in Chapter 6, when we take up the idea of treating ourselves as we would a friend.

Key Ideas from the Chapter

- Curiosity is a resource to help us when we encounter the unexpected or when strong emotions or responses arise within us.
- We can cultivate curiosity through meditation that attends to feeling-tone, that is, whether what is arising is experienced as pleasant, unpleasant, and neutral.
- We can bring curiosity to interactions by approaching them with beginner's mind.
- A complement to curiosity is unconditional friendliness, which we can cultivate through loving-kindness meditation.
- Unconditional friendliness is not the same thing as being nice; acting with compassion may require actions that don't seem nice but that interrupt suffering.

Chapter 4
Setting Intentions to Act Compassionately

"Attention is a limited resource. It creates relationship and intention—attention leads to intention, which leads to action."
—*Robbin Wall Kimmerer,* Braiding Sweetgrass: Indigenous Wisdom, Scientific Knowledge, and the Teachings of Plants

Early in our compassion certificate, we introduce the practice of intention setting. It is a simple practice of checking in with ourselves about our deepest aspirations for how we want to be in life, when we begin our day. A helpful time to set intentions is at the beginning of the day, and intentions, as we will show later, can be set at the beginning of any activity as well. An intention is not the same thing as a daily goal, where we name a task that we want to complete that day and cross it off when we've completed it. Rather, an intention expresses something deeper about how we want to show up for others in our lives. It is not an item on a to-do list, but more like a compass that can remind us of our "true north," our deepest wishes, wherever we are standing. Intention setting prepares us for the inevitable difficulties we face every day, keeping us grounded and able to face whatever arises with an open heart (Jazaieri & Rock, 2021). It is helpful to engage in intention setting regularly—even if our intentions don't change very much—because it's easy to forget our deepest intentions when we are busy or life is challenging.

Deep intention setting work involves orienting ourselves to the values and aspirations that we hold dear and to the reasons we went into education in the first place.

People today often ask, "What is your 'why'?" in your work, to get at the underlying motivation or reason for the work you do. Getting at our deepest intentions might require more time than is given in a professional learning workshop to write down your "why" though. Our deepest intentions are grounded in the values we hold most deeply, values such as speaking the truth, being kind, or affirming the dignity of all beings. Our intentions may not just have to do with work, either. They are likely to apply to all our interactions with others, wherever they might occur. It's hard to maintain integrity to one's deepest intentions if we make a sharp division between how we are at work and how we are at home or with our friends.

Many programs like ours that work with educators use intention setting as a core practice. For example, the Cultivating Awareness and Resilience in Education (CARE for Teachers) program, developed by professor of education, Patricia Jennings and her colleagues, incorporates intention setting at the beginning and throughout the program. The program frames intention setting as a way to align one's actions with a vision of one's "best self" (Jennings & DeMauro, 2017, p. 238). To help set their intentions, program leaders ask teachers to craft an intention and picture themselves acting in alignment with that vision. Teachers then share their intentions with peers in the program and check in periodically on how well their actions are aligning with their intentions in their everyday lives.

For teachers and leaders in programs like CARE, intention setting is taken up as a practice with benefits that are easy to perceive. As one teacher in CARE put it, her mindfulness practice and intention setting practice helped her to be less reactive when she was angry, to ask herself, "Do I really want to say something sarcastic, or do I want to take a moment and think about whether that's really something that I want to express?" (Schussler et al., 2019, p. 516). In a related program for educational leaders, active participants said that practicing intention setting helped them learn to prioritize self-care and to practice generosity (Schussler et al., 2020).

In our own program, teachers report this simple practice can be powerful for helping them to prepare for difficult conversations. For example, one of the teachers who helped co-design our course, Adrienne, was anticipating a difficult phone call with a parent about their child's behavior in her class. Adrienne set an intention to show compassion for the parent and to focus on a wish she imagined sharing with the parent—that the child be happy and successful in her classroom. At the beginning of the call, the parent was upset and screaming at her. Adrienne breathed in, and she reminded herself that she and the parent both wished for what was good for the child. When the parent finished talking, Adrienne then responded calmly, explaining the situation and shining a light on the many successes the student had in class. The two spoke for a long time, and by the end of the call, the parent even thanked Adrienne. Adrienne later reflected that setting an intention prior to the call allowed her to remain calm and keep the focus of the call on the student.

Our intentions really do set the basis for what we think, say, and do, which in turn impact others. An elementary PE teacher in our program, Stephanie, had begun her day with an intention to be patient and calm. When Randy, a student who often runs away from teachers, came running down her hallway near the gym, she asked calmly what he was doing, and if she could show him something. She showed him a picture of her dog and cat on her phone, to which Randy reacted, "Oh, my gosh, they are so cute." The teacher then invited Randy to sit down on the bench to do some breathing in and out with her, and Randy agreed. Together, they took some deep breaths, Randy alongside Stephanie. For the moment at least, Stephanie's intention to be calm benefited Randy. He had stopped running, was able to experience a moment of joy, and practiced breathing with the teacher.

Guidance for Setting Intentions

When setting intentions, it is useful to keep several things in mind. First, pause to connect with what moves you deeply. Perhaps it is the motivation that originally propelled you into education in the first place, or to pursue leadership in schools. Perhaps it is a motivation to serve others through your work that someone in your life inspired you to pursue. It could also be a motivation to become part of a wider effort to make the world a better place not only for young people but for all beings. Our motivation can reflect aspirations that may feel out of reach today—either because we still need to develop skills to realize them, or because they require many people working together over many generations to bring about a more just and sustainable world.

Second, focus on your deepest values. What values—such as integrity, reciprocity, respect, care for others—do you hold? What values guide you when you make important decisions or when you are faced with how to handle a difficult situation? Pausing to reflect on or write about what your deepest values are and why those values are important to you can also help refine your sense of how and why the intentions we set and the actions we take matter to us. Developing intentions that align with our values can bring us closer to what is most important to us. Our values also can remind us that how we go about realizing our intentions matter: we need to be mindful of how our efforts do or don't reflect our deepest values.

Third, when setting intentions, be specific. An intention can be something you hold for a year, a month, a week, a day, or even an upcoming event that is consequential for you in some way. It can serve as a way of priming yourself to be or act in a certain way with respect to a person or situation that matters to you. One of the teachers in our program, Brittany, related the story of how she often journaled about a colleague who had once been a close friend. She and her colleague had lost their trust in one another, and in her journaling, she reflected on all her interactions with her. Through that journaling, Brittany realized she had an intention to repair the friendship. At the end of the school year, a card appeared from this teacher that read, "Thank you for all your patience and compassion with me this year. I know it hasn't been easy." Reflecting on the experience,

Brittany said, "This card is the artifact of everything that I've really intentionally and consciously done, put into practice. That was a beautiful moment. And I really do think we can move forward. That card was it for me."

Formal Practice: Setting Your Intentions for Your Work as an Educator

The Setting Your Intentions for Your Work as an Educator practice is one that we introduce to educators in the first course of our compassion certificate and revisit several times throughout the certificate. We encourage you to do the same; set your intentions through this practice and then periodically revisit the intentions, allowing time and attention to help you clarify your intentions. Following the practice, you may also find it helpful to journal about your experience of this practice, and to capture your reflections and intentions.

Recall a time in your life when you encountered an educator with whom you felt a strong sense of connection. If no educators with whom you feel connected come to mind, you can also call to mind someone who has inspired you in your learning, even if you never met them, or someone from whom you have learned important lessons, even if that person was not a "formal" educator in your life. This person, for instance, could be a coach, a minister, a community activist, or a neighbor.

When you call this person to mind, whoever it is, notice how it makes you feel inside. As best you can, bring up an image, or memory of them, something that brings to mind the connection you feel with them. Allow that and any other memories that come up to just linger in your awareness. Just sit with this memory and sense of this person and their importance in your life.

Now consider the following questions:

> *In what ways is this connection important for me?*
> *In what ways does this connection influence my life and my work?*
> *In what ways does bringing this educator to mind inspire me to be the educator I want to be?*
> *How does bringing this person to mind connect to my deepest hopes and aspirations about my work in my school community?*

Stay with these questions and see what answers come up. If no specific answers surface, that's okay; simply stay with the open questions. If and when answers do arise, acknowledge them and notice whatever thoughts and feelings they may bring.

Working with Intentions

Working with your intentions requires wise effort. Some of us hold tightly to our goals in life, and we use them to beat ourselves up when we don't achieve them. For those of us who hold tightly to goals, it's helpful to remind ourselves that our intentions aren't the same as goals, and hold our intentions lightly and with care, as we might hold a stone in our open palm. Others of us tend to go with the flow, with whatever is happening around us. We might follow someone whom we regard as a leader or adopt the intentions our partner sets for how to live. For those of us who go with the flow, it's helpful to remind ourselves that there are many possible intentions we could set, and we might need to put a little more effort into practice with finding our own intention. We might need to relate to our intention as we might hold a stick in a rushing creek, feeling our strength to keep it still in the face of moving waters. A helpful intention is something that, on balance, nourishes us and helps us move toward wholeness, rather than burdens us or introduces another "should" in our lives.

No matter who we are, it's helpful to work with our intentions by returning to them daily. You might write your intention on a sticky note and post it on your mirror or against the wall in your classroom or office. You might say it out loud as part of a morning ritual. The point of working with an intention daily is to create a relationship with our intentions that we feed and care for. Each day we return to an intention, it may feel a little different. Some days, our intention will truly inspire us. Other days, it might remind us that we feel out of touch with it. By cultivating an ongoing relationship to our intention, it begins to act as a compass, telling us where we are relative to its north pole.

It is useful to share your intentions, out loud, with people you trust. This is one of the roles of a close friend, as described in Chapter 3: to be someone in whom we confide our deepest intentions for our life. If you don't have a close friend or someone you trust to share your deepest intention, you can say your intention out loud in front of the mirror or to an animal companion (a pet). It could be that you share this intention as part of some special meeting with a friend, too, set aside just for this purpose. Some of us may have communities with whom we can share our intentions out loud, as part of ceremony or ritual. Treat the moment of sharing your intention out loud with others as a special moment, set apart from your day-to-day activities. As Robin Wall Kimmerer (2015) says, "Ceremony focuses attention so that attention becomes intention. If you stand together and profess a thing before your community, it holds you accountable" (p. 249). If you are reading this book with colleagues, we encourage you to set aside time to share your intentions with one another.

Sometimes, we feel as though we can't possibly realize our intentions. It's useful to try and work tenderly with feelings of "I can't" as they arise. With intentions, it is easy either to give up on them, or resist taking up intentions that feel beyond our capacities to accomplish. A feeling that we've "lost our way" for days or weeks on end can arise, but it's useful to tell ourselves that we never really left the path once we set our intention. It's just that any path is going to involve some wandering. We can use setbacks and distractions as part of our path to realizing our intentions; all we need to do is view what's happened with friendliness and restate our intention to begin again. The ability to begin again is always there. Sometimes, we are clear in our intentions, but it's not clear how to realize them in a particular situation. For example, we find ourselves in a situation that makes us really upset—maybe it's a familiar one even—and we are not sure we can act in a way that is kind or compassionate, even though that is our intention. In that moment, one intention we can set on the spot is simply not to try and make things worse. And we can see if we can make friends with the feelings that arise when we "don't know if we can" do something that is kind and compassionate when we have completely lost it inside.

Dedication Practice

A complementary practice to intention setting is dedication. A dedication practice involves spending some time each day reviewing your interactions with others with respect to your intentions: In what ways did you realize your deepest intentions today? A dedication can be a tool for routinely checking in on the efforts related to our intentions and for staying focused and committed to our intentions, even when our intentions are not yet fully realized. A dedication practice can involve making a wish that whatever benefit your thoughts, words, and actions may have had on others with whom you interacted impact those beyond your immediate circle. If it helps, you can picture in your mind the people you interacted with and shared a moment of care going on to their next interaction and feeling a bit lighter and more open to that person, and so on (see the following Formal Practice inset).

Taking time also to rejoice in our efforts and actions is another practice that can be undertaken alongside dedication. We can pause after an activity or at the end of the day to appreciate those moments when we have acted in accordance with our deepest intention and, as a result, some other living being has benefited from our actions. It can help to cultivate our own happiness, and it is also an antidote to becoming discouraged by what we did not accomplish or by our sense of having done wrong or failed to do something to rejoice in our beneficial actions. We can consider, too, in this moment, how amazing and wonderful it is—how fortunate we are—to be in the position to act to benefit others. And when we are done rejoicing in our own actions, we can think about all the actions we witnessed in an activity or throughout the day, whether we committed them or others, and rejoice in them. Such rejoicing helps us see the potential for good in others and the potential for good in humanity. It also can help us feel connected to others who perform beneficial action in a way that can inspire us, rather than lead us to be jealous of them or see ourselves as "less than" them.

Formal Practice: Reflecting on Your Intentions Through Dedication and Celebration

Here is an example of a dedication and rejoicing practice that you could try at the end of the day or week.

Take a moment to reflect on the intentions you have set for the day or the week. You might even return to those you set in the Setting Your Intentions for Your Work as an Educator practice earlier in this chapter. See how much alignment there is between daily interactions and your intentions.

It's important not to get caught up in the details of what you did and did not do. Review the alignment between your intentions and the way you showed up for others. Notice any thoughts or feelings that arise from reviewing and reflecting upon your intentions. Stay with these thoughts or feelings for a moment.

Now call to mind something positive from your day or week, something that brings you joy. Maybe it's an uplifting interaction you had, or it could be your engagement with the practices offered in this book, or even how your learning has helped you to show up more compassionately at school. Stay with this sense of joy or accomplishment for a while.

Exploring Intentions and Impacts Together

In our workshops, one of the community agreements we hold is, "We agree to take responsibility for the impact of our words or actions and address those that cause harm." We have this agreement in place because we recognize that our words and actions affect others, and not always in the ways we intend. In situations where we've hurt someone through our words and actions, it's easy to redirect attention to ourselves—and our good intentions—without acknowledging the harm we've done and the pain it's caused someone. It is extraordinarily hard to sit with friendliness and curiosity in the space of seeing suffering that we ourselves may have caused. If we are committed to a life of compassion, we will sooner or later need to acknowledge the possibility that some of our own words and actions could be the source of suffering, no matter what our good intentions are.

Sometimes, we can pay attention to intentions and impacts together as interactions are unfolding, and this can be beneficial for us and the people who are impacted by what we say and do. One of the teachers in our program, Stephanie, a high school teacher, wrote about a difficult meeting she facilitated with a student's father during a parent–teacher conference night. Stephanie had noticed that her student, Leo, appeared to be struggling in her English class. Leo's writing revealed that some of his struggles pertained to his mental health. After seeing Leo's father on her conference schedule, she set an intention to be mindful and caring when sharing "sensitive material" about Leo's mental health.

By the time it was Leo's father's turn for the conference, Stephanie was running behind and felt "pressured to get back on schedule," reflecting that she "jumped into the conference without much tact" and "repeated the same introduction as I had for other families without tailoring my conference to Leo's specific needs." She realized that the impact her words might have had on Leo's father was not in alignment with her intention to treat this particular interaction with care. Partway through her introduction, she recalled her intention and paused, using a strategy she had learned from the compassion course "to give myself a moment to assess the situation and then respond."

Stephanie decided to read one of Leo's writing assignments to his father, an assignment that revealed Leo felt alone and struggled with his mental health. Leo's father began to cry upon hearing his son's struggles. Stephanie, attuning to the father's suffering, also felt saddened. She paused again and checked in with Leo's father about what he needed at that moment. Leo's father wanted to keep talking, and so Stephanie returned to her intention, approached the situation with curiosity, and then asked the father about his son's previous experiences.

Stephanie later reflected that talking with Leo's father helped her to "understand Leo's reality and the challenges he is facing before he enters the classroom" and recognized that "life for many of my students, including Leo, is quite hard right now." As a result of the conversation, Stephanie realized that "Leo needs his support network to extend compassion because he himself is navigating a lot of other challenges" and Stephanie felt that she could "better support Leo and accommodate his needs knowing his history. I can also introduce him to other educators that may be better equipped to respond to mental health needs."

In reflecting on this experience through writing (see the Writing Activity on field noting later in this chapter), Stephanie refined her intention for future difficult conversations with parents: "I would like to set an intention to enter difficult conversations with more tact. I felt that I rushed into the intense topics in our conversation without much context or warning for this parent. In the future, I'd like to communicate directly but also consider that the content may be hard for a parent to hear and thus should be introduced thoughtfully." Stephanie recognized that while she came from a place of care and intended to enter the conversation with the father mindfully, there were moments where she lost sight of her intention. She also recognized that it was painful for Leo's father to hear that his son was struggling, and she felt some distress at causing him pain. Although the conversation was difficult for both Stephanie and Leo's father, she continued to return to her intention throughout the conversation and offer him care. Rather than abandon the conversation, she persisted, knowing that to be compassionate toward Leo meant communicating and collaborating with his father to support his well-being. Despite her reflections on how she might have handled the situation with "more tact," her revised intention did not shy away from engaging with parents about the well-being of their children, but rather to be direct, thoughtful, and caring in her approach and to continue to consider the impact of her approach on others.

Learning to Act with Consciousness of Both Intent and Impact

So much of our interactions involve our projections onto others about what they must be thinking, what their motives are, what their home life is like. This can take us away from our intentions and can show up as deficit thinking about others, but the big problem is that it's really hard for us to actually know what is going on inside people that is motivating behaviors that push our buttons. Asking about them and showing curiosity helps, but even then, people don't always reveal themselves or even know why they do what they do. We are complex, and the things we do are shaped by lots of different causes and conditions, not the singular motive we construct in our heads for what's making us so angry or afraid. Maybe if we hit pause on trying to figure out our colleagues, our students, their parents, we might just be able to see we are all deserving of compassion.

In our program, one of the ways we invite educators to pause is through the practice of taking field notes of their own experiences. Field notes begin as jottings of snippets of interactions that educators have with colleagues, students, family members, and administrators, shortly after they occur. Later, educators transform the jottings into short narrative accounts, and they reflect on the significance of the events through the lens of the ideas and practices of the course.

We emphasize to educators in the course to use low inference statements, or to stay "low on the ladder of inference" about others when developing field notes. The ladder of inference is a metaphor for describing how close we are to what might be called the bare facts of a situation, in making sense of it (Argrys, 1990). Close to the ground are the observable things in an interaction—what people say, how their bodies are moving, what their actions are. But already, as soon as we focus our attention, we're moving up the ladder by selecting some things but not others to pay attention to. Pretty quickly, we get to interpretations—such as about what someone's motive was, or their feelings, or what might be going on for them to make them respond in a particular way. Higher up the ladder further still are assumptions, conclusions, and beliefs about people and interactions that we make. Field noting is a way to discipline ourselves to stay close to what is observable to us, knowing it's already a selection, and filtered by our own interpretive lenses.

One of our teachers, Stephanie, described the effect of stopping finding fault in others from the practice of learning to stay low on the ladder of inference. Stephanie used one field note to reflect on an interaction she had with a student that typically would have resulted in a power struggle over class participation. Instead, she recognized that the student did not feel confident about his abilities, nor did he feel good about himself and therefore showed up to gym class reluctantly and resistant to participating.

Stephanie "understood that he was looking to be treated with dignity," acknowledging that he wanted to "be happy and feel good about himself, just like I and others do."

In practicing staying low on the ladder of inference, we start to see clearly how our interpretations, assumptions, and beliefs color our experience of interactions. This kind of reflection can even lead us to take our own views less seriously, or to question them. This happened to Taryn, who realized after reading an article in the course that her own perspective was contributing to a difficult situation with a student.

> In this situation my perspective was that this student was making my classroom really loud, making it hard for me to teach and difficult for the class to learn. Then I realized that is just my perspective. When I start to think of other perspectives, a wide array of doors opens. Other students could be watching this play out in my math lesson and be learning how we all learn differently. Or see how I react to another student with care and compassion instead of anger or frustration. Or learn how to become resilient and still focus during times that are loud and disruptive. I could also think about my student's perspective and maybe he was trying to communicate something to me that I was not understanding.

Writing Activity: Field Notes for Identifying Opportunities for Compassion in Your School

Field notes are records of significant interactions you have at school. They can include interactions with youth, colleagues, administrators, and/or parents/families. Recall in Chapter 2 the discussion of pain and suffering. In this activity, you will turn toward suffering by naming a "pain point," an unpleasant experience, such as an interaction or event that can be interpreted with curiosity (Worline & Dutton, 2017). The activity of field noting can help you to bring attention to the conditions in your context that give rise to pain, develop awareness of patterns of interaction involving you that offer opportunities for you to cultivate compassion, and reflect on how you might bring intention and compassion to yourself and others. Your field note could focus on an interaction that happened within the context of your teaching, an interaction you had with another adult (e.g., a colleague, a parent) or with a student, or some other interaction that caused pain and led to suffering. Your field note should be a firsthand account of a brief (5–15 minute) interaction. It will likely be challenging to write field notes in the moment, so we recommend jotting a few notes, if possible, directly after the event and then setting aside time later in the day to complete your field notes (e.g., after school, on a break, at the end of the day).

Field Notes Template

I. Narrative

Describe one brief interaction as accurately as you can, including dialogue, actions, facial expressions, body language, or any other details. *Remember to write the narrative using* **low-inference statements**.

II. Reflection/Analysis

Reflect on the interaction you described above from a stance of compassion. Reflections tend to include more high-inference thoughts, feelings, emotions, and sensations that arise as part of interactions. Use the following prompts to guide your reflection.

- Who was suffering in this interaction? How do you know?
- Why do you think this person/people were suffering?
- Describe how your awareness deepened as a result of this interaction.
- How does your identity shape what you notice and how you respond to this interaction?
- Explain how you offered or could have offered compassion within the situation.
- What intention could you set for how you would like to respond to this type of situation in the future?
- Is there something to celebrate about this interaction?

When there was good alignment between one's intentions and impacts of one's actions, educators in our program came to see the power of intention setting for promoting caring interactions. As one teacher, Sara, wrote in her field notes about a call she was anticipating with a parent about a child who was not meeting her expectations in class:

I was feeling slightly nervous and anxious before speaking to Monica (the parent). So before calling, I made a mental list of all the positive behaviors that Emma had this week. I set the intention that I was calling to work with Monica as a team, not to place blame or call out. On the phone, I made sure to stick with my intention and let Monica know what was going on in school. Monica told me that Emma did not act this way at home, and she believed that it was just her adjusting back to in-person learning. Monica's tone was very calm and understanding.

Setting my intention before the phone call helped guide the conversation. It was very helpful to reflect on this prior to and after speaking with Monica. I was able to "stay focused on what was most important to me and to attain my goals of communication." This helped me to set an intention before contacting Emma's parents.

This kind of intention setting is at a different timescale from asking what one's deepest aspirations are in life or at work, but many of our educators have found it to be a powerful thing to do. When preparing for a conversation they know will be challenging, educators think about an intention for the conversation. Importantly, it is always inspired by that deeper intention—whether to be open, to be kind, or to see the best in people. For intentions for specific activity, research suggests that it can be useful to anticipate some of the challenges that might arise and set an intention for how you might respond to different things that come up in the interaction, especially if it is complex. Rehearsals—used often in teacher education in the context of acting out how a lesson unfolds (Lampert et al., 2013)—can just as easily be used when planning for difficult situations with a student, parent, colleague, or administrator.

Some of our intention setting will lead us to become open to people in new ways, and not all that openness will feel pleasant. After all, there is a lot of suffering in the world, and staying open to others who are experiencing it can be challenging. It's not easy to see through that suffering to another being who holds deep intentions for themselves just as we do, and to hold our own intention to be kind and to benefit others. We turn in the next chapter to how we can understand empathy and compassion in a way that can support us in navigating this challenge.

Key Ideas from the Chapter

- Intention setting is a practice we can do for different timescales to prepare us for action in accordance with our values.
- An intention reflects your deepest values about how you want to show up for others in your life.
- Intentions set the basis for what you think, say, and do, which in turn impact others.
- A dedication practice involves spending some time each day reviewing your interactions with others with respect to your intentions.
- Even when you set intentions, it's important to acknowledge when your words and actions could be the source of suffering.
- Writing field notes can help you to develop awareness of suffering and to consider how you can bring compassion to yourself and others.

Chapter 5
Empathy and Compassion

Just simply noticing the difference between empathic distress and compassion, I got my first glimmer of hope.

—Colleen, Middle School Science Teacher

Many educators we have worked with tell us that they have experienced burnout or overwhelm at some point in their career. Sometimes they find their way into our compassion certificate because, as they tell us, they just didn't know what else to do. They are up at night, worrying about students, they feel pulled in many directions, they are exhausted, and their cups are empty. They feel a sense of distress at the suffering they witness. Perhaps you can relate to some or all of these experiences.

When we are faced with another's suffering—a student describes feeling alone or a colleague confides that they have a serious illness—we can feel empathic care or empathic distress (Ashar et al., 2017). Empathic care and empathic distress are two very different responses; and in fact, neuroscience researchers have found that the two responses activate different parts of the brain (Klimecki & Singer, 2014). Empathic care for others is associated with compassion, as it involves a desire to respond to suffering and to do so with warmth and care for the well-being of another. Empathic distress is a negative set of emotions that causes us to withdraw from others' suffering, rather than respond to it, as a way to protect ourselves from negative feelings (Klimecki & Singer, 2014). In this chapter we will review the research on empathy and compassion, specifically as it relates to empathic care and empathic distress and discuss how cultivating compassion can help us to shift from feelings of distress and overwhelm into a wish that another person be free of suffering and an intention to act.

The Value of Empathic Care for Others

One of the greatest human gifts is our ability to take the perspective of others. Beginning in the second year of life, we can begin to discern the intentions of others. Our ability to do so is something that makes us human and helps us to build up cultural ways of life (Tomasello et al., 2005). It is also something that allows us to imagine what it is others are thinking and feeling, and this is a crucial aspect of empathy (Singer & Klimecki, 2014). The ability to discern others' intentions is also key to sharing in another person's emotion or feeling, without confusing it with our own (de Vignemont & Singer, 2006).

An important aspect of empathy is that it requires our imagination (Batson, 2009b). We can't directly know exactly what another person is going through or see through their eyes. How something looks from another's point of view depends, too, on their needs and desires, and our ability to imagine or sense what these are, from where we sit. It's important to remember this quality of empathy because our ability to imagine another's perspective or what they are going through depends partly on how similar or different we are from the other person. Our imagination is always just that—what we think is going on with the other person. Of course, we have lots of experience to go on, and there are cues that we read all the time about what others are feeling, and there's good evidence that we can and do feel things vicariously when in the presence of someone with strong emotions.

We use the term empathy in lots of different ways, and psychologists who study it do too (Batson, 2009a). It's helpful to distinguish, for example, emotional empathy from cognitive empathy. Emotional empathy involves knowing what another person is feeling, while cognitive empathy involves taking the perspective of another person in a situation. These two forms of empathy involve distinct neural systems (Shamay-Tsoory et al., 2009). Another important distinction is whether we are engaging in "forecasting" or anticipatory empathy—imagining what it might feel like in the future for someone to break a bone or experience the loss of a loved one—and more immediate empathy we feel in the presence of someone who has just experienced those things. A third distinction involves whether we take the perspective of someone else who is in need or imagine what things would be like if we were in that person's situation.

This last distinction turns out to matter a lot for whether empathy leads us in the direction toward helping others or withdrawing from them. Developing empathic care for others—that is, imagining and cultivating care for another person from their point of view and with respect to their needs—leads people to engage in more helping behaviors than imagining situations as if one was going through something oneself (Batson et al., 1987, 2003). We can cultivate this kind of empathic care for another by holding a positive regard for others and cultivating an intention to be open to what others are experiencing, whether it is joy or suffering (Jinpa, 2015).

One of our educators, Tina, related what it is to show empathy that is focused outward, that is, on understanding another person's situation from their point of view. She shared her interactions with Izzy, one of the custodians in her school, in field notes she wrote in our program:

> Izzy was experiencing some frustration and was very professional about the situation that they have to deal with at school this year. Having students come back to the building after not being in school for 1.5 years [due to the COVID-19 pandemic] is an adjustment for them. This pandemic has had an effect on everyone.
>
> Izzy told me that they are very busy since one of the custodians resigned, and now there are only two custodians.
>
> Izzy mentioned that students are vandalizing the restrooms, and they showed me a picture of a boy's bathroom that had red food dye squirted inside the bathroom stall.
>
> Izzy mentioned that they have only taken two lunch breaks during the school year thus far. Additionally, custodians need to work weekends and evenings to support sporting events, musical performances, and other after school activities. Many hours are spent at school. Izzy said they would like some down time for friends and family.

As a school librarian, Tina's day-to-day experiences of the school are not like Izzy's. Relative to Izzy, Tina has more autonomy in her job, gets regular lunch breaks, and probably spends less time outside school hours supporting school events. But we see here a genuine responsiveness to Izzy's experience, facilitated by Tina's active listening, as well as her intention setting practice. She wrote, "I feel like my intention setting helped me to be open and to be receiving the words that Izzy had to share." At the same time, she commented, "My heart felt heavy with the huge amount of responsibility and lack of staff to support the work that needs to be done."

The Limits of Empathy

The kind of heaviness that Tina describes can come easily with empathy. Studies of people's responses to training in empathy show that when empathy is aroused, it can lead to empathic distress, activating parts of the brain that are linked to reports of negative affect (Klimecki & Singer, 2015). Empathic distress is when someone witnessing the suffering of others experiences being alarmed, troubled, upset, worried, or perturbed. This is something that is often mislabeled in the literature and in society as "compassion fatigue," and it is often the result of spending time dwelling in the negative feelings of others (Sheppard, 2015). It's a common experience in helping professions like medicine, nursing, and of course, education. Empathic distress depletes us and is linked to burnout and a desire to leave the profession (Wink et al., 2021).

Empathy fatigue is real, and it's a threat to our well-being as people and satisfaction as professionals.

Another challenge to empathy is that we tend to find it easier to imagine the thoughts and feelings of others who are most like us, and so there is a tendency to offer empathy to those closest to us. This is especially problematic if we don't actively seek to be present to how people are feeling and learn about how they perceive a situation and instead project ourselves into their situation. If the person's life experiences are different from ours, thinking about how *we* would feel, think, and act in a situation can be misleading (Jarymowicz, 1992). We might also unknowingly invoke stereotypes that cause harm rather than cultivate compassion (Vescio et al., 2003) that leads to a skillful response to suffering.

While we can work to expand our empathic care beyond those people in our inner circle—and we will share practices for doing so later in this book—there is no getting around the fact that dwelling in the painful feelings of others can be depleting and, if we are not careful, lead us to withdraw from others rather than to help them or to offer our care for others selectively in a way that reinforces inequity rather than address it.

Moving Toward Compassion

As noted in Chapter 1, compassion has four distinct parts, the first two of which relate to attention and empathic care. Compassion, though, involves two additional steps, including offering a wish that the other person be free of suffering. We visualize them as free from suffering, which can help to generate a positive, at times even a joyful state of mind, instead of leading us to feel distress. The last step involves forming an intention to act to relieve another's suffering.

The movement from empathic distress into compassion keeps us from dwelling in negative feelings that another might be experiencing and moves us to a new place. We can try this now: pause and imagine someone in your life who is suffering now, and then really see them as if they are free of that suffering. It might be a memory, but it might also be something they've not experienced—true freedom from suffering. In allowing us to see this possibility for another, our mind shifts, and we may even open our hearts wider to this person. It may bring us joy, to remember or imagine them to be free of fear, anxiety, or whatever else is troubling them. The key here is to think of the cultivation of compassion as a form of *movement,* from becoming aware of suffering, to cultivating empathic care, to seeing the person as free of suffering, to forming an intention to do whatever might be done to alleviate that suffering.

Formal Practice: Movement from Empathy to Compassion

Settle into a comfortable position, whether seated, standing, or lying down on the floor. Take three deep cleansing breaths, in through the nose and out through the mouth. Then let the breath settle into its own rhythm.

Call to mind a close friend who is going through a difficult time now or has done so recently. Notice first what you are aware of when you do so. What calls your attention in the image? This is noticing suffering. Now turn your attention inward to what this image invokes in you. What does it feel like in the body? Is it pleasant, unpleasant, or neutral? What feelings arise? If stories or thoughts come into mind, notice them, too, but see if you can see them the same way you see the passing of clouds in the sky. This is empathic care.

Now see this person in front of you completely free of the mental and emotional suffering associated with whatever they are going through. They are still going through whatever they are going through, but see if you can imagine them approaching all they encounter with grace, ease, and even joy. Say the phrases,

> *"May you be free of suffering.*
> *May you be completely free of fear and anxiety.*
> *May you greet your life with ease and joy."*

Notice now how that feels inside you, to call to mind this image, again noticing the bodily sensations, feelings, and thoughts that arise. This is the turn toward wishing that the other be free of suffering.

Now with this image before you, set an intention to be of help in whatever way you can, to relieve this friend of their suffering. If you are unclear of how to help, that is OK. There is only the need to set this intention to be of help. This is intention setting, motivating us toward compassionate action.

When you are ready, you can release the image of your friend and return attention to the breath for a few moments.

Close this practice by taking a few moments to write down what came up for you. If you have ideas about how you might help your friend, write those down, too.

Setting an intention to do whatever we can to contribute to this person becoming free of suffering by seeing them whole is itself a powerful place from which to act compassionately. It keeps pity—where we feel sorry for someone else—at a distance. Also, seeing someone as whole or helping them "help themselves" to address their suffering is very different from when we think we are trying to fix someone or their situation. Seeing someone as whole recognizes their dignity by calling to mind their strengths and the resources that are available to them when they are happy and well. They may point us to actions we can take as well, even if it is simply to be present to the other person's suffering and let the other person know you are there.

When offering compassion, it is valuable to remember that others may respond to our compassion in different ways. Unfortunately, in our roles as educators, we see this a lot. We try to offer help to a student, and they ignore us. We suggest a way that a parent can help their child out, and they get angry at us. We offer to help an administrator handle a sensitive situation, but they recoil in fear. How do we handle that? When we receive responses like that, do we want to withdraw our compassion? Do we feel hurt because our care is not received or validated by another? And what does that mean when we feel that way? The inset below offers an intention-setting practice to help us work with this reality.

Journal Reflection: Offering Care and Presence to Another

Roshi Joan Halifax is a Buddhist teacher, anthropologist, ecologist, civil rights activist, and hospice caregiver. In her book, *Standing on the Edge: Finding Freedom Where Fear and Courage Meet,* Roshi Halifax (2018) offers a compassion practice that involves setting an intention regarding both how we can offer compassion to others and how we can receive the response to that compassion:

> May I offer my care and presence unconditionally, knowing that it may be met by gratitude, indifference, anger, or anguish. (p. 83)

Take a few moments to say this phrase to yourself, and notice what arises for you—any thoughts, sensations, feelings. Write down what comes up for you, then return to saying the phrase, and again notice what arises. Again, write down what comes up for you. Then take some time to reflect on your beliefs about what it might look and feel like to give up attachment to outcome, as Halifax (2009) puts it.

The Benefits of Shifting from Empathy to Compassion

Colleen, a middle school science teacher, shared that it was a "really big aha moment" to learn about the distinctions between empathy and compassion and that "just simply noticing the difference between empathic distress and compassion, I got my first glimmer of hope." Colleen is not alone in her experience, as many studies have shown. For example, one study by neuroscientists Haakon Engen and Tina Singer (2015) compared trained meditators' responses to short films of people in distress when passively watching those clips, when practicing compassion meditation, and when using a technique called "reappraisal" in which people generate alternative interpretations of an emotional event. They found that when meditators practiced compassion meditation, as compared to the other conditions, they reported experiencing more positive emotions. In addition, fMRI results showed evidence that compassion practice impacted the neural substrates of positive affect. A meta-analysis—that is, a synthesis of several studies—found that interventions that included training in compassion promoted positive emotions, even though compassion practice can often bring up sadness in people as they call to mind loved ones and others suffering (Zeng et al., 2015). Neuroscientists have proposed that one reason why compassion can produce positive affect is that it helps neutralize the negative emotion that arises when being present to or imagining another's suffering through the activity of generating a positive emotion through seeing the other person as free of their suffering; in this sense, compassion is a way of helping us regulate our emotions (Preckel et al., 2018).

The movement from empathic care to seeing others as free of suffering and setting an intention to help alleviate that suffering can help us to get unstuck from our own difficult emotions that can arise when we focus on another's suffering. As educators, we are presented day in and day out with opportunities to notice suffering in others and in ourselves. And we will indeed burnout and lose confidence in our ability to make a difference in our schools if we get stuck in empathic distress. At the end of the day—and the beginning—compassion is an important resource for building resilience and for responding skillfully to the pain we notice.

Key Ideas from the Chapter

- Empathic care for others is associated with compassion. It involves a desire to respond to suffering with warmth and care for the well-being of another.
- Empathic distress is a negative set of emotions that causes us to withdraw from others' suffering, rather than respond to it.
- Empathic distress, not compassion, depletes us and can lead to burnout.
- Setting an intention and cultivating compassion can help us to shift from feeling stuck in negative emotions to responding skillfully to suffering.

Part 2

Embracing
Self-Compassion
and Affirming Dignity

Chapter 6
Self-Compassion Teaches Us to Be a Friend to Ourselves

The only thing I'm certain of is you
Are the best thing that has ever happened to you
Whoever you are

—*Andrea Gibson,* Boomerang Valentine

Have you ever stayed up late worrying about a student?

Have you ever replayed a conversation with a parent over and over again in your head?

Have you ever second-guessed the way you interacted with an administrator or colleague?

Have you ever felt guilt over not intervening when you noticed a student having a hard time?

Have you ever felt pressure to plan and deliver the perfect lesson?

Have you ever felt that you need to solve every conflict that arises in your school or classroom?

If this sounds familiar, you are not alone. Many educators tend to be quite hard on themselves and blame themselves when things don't go as expected. Kaelyn, a high school teacher, articulated what we've heard from many educators: "Teachers give and give and give and give, and educators give and give and give, but we don't give to ourselves or allow ourselves to have struggles." The educators we have worked with over the years have told us over and over again that they are so focused on helping their students that they seldom attend to their own needs. These educators shared with us that learning to be self-compassionate is the most challenging, rewarding, and relevant aspect of cultivating compassion.

In this chapter, we'll define what we mean by self-compassion and dive into ways that you can begin to treat yourself with the same unconditional friendliness that you so readily bring to others in your life. Throughout this chapter and the next two, you might discover that self-compassion comes easily to you, or you might notice that self-compassion is more challenging for you than offering compassion to others. As you read about, reflect on, and practice self-compassion, remember to be gentle on yourself. You can even offer yourself compassion if you find that self-compassion is difficult! It's the perfect opportunity to turn a kind and curious look at your own suffering.

Defining Self-Compassion

Let's briefly review the definition of compassion. The word compassion means "to suffer with." In other words, compassion is when we meet the pain of another, open to it, set an intention to alleviate that pain, and do so without judgment. Self-compassion is extending that same compassion to yourself in the face of challenges. Self-compassion involves recognizing that suffering is present for oneself, that the suffering is worthy of concern, and that others like us suffer too. It also involves offering a wish that we might be free of suffering. When we offer compassion to ourselves, we are greeting our own suffering like we might greet a dear friend's suffering, with concern and attention and a wish that it be relieved.

To better understand self-compassion, it's helpful to distinguish it from some other commonly used terms: self-care and self-worth. **Self-care** is about attending to your emotional, mental, physical, spiritual needs. Cultivating self-compassion is a form of self-care; everyone deserves it, and no one needs to earn it. Even so, self-care does not come easy for many people, if, for example, you identify as a woman or are from a racially minoritized group (Wyatt & Ampadu, 2022). Ben, a middle school teacher, spoke powerfully about coming to realize that he deserved self-compassion:

> It's not one of those things that we as teachers are trained with. And especially in my household, growing up as a Japanese Chinese American, that was not emphasized. And I feel that's been a real revelation for me, just thinking about self-compassion and believing that I am inherently worthy of that.

There is a risk to self-care, when it isn't accompanied by a deep acknowledgement of how our ability to care for ourselves is bound up with how communities organize care and define who is a carer. We take a relational approach to self-compassion, and we take a similar approach to self-care. Self-care is essential to community care; in fact, we cannot think about these in isolation. In this sense, to be powerful and effective as a vehicle for compassion, self-care has to go beyond individualistic conceptions of self-care focused on establishing inner balance (Wyatt & Ampadu, 2022). A different way to understand self-care is as an essential requirement of social justice work. This relationship was articulated powerfully and profoundly by Audre Lorde (1988), who wrote, "Self-care is not an act of indulgence. It is an act of self-preservation and that is an act of political warfare" (p.125). There's a common saying, *we can't pour from an empty cup*; to nurture one another, we must first find ways to nourish ourselves. Here, though, the goals of caring for self and caring for others are tied to one another. By engaging in self-care and self-compassion, we can cultivate our ability to be mindful in our relationships with others. In the context of schools, through self-care, we are able to join communities of care and work toward more just schools together.

Self-worth involves acknowledging and accepting one's value as a human being. Self-compassion can help improve our self-worth, because it helps us care about ourselves even when we experience setbacks or difficulties. Self-worth is connected to dignity—recognizing the inherent worth and value of every human, including yourself. Dignity doesn't have to be earned. Rather each person, including you, has dignity that can't be taken away. Sarah, an elementary teacher, shared that self-compassion helped her to "tap into this idea that I am worthy of being treated [well], just like students are worthy of good treatment." She also encouraged students to see their own self-worth, telling them, "When someone is not treating you the way that you like, then you need to stop and name it and stand up. It goes to that dignity piece. We are all of value. We are all worthy." As the example from Sarah highlights, self-worth is about recognizing your own inherent dignity as a person and your dignity as an educator, which in turn sets an important foundation for recognizing the dignity in others and modeling it for students.

To be sure, in practice, recognizing our own dignity and value can be difficult. For one, we might make our self-worth conditional upon success in areas that are important to us. As a counter to this idea, we can consider that our success in any endeavor can come and go, but our basic capacity to be present and kind to others is always available to us as human beings. Our worth is not contingent on our success. A second obstacle is that we compare ourselves to others, judging ourselves to be better, worse, or equal to them. These comparisons take us out of our own inner sense of value. One response to when this "comparison mind" arises we can adopt is to offer ourselves compassion for such a thought, remembering that most of us do this and do it in ways that can cause us and others to suffer.

On-the-Spot Practice: Checking In with Yourself

Identify a time to check in with yourself each day, such as when you are washing your hands, going from one class to the next, or at the start of a meeting. Bring curiosity to how you are feeling and what you may be needing at that moment. Ask yourself: *What is this I am experiencing now? How could I meet what's arising inside me in this moment with kind attention?*

Being a Friend to Yourself

Self-compassion is about being a friend to yourself and treating yourself, as poet and activist Andrea Gibson's (2018) lines at the start of the chapter remind us, as if "you are the best thing that happened to you." As educators, it is easy to fall into habits of negative self-talk and criticism when things don't go as expected and you might not even be aware that you are doing it. Return to your responses to this chapter's opening questions. When you find yourself in challenging situations, what kinds of things do you tend to say to yourself? Many of us speak much more harshly to ourselves than we would to a friend, or even to a student or colleague. Tina, a high school librarian in our program, spoke to the ways in which educators can be hard on themselves:

> I think that some things we've learned this year have helped me to be kind to myself and not feel guilty. I have a tendency to be hard on myself. I think that intention setting and breathing exercises and self-compassion has really helped me. It's made me more aware of how we treat ourselves and how we treat other people.

When we treat ourselves as we would a friend, we respond to our own setbacks with kindness, understanding, and gentleness.

The good news is that we can cultivate self-compassion and learn to talk to ourselves as we would a dear friend. And, over the last two decades, research has demonstrated that practicing self-compassion improves our well-being, including our mental and physical health. Greater self-compassion has been linked with increases in happiness, connection, curiosity, gratitude, hope, positive affect, and life satisfaction (Neff et al., 2007; Zessin et al., 2015). Practicing self-compassion can support developing greater attentiveness, improving emotion regulation, and decreasing defensiveness and self-criticism when in difficult situations (Kirschner et al., 2019; Leary et al., 2007). Self-compassion has also been shown to help in coping with stress and reducing anxiety (Allen & Leary, 2010; Ewert et al., 2021; Kirschner et al., 2019; Neff, et al., 2007). This means that cultivating self-compassion can be helpful when you encounter stressful situations at school and may help you in responding wisely to such stressful events. And, studies of those in caregiving professions have demonstrated that self-compassion can help protect people in caregiving professions from burnout and fatigue and lead to increased job satisfaction (Gerber & Anaki, 2021; Hashem & Zeinoun, 2020; McDonald et al., 2021; Raab, 2014).

Taryn, an elementary teacher, explained that self-compassion not only allowed her to be gentler with herself, but that she was able to bring new perspectives to challenging situations.

> Self-compassion allows me to be gentler with myself. If I am observed in the classroom or if a lesson doesn't go as planned, I am not as harsh with myself. In times of struggle, I can be reminded that it is ok. This also helps me take a step back when I am feeling frustrated with a student. I have found myself looking at situations differently by naming my emotion and then finding what is lacking. When I know what is lacking, I can find a solution. I find myself reaching out to others and having conversations frequently to check in on how people are doing.

Through cultivating self-compassion Taryn learned to treat herself as she would a friend, recognize and name her emotions, and find new ways to interact with students and colleagues from a place of care and concern.

When we are feeling inadequate, when feelings of failure arise, when we are suffering in any way, rather than ignoring our feelings, or judging ourselves harshly, or comparing ourselves to others, we can recognize that being imperfect, falling down, and experiencing life's difficulties and challenges is inevitable in life. One way to practice self-compassion is to start to pay attention to your internal dialogue, and to practice talking to yourself as you would a friend, with kindness. You may offer words of comfort: "This is challenging", "This hurts", "It's going to be ok." You can bring acceptance to whatever is arising in the moment. You can acknowledge you are not perfect! You can acknowledge your wholeness at this very moment, regardless of your thoughts and emotions telling you otherwise. Stephanie, an elementary physical education teacher, shared an additional benefit of responding to herself as she would to a friend—it supported her to use greater friendliness in her interactions with her students as well as herself.

On-the-Spot Practice: Talking to Yourself as a Friend

While there is good research evidence to support the value of practicing self-compassion, what matters most is cultivating it within your everyday life. Vincent, a high school math teacher who went through our program, shared that in many situations he reproached himself, asking "Should I have said that?" or "Why did I do that?" or he would beat himself up, "I really just messed up there." Through self-compassion practice he learned to notice that "I definitely did not treat my friend the way I treat myself."

We invite you to continue with your own learning and practice and notice what benefits may be showing up in your life. The next time you experience a challenge, bring awareness to how you talk to yourself. See if you can notice and name when you are harsh, critical, or judgmental toward yourself. Just this brief act of attuning to your inner thoughts and feelings can be a powerful way to treat yourself with kindness.

You can then extend this practice by offering yourself words of kindness. Perhaps you say, "I am okay," "I am strong," or "Wow, I'm really upset right now." Imagine what you would say to a friend in a similar situation.

Formal Practice: Loving-Kindness for Oneself

Recall in Chapters 2 and 3 you practiced loving-kindness for others. Now, you'll try cultivating a loving and friendly attitude toward yourself. The key attributes of the qualities of loving-kindness for oneself include warmth, caring, tenderness, connection, and wishing joy for yourself. Loving-kindness is unconditional in its wish for happiness. It's nonjudgmental and open, rather than judgmental or stuck in the past. In this practice, adapted from CCT™, you'll learn to be a true friend to yourself, to be at home with thoughts of self-care, and to honor your worth, dignity, and your own natural aspiration for happiness. If you find self-compassion practice challenging, be gentle with yourself. The recognition that self-compassion practice is hard can actually be an opening to self-compassion.

Find a comfortable posture, one that allows you to relax while staying alert.

Call to mind someone who's helped you or cared for you. It could be someone you know now, it could be someone who loved you into being or an educator who's impacted you, or it could be someone you've never met but who inspires you. This is someone who makes you smile when you think of them. It can even be a pet.

Imagine this person or animal sending you their care, surrounding you in care and kindness. How does it feel when you think of this?

You can bring this same care to yourself, recognizing that the wish for happiness, meaning, and peace are essential aspects of what it means to be human. Silently repeat the following phrases:

> *"May I be filled with kindness.*
> *May I be happy.*
> *May I find peace and joy.*
> *May I be well."*

Feel the meaning of what you are saying, but don't try to force anything. Whenever you find your attention has wandered, it's okay. When you recognize you've lost touch with the moment, gently let go and begin again. Nothing is lost. You can always begin again.

Repeat these phrases with enough space and enough silence so that it's a rhythm that feels helpful to you.

> *"May I be filled with kindness.*
> *May I be happy.*
> *May I find peace and joy.*
> *May I be well."*

Invite care for yourself, exactly as you are in this moment. As you continue on, rest in the repetition of the phrases. Really good feelings, really difficult feelings, it's all okay. Maybe there's no feeling at all, that doesn't matter either, there's nothing wrong with that. The power of the practice is in gathering your attention and its wholeheartedness, wishing yourself well.

Imagine what it would be like if you were to show yourself acceptance and warmth. What would it feel like if you were more caring and tender toward yourself? If you treated yourself as you would a dear friend? If you were to acknowledge more what is good in your life and if you were less harsh with yourself?

Call to mind the ways in which you have been cared for and supported by the people in your life. Acknowledge this generosity toward you. Let this feeling of gratitude touch your heart and stay in it for a little while.

One-the-Spot Practice: Words of Self-Kindness and Self-Compassion

When you are working all day, you don't have time to get a snack, take a sip of water, or even use the restroom, the notion that you could practice self-compassion might seem impossible. But it is possible to do so in brief, concrete ways, without missing a beat. Here is one thing you can do to cultivate self-compassion in the midst of a busy day:

Choose one of the phrases from the Loving-Kindness for Oneself Practice to customize or write your own phrase of kindness and compassion. Some phrases educators have created include:

- I am enough.
- I am doing the best I can right now.
- May I find joy in the small moments.

Jot the phrase on a sticky note. Place the note in a spot where you will see it throughout the day, such as on the side of your computer, in your planner, on your bathroom mirror, or on your refrigerator. Each time you see the note, pause for a moment and offer yourself the wish you wrote.

One educator we worked with set her phone alarm for lunch time, labeling the alarm with her phrases of self-kindness and self-compassion. When her alarm went off each day, she took 30 seconds to silently repeat the phrases to herself. Another teacher we worked with, Crystal, wrote as her self-compassion phrases: "I am okay, this is okay. It's just a little stress." She kept the note on her desk in her classroom, intentionally returning to it during stressful moments to remind herself that she is okay. Crystal shared that this on-the-spot practice has been "so beneficial, just incredible," and helped her to avoid reacting to situations and to let go of the "little things," "which made my classroom calmer, more at ease." We invite you to give this on-the-spot practice a try and see if you notice, like Crystal, any benefits. You may even wish to experiment with different phrases to see what works best for you and when.

Developing the Courage to Be a Friend to Yourself

Sometimes our efforts to talk to ourselves as we would a friend aren't enough. In these instances, it's important to recognize when we do need help from others and learn to accept that help. It can be difficult to accept help in times of need, especially as educators, who are most often in care-giving rather than care-receiving roles. Another way we can be a friend to ourselves is to ask for help and receive that help with an open heart. If you find that receiving help is difficult for you, you are not alone. Clinical psychologist Gilbert et al. (2011) have studied and identified three categories of common "fears of compassion" that people experience, and one fear is receiving compassion from others. It might feel unfamiliar, uncomfortable, or scary to ask for and receive help.

It might also take us by surprise when others offer to help us, as was the case for Raquel, an educator in our program. She had been out of school for a week, caring for her spouse who had gone to the emergency room due to illness. Raquel felt torn between caring for her family and caring for her school community, and worried about the time she had lost at school. When she returned to school on Monday, one of her fellow school counselors called her. Raquel expected her colleague to "ask me to do something or check on someone", as she only received phone calls that "involve a student who needs something urgent." Instead, her colleague asked, "How are you? I know you were out last week because your family was sick, and I wanted to check in and see how you are doing." Her colleague reassured her that "family comes first" and that it's important to take time to care for family too. After the phone call, Raquel reflected that she had been "caught off guard," but when she realized her colleague was calling to express care, "this filled my heart." She reflected, "I realize that sometimes people do not always need something from me, and when I get a little burnt out, this is how it feels." While the phone call caught her "off guard" initially, it helped Raquel to notice her negative self-talk and to realize that she needed the support from her colleague in that moment. Raquel reflected,

> One of the biggest things I have learned in this course through self-compassion practice is noticing my negative self-talk and paying attention to it. Of course, I still do it (negative self-talk) from time to time, and I feel like this daily practice is getting stronger the more I do it. However, even when I did not practice self-compassion, my colleague provided me with the compassion I needed, as she is an incredible team member.

When many people think of self-compassion it is often thought of as being indulgent, self-pitying, self-centered, or selfish. But it is actually courageous to be self-compassionate.

It takes courage to honestly look at yourself in moments of self-judgment, self-criticism, and feeling "less than" and hold those feelings with a curious, open mind and a kind, warm heart. Treating ourselves as we would a friend, with unconditional friendliness, also means we must do the difficult work of forgiving ourselves when we don't live up to our expectations or intentions. Adam, a high school English teacher, spoke about the importance of self-forgiveness:

> You can't think that it's okay for other people to do something that you don't forgive yourself for. It is a really hard pill to swallow for a lot of us, and it's a big calling. It's like, okay, if you really were going to take care of yourself like you would take care of someone who you really cared about, how would that change the way that you care for yourself? You have to take responsibility for that and step up and do those things, and then I do feel myself being better equipped to give to other people when I do that.

As Adam reminds us, self-forgiveness is both hard and necessary if we are to treat ourselves as a friend and show up for other people.

Ben talked about how self-forgiveness was necessary for treating himself with compassion. He used the phrases, "I am a human being. All other people are human beings. People make mistakes, and it is okay to make mistakes because I'm a human being." Ben shared,

> That was really powerful for me. I'd never done that before. It's always been, ruminate on whatever bad situation happened. Then think of all the things you should have done better. Be angry that you didn't do it better and then think about it some more, and just beat down on yourself. That was what I would do. And it's been very freeing to have a way of letting that go.

Forgiving ourselves is different from letting ourselves off the hook, especially when we've caused harm. We can take responsibility for the hurt we've caused *and* offer ourselves forgiveness. This is especially important when we find we have contributed to injustices or upheld inequitable practices within our school systems. Self-compassion has been shown to help reduce reactions to negative events and to help acknowledge one's role in contributing to negative events without becoming overwhelmed by negative feelings (Leary et al., 2007). Thus, practicing self-compassion can help us move out of self-absorption, so that we can take responsibility for our actions without getting centered on ourselves. Realizing that we are interconnected with all those in our school community can help us to take action for hurt or harm we may have caused or contributed to. This can have important consequences for our interactions with our students and other people for whom we care.

Formal Practice: Self-Acceptance and Self-Forgiveness

In this practice you'll have another opportunity to treat yourself as you would a friend by fostering curiosity about your own experience and offering yourself acceptance and forgiveness. The practice, adapted from Jinpa (2015) and CCT™, invites you to differentiate between observations of a situation in your life and your evaluations or judgments of the situation, so that you can approach yourself in a more compassionate way. Instead of instinctively beating yourself up with thoughts like, *"I'm the worst!,"* you can become aware of your feelings and the underlying need you were trying to meet. By remaining curious and gentle, you can begin to accept yourself as you are and tell yourself, *"I'm okay."*

First, you will identify a situation in which you did something that you didn't like or that you weren't proud of. As you first begin, don't choose the most intense situation that comes to mind, but instead choose something that is lower on the scale of intensity for you. You will then investigate the unmet need that underlies your reaction in the situation. An unmet need is a term that we borrow from Nonviolent Communication (NVC; Rosenberg, 2003), and it refers to some condition that we as human beings require to thrive that is not present in our current experience. For instance, unmet needs could include a need for connection, purpose, security, joy, or belonging. Bring awareness to any emotions that arise when you experience that unmet need, such as sadness, frustration, regret, disappointment, or some other emotion. The feelings of sadness or disappointment can help you move away from guilt and self-judgment and open to self-acceptance.

In the second part of the exercise, you will practice letting go of self-criticism or self-judgment, which get in the way of curiosity and connection with yourself and others. The point is not to let yourself off the hook completely, but through curiosity, to move forward by acting in ways that align with your deeper aspirations and intentions. After you've tried the practice, you may find it helpful to record your reflections in your journal.

Recall a time when you criticized or judged yourself for something that you did. This could be, for example, something you said or did to a colleague, a student, or a family member, and then regretted. You don't need to remember all of the details of the event, but rather recall how you felt and how you judged or criticized yourself.

(continued)

(continued)

Now, invite curiosity for your experience. Ask yourself, "What unmet need(s) was I was trying to meet when I said those words or acted in that way?" Recognize that while what you said or did was not necessarily skillful, you had an underlying unmet need. Notice how you feel with this awareness and allow yourself to experience feelings such as sadness, disappointment, and remorse, rather than guilt and shame.

Take a few deep breaths in and out and let go of any tension in the body and mind. Silently say to yourself, "I can let this go. I will let this go. I am okay." Offer yourself words of care and kindness.

Self-Compassion Helps Us to Show Up for Others

Even though we focus on self-compassion in this chapter and in the next two, it is a false dichotomy to think of self-compassion and compassion for others as separate. Being kind, nonjudgmental, and understanding of ourselves helps us to do the same for others, and being compassionate to others helps us to see that we are not alone in our pain and to treat ourselves better. Just a moment of reflection, too, helps us see how the suffering we are experiencing in our body has arisen from conditions both inside us and outside us, including our interactions with others. As we wrote at the outset of this chapter, practicing self-compassion can give us the energy and resources to be of help to others, including offering compassion to them.

In the story of the *Bamboo Acrobat Sutta*, the Buddha reminds us that though we do have responsibilities to care for others' well-being, sometimes the first step is stabilizing and taking responsibility and care for our own minds. In the sutta, an acrobat climbs atop his bamboo pole and asks his assistant to climb up the pole and stand on his shoulders. The assistant shimmies up the pole and onto the acrobat's shoulders. The acrobat tells his assistant to look after him while he looks after his assistant. The assistant replies that instead, they should each look after themselves. It turns out, they were both right, for "looking after oneself, one looks after others. Looking after others, one looks after oneself" (Olendzki, 2005). The first step to looking out for ourselves and others is through paying attention to and taking responsibility for our own minds (e.g., through cultivating mindfulness and thoughts of goodwill to others) and caring for ourselves and others. The key message from this story is that, in the end, protecting oneself and protecting others is the same. By doing one, one accomplishes the other.

When we are in touch with our own suffering and needs, we are more capable of bringing compassion to others because we are more readily available to open our hearts to others' suffering and needs. This can be surprising to educators, who spend the majority of their time caring for others. Adam spoke to this, explaining,

> the whole self-compassion thing, I think, was a life changer for everyone just because most of us in these fields, we have a little bit of this martyr complex in that we have justified our own neglect of ourselves because we're so busy helping other people. And I think that was really shocking and surprising to say that, well, you can't really take care of others if you're not taking care of yourself and looking out for yourself.

As Emma, an elementary teacher who completed our compassion program, stated, "I realized that it starts with me." Emma underscored the necessity of self-compassion so that she could better care for her students:

> If I'm the calm, collective presence in my classroom, then I'm 90% more able to respond to the kiddos who don't have the social emotional skills or who don't have the wherewithal to take the breath for whatever reason it is. I think I'm a lot more aware of what's coming into my classroom and what the kids are coming in with, because I've already dealt with my stuff. I'm not preoccupied with this fight we had last night or this big project that's coming up where I've got papers to grade. I've been able to deal with that myself. And I think that's a huge part of it—that it starts with me and it's not something that I have to put on my students. It's not their job to do this. It's my job to teach them how to respond. But I have to be able to deal with my own stuff before I can even have that conversation with the kids.

By approaching herself with care and compassion, Emma was able to remain calm, present, and steady for her students. Through attending to her own challenges, Emma attuned to her students and in turn helped them to respond to their own difficulties. Emma reminds us just how essential self-care and self-compassion are for alleviating suffering and bringing about healing in classrooms and schools.

There's research that supports this idea, that cultivating self-compassion improves our connections and relationships with others. Cultivating self-compassion helps us to accept our shortcomings, which in turn helps us to accept others' shortcomings (Zhang et al., 2020). One study found that people who are self-compassionate were more likely to compromise and experience less emotional turmoil during interpersonal conflicts than people who lacked self-compassion (Yarnell & Neff, 2013). This means that self-compassion can support you in navigating conflicts and disagreements that arise in your role as an educator, such as those with students or colleagues.

In our own research, educators talked about how self-compassion impacted their relationships with students, colleagues, and family members. Educators noted how cultivating self-compassion actually allowed them to be more present with their students and to reconnect with the joys of teaching (Potvin et al., 2023). Crystal explained,

When I offer compassion to myself, I feel like I'm able to offer it to others more easily. I'm able to offer it more readily and truly stop. I thought I listened to my students, but I realized I didn't always just completely stop and listen to them in the morning because it's busy or in the afternoon when you're trying to leave and that's when they want to have those conversations. But when I did [stop and listen to my students], that was a huge change.

Stephanie, a high school English teacher, not only attuned to her students but invited them to treat themselves with compassion when her students felt overwhelmed, engaging them in conversation and asking them, "What are you doing for yourself right now?"

Being kind to ourselves helps us better take care of others, and so self-compassion is neither self-indulgent nor self-centered, but necessary for acknowledging our wholeness and dignity, accepting ourselves, and sustaining our ability to care for others with open hearts. As educators who advocate for students and work toward justice, you may at times experience feelings of exhaustion or burnout. Adrienne, a teacher who helped us design the digital compassion certificate, told us that the responsibility and connection she feels toward students can exact an "emotional toll" and "lead to burnout." After being introduced to compassion practices, she reflected that "self-compassion is the first step in really dealing with that ... It's been really meaningful to me and helped me be better and more compassionate to my students." This is where self-compassion is important for sustaining efforts to promote healing in schools. To care for students, you must also feel nourished and cared for yourself and self-compassion offers one pathway for doing so. In Chapter 8, we'll look more closely at self-compassion as preparation for action toward justice in schools.

We hope that you return to the practices in this chapter again and again, bringing kindness and gentleness to yourself as you practice, recognizing that even though for some of us self-compassion may be hard, we are worth doing hard things for. We hope that you find strength and courage along your journey to cultivate self-compassion so that you can sustain the important work of bringing healing to your community. And we hope that you treat yourself as you would a friend in good times and in bad, remembering that "you are the best thing that has ever happened to you."

Key Ideas from the Chapter

- Self-compassion means that you extend the same sense of care you give to others to yourself in the face of challenges.
- Cultivating self-compassion is a form of self-care. Caring for oneself is deeply connected to caring for others and helps in sustaining efforts in working toward more just schools.
- Self-compassion can help to improve self-worth, recognizing your own dignity and embracing your value as a human being.
- One way to practice self-compassion is to treat yourself as you would a friend.
- It takes courage to be self-compassionate.

Chapter 7
Making Room for Self-Compassion

You might make it further, if you learn to stay.

—*Brandi Carlile, "The Eye"*

Generating compassion for oneself requires space. We feel as though there couldn't possibly be time for a pause in our day to just feel what we are feeling because our students need us to be "on" all the time. We can't risk feeling what we're feeling in the classroom, in the faculty meeting, or in a parent–teacher conference. And yet there it is, a feeling that we are overwhelmed, stressed, stuck, hurting, afraid, or angry, something that we wish wasn't there but that won't just go away on its own. There's no escape from the fact that this suffering is here.

Self-compassion begins with the decision to pause and make room for something to emerge within this feeling of no escape. As singer-songwriter Brandi Carlile warns her friend in the throes of depression in her song "The Eye," "You might make it further, if you learn to stay." In this context, "staying" means being present to the suffering in our bodies and minds right here and now, without needing to get up and distract ourselves, to avoid the suffering, to try and find some other way to escape it, to fix it quickly, or to ruminate about things. It means transforming this feeling of no escape or this urge to avoid suffering into a sense of confidence that whatever we are going through, the situation is workable for us. This is where developing a compassion practice can be so powerful—it can provide us with the inner resources to stay with suffering. Chödrön (1997) has a beautiful way of putting it, that if we see whatever arises as not just workable, but part of the path of our own learning, then we can learn from suffering.

Obstacles to Staying with Our Own Suffering

Many of us have lots of reasons why we don't pause and learn to stay with our own suffering, beyond making the time it takes to do so. If we are in a helping profession like teaching or counseling, we are always expected to be serving others. This is reinforced by the daily bell schedule, which gives only a few minutes of passing time for students between periods of focused activity and a short lunch period that may be interrupted by students or colleagues who need our help. If we are lucky, we have a common planning period to catch up on work or email or to squeeze in a conversation we need to have with a parent. There's not much in our environment that tells us it would be okay for us to pause, and to take time to attend to our own needs.

Our very jobs as educators present us with a basic dilemma that we can manage but can't escape, a dilemma that creates conditions for suffering to arise whenever we fail to meet the demands of engaging and serving students. As Cohen (2011) writes in *Teaching and Its Predicaments*, the culture of teaching is such that we are each expected to be responsible for both how our students act and for their learning. Coaches and principals observe teachers using rubrics that evaluate them both on what they do and on what students do in the classroom. In many districts, teacher salaries are tied to the growth their students show on standardized tests (Amrein-Beardsley & Holloway, 2019). But despite being held to account for what students do, teachers don't control what students do or how they respond to lessons. Teachers can build productive and inclusive cultures and create conditions for rich engagement and participation in class, but our students have minds of their own. They show up each day with different things going on for them in their hearts, minds, and lives that a skilled teacher attunes and responds to. Teachers may do things that "aren't on the rubric" for evaluation, and they may not succeed in achieving results, even when using "best practices." Teachers aren't the only professionals in schools held to account for students, either. Counselors are responsible for helping students academically, socially, and behaviorally, and instructional leaders like principals are responsible for raising test scores for all student groups. Schools are set up for us to readily feel as though we are failing in our responsibilities to students whenever we can't accomplish these goals, even though all educators depend both on students' own actions and on having the resources and conditions to promote learning and development to succeed.

But we don't have to think about these challenges simply as failures. We can recognize that the systems we are working in are complex and difficult, the demands made on us are actually not attentive to the ways that learning occurs, and that the important work we are doing—tending to students' hearts and minds—is not always straightforward and simple. We can also choose to see that "failing" is part of what it means to be human; it's part of our common humanity. Embracing dilemmas and struggles we face as part of our growth and learning processes isn't easy. Many of us learned along the way that when we can't accomplish something that others expect us to do or that we set out ourselves to do, it says something about our worth and dignity. But we know that's not true. Dignity isn't earned through achieving success or taken away from us when we fail. Dignity is something we all have because we are human, and we can choose to recognize our own dignity and others' even when we can't figure out how to manage the dilemmas and contradictions we face in our work or when we don't live up to expectations set by the system.

Embracing challenges and contemplating them can provide us with important information that facilitates our growth and learning. This is a key part of the practice of self-compassion—reframing ways we fall short in accomplishing something important to us as opportunities for growth, learning, and care for ourselves. Ben, a middle school teacher in our program, found that self-compassion helped him to reframe challenges as setbacks rather than failures, allowing him to continue working toward equitable policies and practices within his school and district. He shared how self-compassion helped him to "be more at ease when things didn't go how I wanted them to", explaining:

> I feel like when there were setbacks, I didn't take it personally, and I could see that there's other things at work here. I'm definitely giving what I have. Definitely offering what I can to this issue, but not having that sense of failure if it didn't go how I wanted it to ... It was a little less frustrating for me.

As Ben points out, we don't have to absorb blame when we experience setbacks, and in fact we might learn more from seeing that whatever feelings arise from such setbacks—such as frustration, anger, guilt, or shame—are common to others in whatever "predicament" we find ourselves in. We don't have to fight with the fact that these setbacks happen or with the fact that feelings of frustration and anger co-arise for us. They just are, and the question is: how can we respond skillfully when they do arise and what can we learn? Self-compassion can be part of a skillful response in the situation, especially when the feelings are so strong, we can't seem to come up with what to do and we feel like there is no escape.

Learning from setbacks, as Ben calls them, may also point us to parts of the system that are causing suffering and need to be addressed through compassionate change. We may come to see that some of the ways our schools are organized actually cause suffering. We'll return to this idea in the final section of the book and provide guidance for making compassionate change.

Another obstacle to self-compassion is our tendency to generalize from our experiences. It's hard for us to see this moment as just a moment of suffering we are experiencing, especially when we feel as though we are not in control of the situation. We tend to turn experiences into "the way things always are", and that can lead to despair and hopelessness. Maggie, a high school counselor in our program shared, "the world is stressing me out right now. There's so much that it feels hopeless so much of the time." She went on to say that the compassion practices helped her with these feelings: "the meditations are really helpful and important to do right now." But sometimes, we generalize from our experiences to our character. Think about the last time you began the sentence, "I am the sort of person who ... ." and ask yourself: Do you always think, feel, and act in a manner consistent with the statement that follows? What do the exceptions say about you? It's hard to see experiences as experiences, without adding something extra to them by telling a story about them that is also wrapped up in how we see ourselves. But doing so—holding lightly our sense of self in light of present experiences, can help us (see "Not Only That" later in this chapter).

Especially challenging for self-compassion is when our thoughts, feelings, and actions fall short of who we expect ourselves to be. We lose our temper with a student, but we value being calm and communicating nonviolently with others. We gossip about a colleague, but we also value speaking only words of truth and not speaking about others behind their backs. We don't finish all the paperwork owed to the district about our caseloads, but we see ourselves as conscientious and always getting things done on time. At these moments, many of us turn to blame ourselves. A voice inside—maybe barely discernible, but maybe also loud and angry—tells us we have fallen short of our ideals. How could we possibly have a right to feel any self-compassion, given that we are responsible for hurting others or letting others down?

In such moments, it is helpful to pause and acknowledge the sensations that arise when we realize we've fallen short of our intentions. As Chödrön (2013) explains, for a moment we can "feel the feeling and drop the story" that either justifies our actions in light of our circumstances or blames ourselves for being a "bad person." We can just feel whatever is happening in our bodies when we acknowledge our actions. We might call to mind the person we harmed and feel what it is like just to invoke their image. While this can be hard to do, it is part of learning to stay with our own suffering, but in a way that doesn't keep building up a story of what a bad person we are, or of how we can't possibly do the right thing because of external circumstances. We can also open up and see how others—just like us—experience falling short of intentions from time to time, maybe a little bit every day, and that it hurts to do so. We can offer an intention or wish that we all be free of the hurt that can arise in us and in others, when we don't live up to our expectations for ourselves.

Sarah, an elementary Spanish teacher, who values positive relationships with her students, had several interactions with a student that fell short of her expectations. When she greeted the student in the hallway, he ignored her and when she followed up to ask how he was doing he brushed her off, replying "Ugh, I am fine." Despite Sarah's best attempts at connecting with her student, he continued to ignore her during class and argued with her when she asked him to join the class activity. Sarah shared that in the moment she interpreted his actions as "disrespectful" and she felt "annoyance, frustration, anger, disappointment, and sadness." She shared that "I had the underlying thought that I am a failure because I don't seem to connect with this student."

She explained that later, "When I slow down, I notice that his actions and words are not unique to only me, many teachers experience similar interactions. This helps me to see that it is not personal, not about me." She was able to cultivate compassion for herself and "drop the story" that she was a failure or that she "was not good at my job." Cultivating self-compassion allowed her to "look at my inner critic that is judging me for not having a positive relationship with every student." Instead, she was able to "come back to reality and notice that not all interactions have to be perfect." Through offering herself compassion, she was able to see that it's also possible that her student felt "frustration" and was suffering, noting that she had "a growing sense of compassion for him."

None of this is to say we should let ourselves off the hook for not acting ethically. Our intentions to be kind to others, to refrain from hurting others with our anger or gossip, and to show up at work in a way that allows others to depend on us to get things done are all worthy intentions. But we can recognize that it's often hard for us to meet these intentions, no matter the reason, and that internal and external conditions make it easier or harder for us to act in a way that aligns fully with our intentions and values. We don't have to beat ourselves up about it. In fact, doing so takes us away from learning to see and stay with the consequences of our actions for both ourselves and others. Similarly, praising ourselves for our own good deeds can easily take us away from learning to appreciate how good it feels in our hearts to act compassionately and observe the effects of compassionate action on others.

It is helpful to remind ourselves that we live within a society that undervalues the labor of care and that makes little room for replenishing ourselves when we have exhausted ourselves from caring. As sociologist Dowling (2021) writes, "The imperative to take care of oneself is a response to the experience of a growing care deficit in society: people cannot keep going forever without the chance to replenish their physical and mental resources" (p. 185). In this connection, it is especially critical to ask ourselves whose care is undervalued or even rendered invisible, and to encourage ourselves collectively to both acknowledge that care and its toll on those who bear its burden.

Wise Perspectives for Preparing the Heart for Self-Compassion

This chapter presents three perspectives or ideas to help motivate the practice of self-compassion: dignity, common humanity, and interdependence. While we present each of these three ideas one at a time, they are actually interconnected. Emma, an elementary teacher, highlights how each of these ideas helped her to turn toward self-compassionate thoughts and action.

> Checking in with other teachers has been huge. Just reminding myself that I'm not the only one going through this, that there's other people here who probably are having the same emotions or feelings [*common humanity*]. So checking in with them, making sure they're doing all right [*interdependence*]. And then just seeing myself reflected in that, it's affirming to feel like I'm not the only one, it's okay to have these feelings, we're going to be all right [*dignity*].

Each idea—dignity, common humanity, interdependence—mutually strengthens and informs the others. They can help us to build skills for caring for ourselves when practiced individually and in combination.

Dignity

Each and every one of us has dignity, an inherent quality of worth as human beings that is our inheritance. Our dignity allows us to be in our bodies as they are in a way that allows both ease and presence, and it invites us to see that all are deserving of compassion. Honoring our own dignity helps us establish that we, too, like all human beings, are worthy of compassion.

Many of the teachers in our certificate program come to see dignity as something that is a characteristic of being human, something that is critical to bring forward in our relationships to ourselves and others. For example, Kendra reflected, "People should be treated with some dignity just because they're people, right? It's part of being human." After completing the certificate, Adam said that dignity was "honoring people just for being human but realizing also that there's something about them that is really magical, and trying to figure out what that is, in every single person." Ben indicated that the dignity inherent in others calls for a response of the self, to honor the dignity of others: "The dignity inherent in other people calls on the dignity in me for a response. There's like this pinging and we're all pinging off each other and dignity is when I can honor the same spark in them that I know is in me."

Within schools and classrooms dignity is always at stake (Espinoza & Vossoughi, 2014) because our interactions, routines, and policies can either affirm or undermine the dignity of those within the school community. Even though dignity is something that we can say inheres in someone because they are human, in fact our experiences of it are highly contingent. Sometimes, we treat one another in ways that affirm one another's dignity as a human being. Other times, we deny others' dignity by how we treat them. Speaking in demeaning ways about another, humiliating someone, verbally abusing someone, and repeatedly ignoring someone are all forms of speech and action that are dignity-denying. The contingency of our experience of dignity reminds us of our deep vulnerability as people to suffering—suffering that we cause, as well as suffering that we experience at the hands of others—and the need for care to safeguard our own and others' dignity (Gustin & Wagner, 2013).

The concept of dignity is relevant to many of the activities and roles of people in schools. At their heart, educational experiences seek to promote dignity by cultivating "one's mind, humanity, and potential" (Espinoza et al., 2020, p. 326). Counseling students in need requires us to see students as whole and with dignity, even as they require our care. Dignity is something we often ascribe to work—though it is not always conferred for all forms of work equally in the school. Nonetheless, we can take care to ascribe dignity to any work involving care and compassion. For those of us who engage in research with human beings, respecting the dignity of participants is a key ethical obligation in what we do.

An affirmation of the dignity of human beings prepares the heart for self-compassion in two ways. First, an acknowledgment of our own dignity can provide us with the reason or justification we need to pause and name our own suffering. Affirming our own dignity says, "We're worth it" and "Our suffering matters." Second, being conscious of dignity as a human inheritance connects us with others, helping us to see that we are not alone in our suffering, a key part of self-compassion. Recognizing our own dignity can also help us see the dignity in others, as was the case for Stephanie, a high school English teacher in our program. Stephanie shared that after noticing a student was upset about their grade, she decided to hold an impromptu conference with the student, during which she offered compassion to her student. Stephanie reflected that "I would not have held such empathy for my student ... had I not been on a self-compassion journey myself." Stephanie had been inspired by a video from the compassion certificate created by one of the teachers who helped co-design the course sequence, quoting the teacher as saying, "as I softened toward myself, I softened toward others." Stephanie reflected that "this is what happened to me at this moment. I was able to recognize and dignify my student's experience because I am working on recognizing and dignifying my own varying experiences."

Dialogue Practice: "Not Only That"

One of the things that can get in the way of recognizing our own dignity is our belief about who we are and who we should be. When we fall short of our expectations, we may feel as though we don't deserve compassion or that we are not worthy. This "not only that" practice can help to loosen our relationship with conceptions of who we are, helping us make room to recognize that who we are is much bigger than our ideas of who we are.

For this practice, you will need a partner. The partner whose name comes first in the alphabet will start as the questioner for this activity, and the other person will respond.

Take a few moments to find a comfortable seated position a few feet opposite your partner. Close your eyes and settle the mind by taking three deep cleansing breaths.

The questioner asks, "Who are you?"

The respondent offers the first thing that comes to mind.

The questioner responds by saying, "Not only that. Who are you?"

And the activity continues for three minutes in this way, before switching.

(continued)

(continued)

During the pause when partners switch roles and after both partners have shared, close your eyes and notice how you feel. See if you can feel what it is like to acknowledge the statement, "not only that." If it helps, you can say to yourself a sentence like, "I am _____, but I am not only that."

Write down any reflections you have from the exercise, including thoughts and feelings that arose for you during the activity. How, if at all, have your feelings changed about your ideas of who you are? Can you recognize your own dignity? Can you tap into compassion for your own suffering more easily now, in relation to one of these ideas of who you think you are?

Common Humanity

Common humanity refers to the idea that each of us wants to be happy and free of suffering. Common humanity acknowledges that we all suffer: that it is a part of being human to get sick and experience things that hurt us emotionally (Ling et al., 2020; Strauss et al., 2016). We are, from the standpoint of common humanity, all the same in this respect. Common humanity is the very foundation for cultivating compassion and can serve as the basis for acts many of us would consider truly altruistic, such as risking one's life to help save the lives of people who are not one's close friends or family (Monroe, 1998). Conversely, if we see others as fundamentally different from ourselves, we can dehumanize others (Jinpa, 2015). And if we see our own capacity for suffering and desire to be happy as particular to us or as the result of our own unique shortcomings, then we can feel a sense of isolation (Neff, 2003).

There is evidence that cultivating the view of common humanity can help us feel connected to others through our suffering. It helps us to replace feelings of isolation by normalizing the idea that we all experience suffering in life (Alasiri et al., 2019) and that others—just like us—are imperfect (Neff & Pommier, 2012; Neff et al., 2021). It helps direct attention away from our own internal experiences, and toward others who share challenges with us, while reminding us that we are all part of this human experience (Slivjak et al., 2022). The heart of common humanity might be summarized in the short phrase that we can use to remind ourselves that we share with others the desire to be free of suffering, "Just like me" (Jinpa, 2015, p. 159). We will return to the idea of common humanity in Chapter 9.

Journal Reflection: Common Humanity

One way to strengthen our sense of common humanity is through writing about an experience of a painful event. You can try this exercise, adapted from Aljoscha Dreisoerner et al. (2021), psychologists who studied how to increase self-compassion among a sample of 80 adults in Germany. For participants who did this writing exercise, their self-compassion increased, and they ruminated less on their own suffering.

Think about a recent event that was painful to you. How does this event connect you with other people? Write down any ways you see this event as connecting you to others. When you remember this event and emotions you felt, consider how other people may have felt or behaved in a similar fashion. Consider how events like these are a part of life and consider that people in your situation might have felt similarly about their own actions and responses. Also consider the reasons and circumstances of the difficult events, emotions, or self-criticism associated with the event. What has brought you to behave and feel like this?

Over the next week, remind yourself that everyone has setbacks or unpleasant emotions from time to time and that you are not alone in your experience.

Adopting the view that we all share the desire to be happy and free of suffering does not require us to erase or negate the diversity and richness of our experiences and life trajectories. Larry Yang (2017) writes beautifully about the relationship between common humanity and difference, when he writes:

> Like any manifestation of nature—like any snowflake, leaf on a tree, or shape of a cloud—we all have attributes that are unique and characteristics that are common. It is through seeing the deep nature of our differences and how they are part of our lives that we can also see the deep similarities of our human experience. We all feel different at some point in our lives; in that experience of difference is a similarity common to us all. (pp. 52–53)

In addition, acknowledging our common humanity requires us collectively to transform beliefs about others as "more than" or "less than" us, or as more or less deserving, beliefs that may be grounded in racism, sexism, heterosexism, and ableism, among other beliefs (Pasquerella et al., 2019). The Poor People's Campaign, the very last campaign led by Dr. Martin Luther King, Jr. before his assassination, brought forward claims of dignity for Black workers in the form of signs such as "I am a Man," a statement that is at once an assertion of dignity but also an acknowledgment that from the standpoint of white supremacy, the view is that we are *not* all the same in this respect. The claim of common humanity can be seen as a claim for radical equality, as well as an acknowledgment that through acts of power—social, economic, and political power—differences can be made into deficits and made into justifications for acts of oppression. We will return to the theme of self-compassion and self-care as "radical acts" (Lorde, 1988) that stand against the dehumanizing forces of racism in the next chapter.

Interdependence

Sometimes when we are suffering, we can feel alone in that pain and suffering. We can focus on our own pain in a way that narrows our attention, and we need a little help with seeing how we are connected to others. Just a little bit of reflection on our own daily lives helps us see that we are dependent on others for our well-being. Most of us depend on others to grow our food, to bring it to the grocery store, to pay us money so that we can buy groceries to feed ourselves, to make and install the oven where we cook, to make and sell the plates and silverware with which we eat, and so on. And all of us have been dependent on another being for our very survival as infants when we first came into this world. Our very bodies are not the same as "us" even, as we are host to some 39 trillion cells that are bacteria, fungi, and viruses. And most of our very own human cells are much younger than we are (Spalding et al., 2005). If all these things are true, where do "we" end, and where does the "world" begin?

In his book, *The Art of Living,* the late Vietnamese monk Thich Nhat Hanh (2017) describes a word that he came up with to communicate just how we are in this world: interbeing:

> About thirty years ago I was looking for an English word to describe our deep interconnection with everything else. I liked the word "togetherness," but I finally came up with the word "interbeing." The verb "to be" can be misleading, because we cannot be by ourselves, alone. "To be" is always to "inter-be." If we combine the prefix "inter" with the verb "to be," we have a new verb, "inter-be." To inter-be and the action of interbeing reflects reality more accurately. We inter-are with one another and with all life. (p. 13)

The awareness of inter-being can be a little frightening, if we are used to thinking of ourselves as fully responsible for all that we do and all that happens to us, and if we think we are in control of all the circumstances that affect whether we feel pain or joy. But it can also help us—like contemplation of dignity and common humanity—feel more connected to others and to feel less alone. And it can make us feel a sense of tenderness in our hearts and also awaken an appreciation for all the causes and conditions that have to come together, that have enabled us to work with students and to be members of our school community. Kaeyln, a high school teacher, shared that in "thinking about the interconnectedness of our humanity" she realized "we are all part of a community made of smaller communities."

The Bantu word *ubuntu* also captures this quality of interdependence. One translation of this word is that "I am because we are," and it characterizes the bond that connects all people to one another. Ubuntu is more than just an idea, it is a set of values and practices that help to embody this sense of the "I" being part of a larger "we" and that support the thriving of human communities (Gade, 2012). What it means for interdependence to be more than a fact, but a guide for how to live our lives in community is a question that we can hold and even write about, just as we can write about how our pain connects us to others (see "Journal Reflection: Common Humanity" earlier in this chapter).

Key Ideas from the Chapter

- We can learn to stay with our own suffering so that we can make room for self-compassion.
- Dignity, common humanity, and interdependence are distinct yet interrelated concepts that we can practice to build skills for caring for ourselves.
- Honoring our dignity helps us to remember that we are worthy of compassion.
- Common humanity and interdependence allow us to see that we are not alone in our suffering.

Chapter 8
Self-Compassion as Preparation for Action Toward Justice

Ours is the struggle of a lifetime, or maybe even many lifetimes, and each one of us in every generation must do our part. And if we believe in the change we seek, then it is easy to commit to doing all we can, because the responsibility is ours alone to build a better society and a more peaceful world.
                    —*Honorable John Lewis,* Across that Bridge:
                    A Vision for Change and the Future of America

I (Bill) have had a difficult relationship with hope. Much of my career has focused on promoting systems-level change in school systems, specifically related to making quality instructional experiences available to all students, and to improving the experiences of racially minoritized students and LGBTQIA+ students in classrooms. While I've seen small-scale shifts, large-scale change remains elusive. The past few years have been especially discouraging, with laws passed that make it impossible for many teachers and school leaders to talk about racial equity without fear of losing their jobs. I've been at this kind of work for close to thirty years, and from time to time, I lose heart. I reconcile myself regularly to the reality that the late Honorable John Lewis (2012) reminds us of, that "ours is the struggle of a lifetime, or maybe even many lifetimes, and each one of us in every generation must do our part" (p. 66). And often I still feel I need something even more than these words to keep me going.

    Hope matters, because as we move from empathic concern to intention to responsiveness, we can easily get caught up in our distress over what we see in the world, and we can also get stuck in between intention and action. If we don't see a sense of possibility, it is hard for us to act. And for many of us, the idea that hopefulness requires an openness to the unknown is a difficult thing to accept. How, then, can we orient to hope in a way that facilitates our responsiveness to the suffering we see in ourselves and in the world?

Others have written discerningly about the kind of hope that can motivate us to work toward more equitable and just schools. For example, the poet, teacher, and professor Duncan-Andrade (2009) writes about the difference between *hokey hope* and *audacious hope*. In hokey hope, we are asked to see the resilience of individuals as evidence that it is possible for individuals to pull themselves up by their bootstraps, and to ignore "the laundry list of inequities that impact the lives of urban youth long before they get to the under resourced schools that reinforce an uneven playing field" (p. 182). By contrast, audacious hope sees the reality of suffering and sees how systems perpetuate suffering, for example, through the ways schools police and surveil Black and Brown bodies in schools. Audacious hope shares in that pain—seeing it as collectively shared by us—and imagines creative ways to respond to the presence of suffering in the crucible of our classrooms and schools in ways that honor the dignity of the young people before us. As Duncan-Andrade (2009) writes, "Audacious hope stares down the painful path; and despite the overwhelming odds against us making it down that path to change, we make the journey again and again" (p. 191).

Halifax (2021) calls audacious hope "wise hope," which is "sourced in the heart of imagination and surprise," with a genuine sense that we don't actually know what's going to happen next, and so clear seeing demands that we open rather than foreclose a sense of possibility. By contrast, "ordinary hope" in which expectation is always "hovering in the background" is itself a form of suffering. That is because we are always looking at what is arising for us now as something that should be different from what it is, and our expectations keep us from seeing both what is and what is possible that falls outside what we might expect. Seeing possibility, we can face the world in a way that is more resilient and have the capacity to address the issues that are most important for us to confront (Halifax, 2021).

Working with the Edge State of Moral Distress

One of the most challenging obstacles we face to feeling a sense of possibility in our work as educators is moral distress. This is one of the things Halifax (2018) calls an "edge state," where our identities are challenged, and where the boundary between suffering and well-being can be seen. Many of us know the edge state of moral distress well: when we see that a student needs something from us or the school, but we can't provide it, when we feel a sense of outrage when others treat us unfairly or when we see others being treated unjustly, when we are shown disrespect by others for who we are or how we appear, and when we experience burnout when our institutions place demands on us that exceed our limits and deplete us.

Anger and outrage are responses that are common within the edge state of moral distress. On the one hand, such outrage arises whenever we have an open heart to seeing the suffering around us and inside us. Such anger is a valid response and can support us to move toward action when something we value is being threatened (Linehan, 2014). And as His Holiness the Dalai Lama (2019) says, it is actually wrong to remain indifferent to injustice. He writes, "Anger toward social injustice will remain until the goal is achieved. It has to remain" (p. 34). There is nothing at all wrong with the anger we feel, and we can greet anger with the same approach we do other states that arise, with curiosity and friendliness.

Problems with anger can arise from how we respond to its presence in us. The anger we feel inside doesn't tend to stay as raw energy, but it instead gets bound up in stories, thoughts, and motivations that are more complicated and that cause us suffering. Our anger can hurt us inside, lead us to feel numb and hopeless, and lead us away from action. In the end, our anger alone cannot sustain our fight for justice for our students and their families and communities. We need to practice compassion for ourselves and do so in a way that connects us materially to others with whom we share common cause. We need a way, too, to stay at the edge where we neither become numb to suffering nor fall into despair.

Stepping Back from the Edge to Practice Self-Compassion

Sometimes, the most self-compassionate thing to do is to temporarily step away from the edge where we find ourselves. We can dance at the edge—where we are working to transform ourselves and work for justice—when we ourselves have more stability. The idea is not to completely withdraw, but to step back and to find a place inside, where we can tune into a quality of peacefulness and stillness. We do that in the same way we've been writing about: by becoming attentive to and curious about what is, perhaps touching into the feeling of our own breath, so that we can become more grounded and prepared to meet the world with more light-heartedness. We can pause—recognizing that we feel some sense of overwhelm, acknowledge the feeling, and sense that others, too, might be overwhelmed, and offer a quiet wish that we might find some calm and peace inside from which we can do what we need to do in the world. For those of us active in efforts to promote justice and equity, this momentary act of self-compassion can build a sense of confidence (Stevenson & Allen, 2017) and help us fight burnout (Eaton & Warner, 2021).

One of our collaborators in our program is Carla Burns. She is a professor at Naropa University, and she has served as a meditation coach in our certificate program.

She spoke with us about how challenging it can be especially for Black people to step back and practice self-compassion. Internalized oppression, she said, can lead Black educators to feel the pressure to dedicate their minds and bodies to be in constant service to others, pressures rooted in and perpetuated by continuing legacies of slavery and intergenerational trauma held in the body. When awareness of resistance to stepping back arises, it can be powerful to say internally, "I have the right just to be here and rest. I don't have to be doing things for others." In her book, *Rest is Resistance,* Hersey (2022) writes an affirmation that could be helpful to Black educators who hold the belief that they do not deserve rest, "You were not just born to center your entire existence on work and labor. You were born to heal, to grow, to be of service to yourself and community, to practice, to experiment, to create, to have space, to dream, and to connect" (p.72). For Black and other educators of color, self-care can, as Lorde (1988) writes, be a radical act that resists oppressive systems' perpetual pull.

Caring for oneself can help sustain hope and care for others, but it can also remind you of your own dignity and worth. When we met Ben, the middle school language arts teacher in our program whose insights we've been sharing throughout this book, he was pulled in many directions, teaching, coaching, supervising clubs, and driving the school bus in a rural community. After reading an article assigned in the compassion certificate by Jamilah Pitts called "Self-care Can Be Social Justice," (2020) and cultivating self-compassion he reflected,

> I have a responsibility to take care of myself. As the only Asian teacher in the county, I need to do whatever it takes to keep myself as a presence in the schools. There are Brown kids who look to me as their role model and they need to see that we are worth taking care of. Racial justice is Brown teachers standing up and realizing that we have a worth that is intrinsic and valuable.

Activity: Pausing and Resting

All educators may feel the pressure to keep going and to "give it our all" for our students. We can notice and write down the times when we say to ourselves that we need to keep going, even though we are tired. If we can see the situation fully and clearly—both our own needs and those around us—it's likely we'll discover that a lot of the times we say this to ourselves, we do need to stay present and show up for other people on the job, whether that's getting out of bed when we are tired to get to school, or bearing witness to a student who is sharing a distressing experience at the end of our day. But it's also possible we'll see occasions when we don't need to respond based on the belief that we "have to be there."

- Create a list of instances when you told yourself that you needed to keep going, even when you were exhausted.
- Review your list. Reflect on the instances when you didn't need to respond.
- Set an intention to pause and rest. Identify a time in your week where you could pause and rest. What will you do to rest?

Sometimes we can help one another with this practice: if you have a hard time seeing any possible places of pause, show your list to a colleague you trust or a loved one who cares about your well-being, and ask them to say which of those moments could be opportunities for pausing and resting.

Getting Close to Discomfort and Stepping Back

We don't always have the ability to withdraw or pause in our work during our workday. We need skills to help us with being open-hearted and staying with suffering during challenging situations that we can't escape. We need skills to help us cope with uncertainty, of not knowing what the right thing is to do, and use uncertainty as a motivation to open up to possibility. We also need to cultivate dispositions that can help us with seeing and working to transform the injustices we see in our schools. We need to find a rhythm of stepping back and stepping forward to face what is before us.

For instance, when it comes to creating more inclusive spaces for LGBTQIA2S+ young people, it is critical to be able to engage with uncomfortable feelings in ourselves or in other people with whom we interact without shutting down our hearts and minds. Some of what prepares us for those moments are our efforts to learn to tune into our own suffering and greet it with kindness, as well as the time we take to rest from being at an edge state. But we also need to practice within loving and supportive contexts for what Sara Staley and Bethy Leonardi, professors and co-founders of A Queer Endeavor, drawing inspiration from Pema Chödrön, call *leaning into discomfort*. By that, they mean being willing to look at our own practice for ways that it excludes LGBTQIA2S+ young people's experiences or reinforces heteronormativity. Whatever we take to be "normal" or "typical" are things we've taken for granted as "the way things are," and normal or expected don't work for many of the children and youth in our schools. To see that clearly and see that what we do in schools contributes to that requires shifts away from doing things we've been prepared to do and see as normal.

When it comes to interracial conversations about race, we need to cultivate similar kinds of capabilities. In the Courageous Conversations protocol for discussions about race, Singleton and Hays (2008) offer a set of agreements they argue are critical to facilitating such conversations and having them lead to insight and to preparedness for action. Two relate directly to leaning into discomfort, and both require mindfulness and self-compassion. The first is "Stay Engaged," and by that, they mean that we need to stay present in conversations that may feel uncomfortable and unfamiliar, taking care both to "step up" to share thinking that we don't know how it will be received and to "step back" so we can be sure to hear the perspectives of others. This requires us to pay attention to our own and others' contributions, as well as to silences. The second agreement, "Expect to Experience Discomfort," requires us to feel our discomfort, and possibly to see that for everyone, conversations about race may be uncomfortable, although in a different way for each participant. We will find there are disagreements, or places where our own beliefs and actions don't align. We may recognize things we have said or done have possibly harmed others or been said or done out of a motive for self-protection. In those moments, to be able to experience the discomfort that is accompanied with seeing clearly, we need a tender heart that we extend in all directions, including to ourselves. The resolve to speak and act differently can be easier when we soften our hearts rather than withdraw or retreat into comfort. In these moments, practicing self-compassion actually can help us to face up to the work we need to do for our own healing and to contribute to the transformation of society. As law professor Magee (2019) writes, "Self-compassion helps us to bear the pain of seeing our own biases and the work we need to do to minimize their harm … . Self-compassion sustains us as we do the painful work of seeing ourselves and our circumstances rightly, and this is the first step in personal healing and societal transformation" (p. 86, 91).

What can be especially challenging to us as educators is that we find ourselves feeling powerless or hopeless in a given situation, confronting a feeling or experience that we had not planned for and do not want. We might not be able to control the times when we step back or step forward. Lingo (2021), a Buddhist teacher who integrates mindfulness and social justice work, writes:

> What can be so stressful in moments of change or challenge is feeling unprepared, caught off-guard, somehow out of control. But if we shift our perspective right in the middle of this falling and losing control, we can maintain our balance *inside of us* and touch the many resources we *already have* to meet the unexpected. (pp. 112–113)

Staying with discomfort—or even just bearing witness to or being present to it in our bodies—requires us to develop an appreciation for feelings that we might judge within ourselves or wish we could push away. Self-compassion welcomes all feelings, no matter what they are. This is a lesson consistently taught by Mister Rogers to the four- and five-year olds to whom he ministered through his daily television show on PBS. For Rogers (1995), "There's no 'should' or 'should not' when it comes to having feelings. They're part of who we are, and their origins are beyond our control. When we can believe that, we may find it easier to make constructive choices about what to do with those feelings" (p. 128). With that understanding about feelings, we can develop the capacity to talk about any feeling, whether we feel it is "mentionable" or not, and thereby our feelings can become more workable, less overwhelming, and less scary to us.

Supporting Each Other in Self-Compassion

While self-compassion is an important resource for us, whether we are stepping back or exploring our discomfort, we may need help from others to practice it and to reconnect with hope. Our own experiences of self-compassion and our understanding of self-compassion are shaped by who we are. If we have faced discrimination in our lives because of who we are, self-compassion may be difficult, but it may be especially necessary and healing. Raquel, one of the educators who has been part of our programs, said this about self-compassion:

> Self-compassion through social justice has been amazing for me because inclusion and equity have been topics that I've always been curious about. I always think of myself as a social justice warrior, thinking of ways I can use my voice when I can for our underserved population. And thinking of my own experience as a Latina woman and how subconsciously you can carry so many things and living in the society and in the U.S., I think the self-compassion piece has been huge for me in learning and how I can support students and families too.

Importantly, Raquel had support—from other educators in our program—to come to this place of appreciation for the value of self-compassion. We all need that kind of support. With support, we can overcome our tendency to disengage, push away discomfort, or go numb. With support, we can remember to pause and acknowledge what we are feeling. With reminders from others, we can recognize that this kind of feeling is something lots of people might feel in this situation. Others can tell us what we forget to wish for ourselves, that we be free of whatever suffering we are feeling that is "extra" in this moment, and that we might find grace and ease in meeting the moment we find ourselves in.

A community can make a difference for all of us in supporting us with self-compassion and in the cultivation of wise hope, the topic that we introduced at the beginning of this chapter. A community can remind us of our intentions to care for ourselves and others.

A community can remind us to pause, to step back, and then to step up again when we are ready again to engage in action. A community can also remind us that what we are working for together shows us that another world is possible, and that we don't actually know the future. We can feel that we are part of something bigger, spanning generations. We can embrace our journey together, without knowing where it will lead. And we can be all right with that uncertainty, because we have each other, wise beings imagining and working together toward a more just world.

Key Ideas from the Chapter

- Hope can motivate us to work toward more equitable and just schools.
- Audacious hope, or wise hope, allows us to open to a sense of possibility and to imagine creative ways to respond to suffering by honoring the dignity of those in our school communities.
- One of the most challenging obstacles to feeling a sense of possibility as educators is moral distress.
- We can cultivate skills and dispositions that allow us to remain open-hearted and present, and that help us to notice and transform injustices we see and experience in our schools.
- Sometimes, the most self-compassionate thing to do is to temporarily step away from the edge where we find ourselves and to pause and rest.
- We may need help from others to practice self-compassion and to reconnect with hope.

Part 3

Widening the Circle of Compassion

Chapter 9

Recognizing Common Humanity and Interdependence in Our Everyday Interactions

In Lak'ech
Tú eres mi otro yo. / You are my other me.
Si te hago daño a ti, / If I do harm to you,
Me hago daño a mi mismo. / I do harm to myself.
Si te amo y respeto, / If I love and respect you,
Me amo y respeto yo. / I love and respect myself.
—From Pensamiento Serpiento by Luis Valdez

The Mayan greeting of one person to another, "In lak'ech" means "You are my other me." It is a statement about unity and oneness, reminding us that our humanity is bound up with one another's humanity. Embedded in this beautiful greeting is a deep sense of belonging and community, of commitment we have to one another. As Valdez's (1973) poem asserts, "If I love and respect you, I love and respect myself." As an educator, you likely have a deeply felt sense of the importance of community for your students and for yourself. No doubt you have even experienced how, when a student in your class is having a tough time, that can impact the rest of the class, including you. Vincent, a high school math teacher told us, "No matter what you're doing, when we're suffering, we share that suffering. When I'm suffering, I'm sharing that with others. And when they're suffering, it's shared with me."

Consider for a moment the ways in which "you are my other me" shows up during your day. It might show up, for instance, when a student tells you about a conflict they are having with a friend, or when a colleague reveals that they have been caring for a sick loved one, and you share in their distress, sorrow, and pain. You might also realize that in the everyday world of schools, amidst the hectic pace and focus on test scores, it can be challenging to recognize "you are my other me" in the faces of students, colleagues, parents, and administrators. And yet greeting others with this spirit in everyday interactions is a necessary gift to offer toward building more compassionate schools. And as the saying reminds us, it is a gift to oneself as well.

In this chapter we begin to expand the circle of compassion to include people beyond our loved ones and practice offering compassion to people we don't know well and to people who push our buttons, and we will continue to expand the circle even further in the next chapter. We pick up the concept of *common humanity* introduced in Chapter 7, that we all share a vulnerability to suffering and we all want to be loved. In this chapter, we look at common humanity as it relates to compassion for others and as a vital aspect of cultivating a caring school community. We also return to the concept of *interdependence* introduced in Chapter 7, that our survival and well-being is intricately connected and dependent upon many others. We invite you to consider how interdependence shows up in your school and how it can support you in offering compassion to others. We identify some of the challenges to common humanity that can undermine a sense of belonging and leave us and members of our communities feeling isolated. We offer tools and practices to support your capacity to recognize common humanity and interdependence within your everyday interactions and to develop appreciation for others' contributions in our lives and school communities.

Just Like Me

The notion of common humanity connects us with all other humans, for "just like me," every person I meet wants to be happy. We all have a desire to be seen, recognized, valued, and treated with dignity. All people have a need for human connection and belonging. This is true for the people with whom we get along, as well as for those who push our buttons. The phrase, "just like me," captures the heart of common humanity, and can be a useful tool. When we find ourselves in challenging situations, as educators often do, we can silently remind ourselves that just like me, the person before me is human and wants to be safe and happy.

Educators in our course have applied this phrase in their interactions with students, colleagues, parents, and administrators.

- "These kids may be struggling, just like I have in the past."
- "Just like me, my colleagues want to feel safe and comfortable and not suffer."

- "Just like me, these parents want their kids to be happy, healthy, and successful."
- "My principal is a person, just like me, and I don't have all the answers either, even in the things that I consider myself an expert in."

Remembering, in the moment, that the person in front of them is human too has helped educators to shift their perspectives and to relate to their students, colleagues, parents, and administrators with more care. Sarah realized that "we all have our struggles, we all have our points of happiness, and it just might look different. So, really trying to look at things from different perspectives, and just like me, I can relate to that student." She continued, "It might not look the same, and we're all experiencing something, and just keeping that in the front of my mind [when interacting with my students]." Sarah reminds us that interacting with students from the lens of common humanity can help us to relate to our students with care and compassion. Recognizing and embracing another's common humanity can support us in offering compassion in difficult moments, showing up with more patience, and attuning to another's suffering.

Cultivating a sense of "just like me" for those in our school community isn't always easy, especially when we find ourselves in difficult situations. Nonviolent Communication (NVC) offers helpful concepts for invoking a sense of "just like me" in these situations. A key assumption of NVC is that all people experience similar feelings and needs (Rosenberg, 2003). These universal needs include physical and emotional conditions, such as connection, autonomy, peace, interconnection, meaning, celebration, competence, and basic survival (Rosenberg, 2003). When our needs are met, we thrive. But when our needs are unmet, we experience suffering. Acknowledging and expressing our own needs can help us to recognize the needs of others. And appreciating the universality of needs and feelings serves to connect us with common humanity.

On-the-Spot Practice: "Just Like Me"

When you find yourself in difficult situations this week, remind yourself that *just like me*, the person in front of me wants to be happy and to belong. Extend compassion to them, silently saying "May you be happy" or some other phrase that resonates with you. Notice if anything changes or shifts as a result of recognizing common humanity in the present moment.

You might also reflect on for whom it's easier to remember "just like me" and for whom it's harder. In the formal practice introduced later in this chapter we will begin to practice with these various groups of people, and we will continue working with these groups of people in the practices introduced in the next chapter.

Strengthening Our Capacity to Embrace Common Humanity

Consider how you naturally feel a sense of concern for the well-being of some of the people you encounter, but perhaps not to all the people you encounter. You are not alone if you find it more challenging to extend care and concern to all people. It is easier to feel a sense of warm-heartedness in response to the pain and difficulties that our loved ones experience than it is to feel open-hearted toward the suffering of a stranger or someone who is not close to us. With such people, you might find you feel a sense of distance or even indifference. With others, you might feel anger or judgment arising. You might experience something like this with the students or colleagues with whom you are working this year. You might find it is easier to extend compassion to some students and harder to extend that same compassion to others. You may struggle to understand the experiences or actions of some students or colleagues, or jump to conclusions about their behavior, in ways that are actually quite far from what they intended. This can be true for a variety of reasons—we may not understand their experiences, or we may lack the tools to recognize how our own experiences and identities filter how we see others.

Building from a basic understanding of common humanity as a principle, we develop the *practice* of common humanity as a key aspect of extending the circle of compassion beyond those who are dear to us and those who are easy to greet with compassion. Research indicates that when people are exposed to scenarios where they are invited to explore common humanity, their motivation to act compassionately increases (Ling et al., 2020). We introduce the practice of Embracing Common Humanity (see "Formal Practice: Embracing Common Humanity" later in this chapter) as a step toward extending compassion to people whom we see every day, whether we interact with them with ease or whether we experience them as difficult. In the practice, we first call to mind someone who is dear to us and bring attention to what it feels like to offer compassion for someone who it is easy to do so for. Next, we begin to realize the common humanity for a "neutral" person, someone whom we recognize but don't know well and we begin to see the humanity of a person we don't often think about. In your school community, this might be a parent volunteer, a substitute teacher, or a student in another grade. We then extend compassion to a person who is difficult for us in some way, someone who "pushes our buttons." In your school community, this might be a colleague whose work ethic differs from yours, an administrator who sets policies you disagree with, or a student who repeatedly calls out in class. As you get started with the practice, avoid selecting the most difficult person in your life. Rather, select someone with whom you wish your interactions were smoother. This will allow you to begin to strengthen this skill before applying it in more challenging situations. It's important to note that practicing compassion for this person is not about approving of or condoning problematic or harmful behaviors and we'll explore this idea further in the next chapter.

Finally, in the practice we picture the three people together and relate to each of the three people from the perspective of common humanity. Through the practice, we begin to see that "just like me" the three people—a loved one, a neutral person, and a difficult person—have needs. We recognize that they all want to be happy and free from pain. And we begin to see that all people, regardless of our relationship to them, are deserving of compassion.

Educators have found the formal practice of Embracing Common Humanity to be supportive in their day-to-day interactions, helping them feel more connected to others in their school. Sarah, for instance, worked with the same three people repeatedly in the common humanity practice, noting that doing so was "super impactful." Sarah practiced with the head of the school's cafeteria as her neutral person, the person she recognized but didn't know well. As the weeks went on, Sarah noticed this person more often during the day and this person "became a loved one [to me], even though I may not have gotten to know her." As a result of consistently engaging with the Embracing Common Humanity practice, Sarah also reported a small shift in the way she viewed a challenging colleague. She began to see her colleague as more than just a difficult person, but she saw him "as a son, a father."

As Sarah's example illustrates, we can strengthen our ability to recognize common humanity with the various people we encounter within our school communities, but it's not always easy, and it requires practice. We can deepen our ability to recognize the common humanity of those before us through formal compassion practice and through inquiry into our daily interactions. Our research demonstrates that engaging in both practices—formal compassion practice and inquiry into daily interactions—supports educators to develop skillful ways of caring for themselves and others (Potvin et al., 2023). Therefore, we invite you to try out the formal practice of Embracing Common Humanity in the next section, *and* the inquiry practice of writing field notes (at the end of this chapter) and notice how they work together to support you in deepening your felt sense of common humanity and expanding your ability to embrace the humanity of those in your school community. In the next chapter, we'll focus on working with our difficulties and limitations when widening the circle of compassion.

Formal Practice: Embracing Common Humanity

In the Embracing Common Humanity practice, adapted from Jinpa (2015) and CCT™, you will extend compassion to a loved one, to someone you don't know well, and to someone who pushes your buttons. This practice invites you to not only develop appreciation for common humanity, but to also see where you have some resistance and where there are opportunities to grow in compassion. You may decide to work with the same people, or you might decide to call to mind

(continued)

(continued)

different people each time you practice. Listen to yourself and trust that you know what you need on any given day. You might find that someone whom you called to mind as a loved one is now showing up as someone who is challenging for you. Or you might find that when you sit down to practice on a given day, there is someone who is too difficult to practice with at that moment. That's okay! You can return to practicing with that person *if* and *when* you feel ready. Remember to be gentle with yourself as you practice. Hold yourself with kindness as you practice cultivating the knowledge and disposition to recognize that all people have a desire to be seen, recognized, valued, and treated with dignity.

Imagine a student or colleague you find it easy to care about and love or feel connected with. Notice how it feels to call to mind this student or colleague. Imagine being with this person. See how easy it is for you to recognize that like you, they wish to be happy.

Now bring to mind another person, such as a student, a student's parent or family member, or colleague, whom you recognize but with whom you do not have significant contact or connection, someone with whom you have no special sense of closeness. Think of a real person you see quite often, perhaps someone you see in the hallway or the office, in the cafeteria, at recess, or before or after school.

Notice any feelings that arise as you picture this person. These feelings may be different from the ones you felt in relation to the student or coworker with whom you had a special connection. Even when you interact with this person, you may not give much thought to what their situation might be or whether or not they are happy.

Now imagine being this person, walking in their shoes. Imagine their hopes, their dreams, and their fears. Recognize that this person shares the same basic wish for happiness as you.

Next, bring to mind a student or colleague with whom you may have some difficulty, someone who irritates you or annoys you, someone who may have done you harm, or someone who pushes your buttons. Notice any feelings that arise when you picture this person. Uncomfortable feelings might arise; as best you can acknowledge them without pushing them away or without dwelling on them.

Now, if you are willing, and just for a moment, put yourself in this person's shoes, recognizing that this person is someone's child, friend, parent, loved one—this person is cared for by someone. Acknowledge that this person shares the same basic wish for happiness as you.

> *Finally, picture the three people together in front of you, and reflect on the fact that they all share a basic desire to be happy and free from pain and suffering. On this basis, there is no difference between these three people. See if you can relate to each of these three people from this sense that you all share a wish for happiness and a wish to be free from pain and suffering. This is what unites us with all other beings. Notice how this feels in your heart and rest here.*

Embracing Common Humanity and Appreciating Difference

Common humanity means acknowledging that all people share a vulnerability to suffering and all people want to be loved and cared for. All people have a need for human connection and a sense of belonging. That said, common humanity does not suggest that we all experience the world in the same way. It also does not negate the differences among people, as individuals and as communities, that are so important for our beautifully diverse world and so important as aspects of personal identity for many people. Compassionate communities can embrace common humanity as well as appreciate differences. As Hooks (1996) wrote, "Beloved community is formed not by the eradication of difference but by its affirmation, by each of us claiming the identities and cultural legacies that shape who we are and how we live in the world" (p. 265).

The invitation to embrace common humanity, in fact, requires explicit contemplation of suffering experienced by specific groups of people due to systemic bias, discrimination, and marginalization. In our capstone course, we ask educators to do just that—contemplate suffering experienced inequitably by specific groups of people— and then set an intention for alleviating suffering caused by or exacerbated by school policies, routines, or practices. One team of teachers working at an alternative high school set as their intention: "May all students, regardless of ability, identity, neurodivergence, and educational experience be free from the suffering caused by the inequitable expectations, and oppressive system of standardized threshold grading, that has marginalized and limited students' agency to co-create their own pathway towards growth and learning, as well as their progression towards educational success." This team was acutely aware of their students' humanity and the ways in which the grading systems were causing suffering for their students and for the teachers. They envisioned their school as a place that "supports compassion, growth, and healing" that is "vital to human dignity" and as a place that helps students feel a "sense of belonging and agency over their own lives." All people share basic aspirations to be happy and free of pain, and our experiences are shaped by social, cultural, and historical contexts. Thus, there is a direct and powerful relationship between embracing common humanity and appreciating and honoring differences.

Genuinely connecting with someone through shared humanity does not iron over the important differences that define us. In her book, *The Inner Work of Racial Justice,* Magee (2019) wrote, "Particularity and common humanity are two sides of the same coin. By being lovingly present to the real and perceived differences between us, we create pathways toward meeting in our rich and full humanity together" (p. 194). Thus, if we are serious about compassion, it is necessary to get to know other people who may be very different from us, based on respecting and honoring the person's sense of who they are.

Raquel, a school social worker explained, "We just see so many different types of people and families and being more flexible with ourselves, and learning about the human experience allows us to accept people fully and completely, not be so rigid with our ideas of what people should be." Raquel's reflection tells us that we can strengthen our ability to see students and their families and to open our hearts to their experience.

Adam, a high school English teacher, shared how recognizing common humanity *and* honoring differences allowed him to approach his students with compassion and dignity: "There are people who are difficult to deal with on the outside. But when you remember to honor their dignity, then you're honoring something that is timeless and universal inside of them." He explained,

> Compassion is more of an action. It's more of a way of responding to people around you and an awareness of what I think of as a difference. I think that it's just so easy for us to think that other people think like we do and that their experience overlaps ours in some decently grand way. Whereas now the more I learn about compassion, I realize that other people's experience of being an alive person on the planet is completely different than mine. Everything that they see, and feel, and think, and do is nothing like what I am doing. And so, compassion to me is like a curiosity about that, what is your reality? And where are you coming from? And then the dignity is just honoring that it's good, and that they are doing the best they can with the tools that they have.

Adam shared that this sense of seeing someone's humanity and recognizing that they are doing the best they can helps him to remember that "every kid in my class wants to learn, they want success, they want love, they want validation, and everybody deserves that." As Adam's reflections highlight, it's possible to honor differences and value common humanity among students.

A focus on difference does not mean distancing ourselves from others, and it does not mean reducing people to only the identity statuses that are unfamiliar to us. This kind of distancing and over-simplifying can be understood as "othering." Othering happens when we make assumptions or judgments based on difference alone, and we fail to see a person's or group of people's humanity. john a. powell, law professor and director of the Othering & Belonging Institute, explains that othering "can happen across any dimension. Race, gender, sexual orientation, disability, language, height" (Hasenkamp, 2020) and it can lead to students and staff feeling isolated and lonely.

Research suggests that just as we have the capacity to show compassion for others, we also have the capacity to "other" people who are different from us, and this "othering" makes us less likely to act with kindness toward them, and more likely to act with hatred or animosity toward them. Sometimes, this othering involves denying that people have minds or feelings of their own (Harris & Fiske, 2006). Othering can also involve seeing people's intentions and beliefs in such a way as to make them into an other, not worthy of our care and concern (van Loon et al., 2024). When we deny that people are like us, it makes it easier to ignore their experiences and neglect their feelings, thus making mistreatment, discrimination, and violence more possible (Bandura, 1999; Nussbaum, 1999).

Embracing common humanity can be a powerful antidote to the othering that can happen in schools and elsewhere. Emma, an elementary teacher in a rural community, realized that when you can "allow everyone in your space or in all spaces to truly express who they are" even if "that clashes with you and your beliefs and how you identify, that's okay" because you can then "come back and find the common humanity that you hold." For Emma, honoring difference meant making space for a variety of beliefs to exist, and then from there working to find common ground. She explained, "We don't agree on *this*, but we do agree that *this* is important, and we can meet here and go from there. And we don't have to do this othering. Just because I don't agree with you doesn't mean I have to shun you and push you away." Emma powerfully asserted that in her classroom and school,

> The only way we counter this whole isolation of "us versus them" thing is by opening up and saying, you know what? I don't agree with you, but we do have things in common and you have every right to feel safe and comfortable and loved as I do. And so where can we meet in the middle there?

For Emma, recognizing her students', colleagues', and families' common humanity, even during intense moments of disagreement, created an opportunity to move forward together and to foster belonging in her school.

Journal Reflection: Noticing Othering

As you go about your week, notice when someone or a group of people in your school community is othered. You might notice, for instance, when you refer to people as "you" or "they," you might be othering. Bringing awareness to when people in your school community are othered is an important step in identifying where a sense of common humanity can be strengthened.

- What forms of othering are you aware of, have witnessed, or have engaged in within your school community? Have you noticed people using the language of "they" or "you" that others people in your community?
- Choose one example from the week. How was the person or group of people othered? Was it through actions, words, policies, routines?
- Take a moment to consider the humanity of the person or group of people who were othered. How do you feel when you think about their common humanity?
- How can the concept of common humanity facilitate more compassion within your school?

Appreciating Others Through Recognizing Interdependence

Another important resource for us in deepening our capacities to offer compassion to others is recognizing interdependence. Recall that we introduced the concept of *interdependence* in Chapter 7, that is, the idea that we all depend upon others for our survival and for our well-being and as a result we are intricately connected to one another. Calling to mind the ways we are connected can help foster self-compassion by reminding us that we are not alone, that we are part of a community, and that our pain connects us to others. Acknowledging our interdependence can also help us to appreciate the vital role that others play in our lives. Bringing awareness to the ways we are interconnected can help us to broaden our circle of compassion for all the people who have touched our lives (see "Formal Practice: Appreciating Others").

There are many ways that the members of a school community are connected. Consider all the people you rely on throughout your day to do your job well or consider all the people it takes to support a student to be successful—from their network of friends to their counselor, to their teachers, to the librarian, to the cafeteria workers, to the custodial staff, and many others. Educators in our program have found the practice of recognizing interdependence helpful in acting with compassion. Maggie, an educator at an alternative high school, for instance, felt angry and frustrated with a couple of colleagues who were failing a large percentage of seniors at the end of the school year. During a faculty meeting, her two colleagues blamed the students and described them as "lazy." Recognizing the ways in which staff and students were interdependent, as well as interconnected in a system that relied upon grading and accountability, allowed Maggie to notice her anger and frustration, to "step back" and "realize that we all work here, we all care about kids, and we are all in this together," and then advocate for a solution that gave students the opportunity to graduate through a system of supports. Instead of "shutting down" in the meeting as she tended to do in the past when upset with colleagues, "I expressed my thoughts on grades and grading, and shared what I have learned and what I think." Maggie advocated for students by sharing, "while academics are important and vital to move forward in the world, bonding and caring about kids is what really matters."

Formal Practice: Appreciating Others

After you have worked with the Embracing Common Humanity practice, try the Appreciating Others practice. In this practice you'll recognize how deeply interconnected our lives and well-being are. Notice if this practice supports you to expand your circle of compassion beyond the people to whom you often offer compassion.

For this practice you'll need a glass or cup of water. We often engage with everyday items, such as a glass of water, with a sense of automaticity, and we don't often stop to consider how these seemingly simple items connect us with many other people and with the world around us.

Consider this thought: "I share with others the wish to be happy and to overcome pain. My life and the lives of countless people around the world are connected in a network of relationships. We depend upon one another for our survival and well-being."

Consider the glass or cup of water in front of you. Think about how the energy of the sun drove the movement of water from the oceans, to the clouds, into rain that falls into rivers and lakes, how people built ways to transport that water through pipes; the materials and the people from so many different backgrounds that contributed to making the glass or cup you are holding, who sold it to people in different stores, and from whom you bought the glass or cup from which you are drinking this water.

Let your mind rest in this awareness of deep appreciation of interconnectedness.

(continued)

(continued)

As you reflect on the benefits received from the sun, from the water itself, and from such a wide range of different people, including countless strangers, open your heart so that a deep sense of appreciation and gratitude may begin to arise in you, replacing whatever indifference or conflict you might have felt toward others before. Let this feeling permeate your entire being.

Through our wish to be happy, and our desire to be free from suffering, we share with others a common humanity. We can feel happy when others wish us well, and we can feel touched when others show concern for our pain and sorrow. We can delight in others' joy and feel concerned for their pain and sorrow. We can develop a sense of loving concern for others, taking sincere interest in their well-being.

Let your heart be touched by this feeling of warmth, tenderness, and caring for others.

Journal Reflection: Interdependence in My School Community

Contemplate the ways in which you are interdependent and interconnected with members of your school community.

- Make a list of the major activities you did today at school.
- Consider how you depended upon other people to carry out each activity.
- Create a list or visual diagram to make visible the ways in which you are connected and dependent upon members of your school community. See if you can move beyond the obvious people (e.g., your teaching partner), to consider those people to whom your connection is often less visible (e.g., bus drivers who bring students to school safely or the custodians who clean the school after hours). See the diagram below for an example.
  - Now take a moment to reflect on the following questions:
    - What do you notice about these connections?
    - What, if anything, is surprising?
    - In what ways, if any, does this activity help you to appreciate the contributions of these people in your life and in your school community?
    - What, if any, connections could be strengthened?

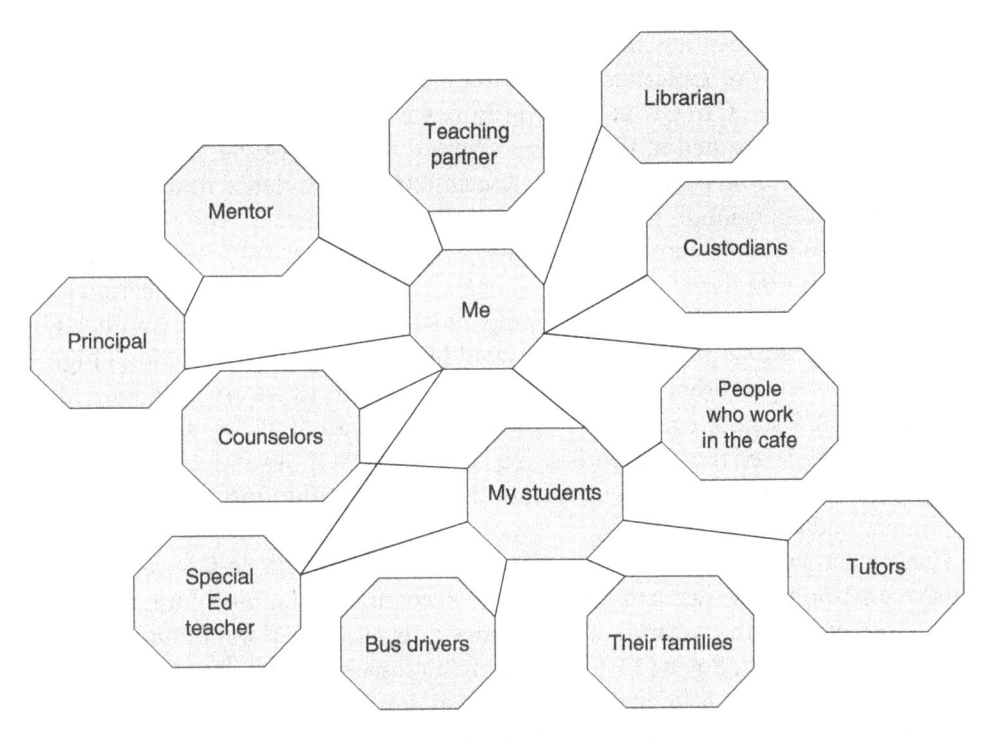

Figure 9.1 Example of Connections in My School Community Diagram

Creating Connected Environments

Embracing common humanity and recognizing interdependence can be important tools for addressing loneliness and isolation that can be so prevalent in schools (Jefferson et al., 2023; Murthy, 2020). Even within busy and full classrooms and schools, students and educators can feel alone and disconnected. Embracing our common humanity provides a pathway toward creating welcoming and inclusive environments. Archbishop Desmond Tutu said in the *Book of Joy*, "You want to make the person feel really as they are, special. And accepted as they are and help to open them ... It's wonderful to see people who were closed down open up like a beautiful flower in the warmth and acceptance of those around them" (p. 191). Through treating another, such as a student, as special and opening your heart to them, it's possible to feel connected to them, long before they open their heart to you. When we recognize our own and others' humanity and embrace those aspects of ourselves that we have in common, we can strengthen our connections.

As educators, we can find common humanity with our students, but we can also help our students get to know one another, seeing the common humanity and interdependence that exists within the classroom and school. In doing so, we can foster a sense of belonging and connection that's so important for healing and thriving. Through cultivating awareness of suffering, Tina, a high school librarian, noticed that students who were part of the LGBTQIA2S+ community were often othered within her school, and this othering happened in the library where the LGBTQIA2S+ literature and displays were separate from other literature. Recognizing her students' humanity, and that they are "multidimensional, just like anyone and everyone else," she set an intention to develop a safe and welcoming space in the library for her students, by reconfiguring the library so that the LGBTQIA2S+ books were part of the full collection and by creating resource lists of these books to help all students recognize one another's multidimensionality. She shared, "I feel like I wouldn't be doing my job if I didn't highlight the multiple dimensions that people have. We all have this as we are deep individuals." Tina envisioned a school community where students can "flourish and expand their horizons." She believed that this flourishing could happen if the educators who care for students feel "more certain of our own emotions, practice mindfulness, and treat others with dignity and respect."

Tina's example demonstrates that we don't have to wait to create welcoming and inclusive environments—we can begin today. Recognizing common humanity doesn't require us to wait for the warmth or acceptance or even recognition of another person. In *Tattoos on the Heart*, Boyle (2010) observed, "Compassion isn't just about feeling the pain of others; it's about bringing them in toward yourself" (p. 75). We have the capacity and agency to become aware of suffering and embrace the common humanity we have with those who are suffering, which taps into our natural capacity to care for others (Jinpa, 2015). When we feel we have something in common with someone else, we are more likely to care for that person. As we discussed in the previous section, it's so important to honor and value differences, but if we *only* focus on differences without also acknowledging what we have in common, we run the risk of dehumanizing people or groups of people we encounter.

In our own lives, this means we have important choices to make. We can choose to see how the person before us is "my other me" while also honoring differences. For instance, rather than dismissing students whose behavior challenges us in some way as "troublemakers," we can choose to see that they, like us, wish to be happy and to belong. We can choose to see the humanity of these students, and recognize that they have unmet needs, such as a need for safety, understanding, belonging, or autonomy, and that they are communicating these unmet needs through their behavior (Rosenberg, 2003). At the same time, we can recognize the rich experiences, strengths, and histories that these same students bring to our classroom. Recognizing the humanity and dignity of these students can help us to remember that they too are deserving of our compassion. Thus, we don't have to wait for students who challenge us to offer us warmth or kindness, but rather we can take the first step in recognizing their dignity, connecting to them as humans, and even shifting routines or pedagogical practices that might be isolating them.

Relating to others through a lens of common humanity doesn't just help students to feel less lonely, but we come to feel more connected too (Jinpa, 2015). Adam describes how seeing common humanity in the people around him helped him to feel less alone in his struggles. He observed,

> You look at people's faces, and I sometimes do this when I'm on the bus or in groups like staff meetings, you look around and you can see on people's faces how they're doing. Nobody's comfortable. Everyone is struggling almost all the time ... Which means also that when I'm struggling, I'm not alone in that either. And so, it's like this solidarity with whatever room of people you're in with. We're fighting through this together, and so that's cool to know.

As Adam noted, it's the sense of solidarity that we all struggle that helps us to feel less alone and more connected.

Writing Activity: Field Notes for Opportunities for Embracing Common Humanity in School

Through the practice of field noting, we invite you to pay attention in everyday interactions to opportunities to recognize that "just like me," the person in front of you desires happiness and wishes to be free from suffering. Field noting helped middle school teacher, Karen, to cultivate a sense of common humanity, even in moments where she felt as though she could have acted more compassionately, such as when she felt challenged by a student who was showing up late to class and consistently not turning in work. Karen was able to pause and recommit to engaging with her student with compassion, "to step back in and let's try this again, or let me just frame this in a different way." For Karen, perceiving her student's common humanity helped to "dissolve judgment" and to approach her student from a "place of compassion rather than frustration." She noted that she worked to recognize common humanity with "any students who are struggling ... viewing those who struggle in some way with more awareness."

In this next field note, you are invited to document and reflect upon an interaction you had or witnessed which offered an opportunity for embracing common humanity in your school. You may write about an event in which you or someone else recognized the common humanity present in the moment or after the interaction transpired.

As a reminder, your field note should be a firsthand account of a brief (5–15 minute) interaction. It will likely be challenging to write field notes in the moment, so we recommend that you set aside time after the event to record what happened (e.g., after school, on a break, at the end of the day). You may wish to return to Chapter 4 to review more detailed instructions on writing field notes.

Field Notes Template

I. Narrative

Describe one brief interaction as accurately as you can, including dialogue, actions, facial expressions, body language, or any other details. *Remember to write the narrative using **low-inference statements*** (see Chapter 4 for an explanation of low-inference statements).

II. Reflection/Analysis

Reflect on the interaction you described above from a lens of common humanity. Reflections tend to include more high inference thoughts, feelings, emotions, and sensations that arise as part of interactions. Use the following prompts to guide your reflection.

- Who was suffering in this interaction? How do you know?
- Why do you think this person was suffering? Consider if the person suffering experienced suffering due to othering.
- What might the person have been feeling during this interaction? Why do you think this?
- How do you feel when you consider this person's experience?
- What aspects of common humanity are now visible to you in reflecting on this interaction?
- How does an awareness of common humanity affect your interpretation of this interaction?
- What intention can you set for the next time a similar situation arises?
- What can you celebrate about this interaction?

Key Ideas from the Chapter

- Embracing common humanity and acknowledging interdependence are powerful practices that can help extend our circle of compassion to include not only people we are close to, but also people we don't know well and people we experience as difficult.
- Embracing common humanity and recognizing interdependence can be important tools for addressing loneliness and isolation and for countering othering that can be present in schools.
- The notion of common humanity connects us with all other humans, for "just like me," every person wants to be happy.
- Common humanity does not suggest that we all experience the world in the same way; compassionate communities can embrace common humanity as well as appreciate differences.

Chapter 10
Working with Our Difficulties and Limits

We cannot love ourselves unless love propels us beyond ourselves, to the furthest corner of the cosmos, and then back to us.
— *Omid Safi,* "Widen the Circle of Love"

We all have a colleague or student who we just don't get. They say things that confuse us, make us angry, put us off balance. They "push our buttons," and when we interact with them, we feel prickly inside. We anticipate planned interactions with them with fear or dread even. We know we're not our best selves with them either. We notice we are reactive, possibly even unkind. There are also many people in our buildings we see every day, but we barely know. Some are teachers on the other side of the building; others might be custodial staff. Some of them might be students who come into our library or show up in the office. Some of these students are in our classrooms everyday—they are quiet, and if we pause and reflect, we realize we don't know what they are thinking about or how the material we are teaching is landing with them.

This chapter is about how to widen our circle of compassion, to "love beyond ourselves to the furthest corner of the cosmos, and then back to ourselves" (Safi, 2016), to include groups of people in our school community—that is, the people who push our buttons and people whom we barely know. In the meditation practices we introduce here, we will refer to these groups of people as "difficult" and "neutral" beings in our lives. By "difficult," we mean "difficult *to us* at this moment in time." We write this chapter from the perspective that no one is inherently difficult—but that difficulty is something that always partly has to do with our own reactions to what someone says or does. We like the term used by Pema Chödrön to describe "difficult people" when it comes to developing compassion, that they are people who push our buttons, that is, the things they say and do and maybe even the ways they simply show up bother us in some way, either subtly or profoundly. Some of those people push more than one button, and we come to fear them, avoid them, dread our interactions with them, or perhaps even feel resentment or animosity toward them. By "neutral," we don't mean that they are neither kind nor unkind people, but that we haven't formed the kind of bond with them that allows us to know much about them, and to care whether or not they had a good or bad day, or ask if they have recovered from the cough that has been bothering them, a cough that we might have noticed if we had a connection to them. In schools and other workplaces, people who push our buttons and neutral people can almost always be found.

While it may be easier to feel compassion for loved ones, we may find it challenging to offer compassion when it comes to strangers or those with whom we struggle to understand their experiences or actions. One challenge is that we may not see their suffering. We don't know about the quiet child's struggle to help their younger sibling keep up in school, and how worried they are about their sibling. We may not know about a regular substitute teacher's housing and food insecurity, or their situation of having to care for a mother with dementia. And for the people who push our buttons, we might not see their anger at us or others as expressions of unmet needs, that is, of their own suffering.

One of the teachers in the compassion certificate, Ben, got to ask His Holiness the Dalai Lama a question over Zoom, as part of a special conversation between His Holiness and several educators from the U.S. (https://www.colorado.edu/crowninstitute/join-his-holiness-dalai-lama-along-world-renowned-scholars-and-k-12-educators-virtual-conversation). Ben explained to His Holiness:

In moments of stillness, it is easy for me to remember my intentions, such as being patient with difficult students. But when it gets stressful, I often fall back into my old habits. How can I keep my intentions at the front of my mind, even when situations are difficult, and I feel frustrated?

His Holiness gave Ben something to think about that he said he turned over a lot in his head in the following months:

Patience, tolerance on the basis of compassion, is most needed when we are passing through a difficult situation. When you are relaxed and face no challenge, "When the sun is shining and your belly is full," as a Tibetan saying goes, there is no immediate need of compassion or patience. Compassion and patience are really needed when you are facing a problem. Just like you need medicine when you are afflicted with an illness. Similarly, when we are passing through difficulty, at that moment, compassion is not only relevant but can also be powerful.

Ben interpreted His Holiness to be saying that the easy part of compassion is loving people who love us back, but that the true test of our compassion is offering it to those to whom it feels harder for us to love. That is, developing compassion requires extending it to people who are suffering and experiencing difficulties, with whom we don't feel a strong, positive connection. Ben's own interpretation motivated him to develop compassion for the neutral and difficult students in his classroom.

What Gets in the Way of Extending Compassion to Neutral and Difficult People

Some of us have probably heard that extending compassion to neutral people "isn't natural." After all, some of us might have learned in science class that evolution rewards behaviors that ensure that our own genes live on in our children or in others who share a portion of them (Dawkins, 1976/2016), and that means it's natural to show more compassion to people we are related to. In fact, the past three decades of scholarship in evolutionary biology have shown that our altruism toward others—including those in our community with whom we don't share close relationships—is what provided us with advantages in a changing African climate over millions of years (Silk & House, 2011, 2016). And one of the most important altruistic things human beings do that even our closest primate relatives don't is to intentionally *teach* their young and others in their communities how to do things they need to survive, at some cost to ourselves (Tomasello, 2008). Often this teaching involves noticing where someone is struggling and helping them to do something. Tapping into our motivation to act to alleviate the suffering of the colleague we don't know that well or the quiet student is actually a deep part of our humanity, a motivation we can tap into and cultivate.

One of the things that several studies show interferes with extending compassion to difficult people—that is, the people who push our buttons—is our sense that they may not *deserve* our compassion. For example, psychologists have found that when we feel sympathy toward someone who is suffering to begin with, we are quick to come up with reasons why that person needs our help (Loewenstein & Small, 2007, p. 113). A sense that someone is deserving of our help itself independently shapes our sympathy and our actions to help others (Gross & Wronski, 2021). Judgments of deservingness also are tied to our biases about particular groups' intentions or qualities we see as inherent in groups (Yu et al., 2023). We may also attempt to convince ourselves that victims who cannot be helped in fact deserve their suffering (Lerner, 1980). Our judgments of deservingness extend to more-than-human realms, including to animals (Wallach et al., 2020).

Our views about deservingness often lie just below the surface of our awareness, but they show up everywhere in the life of a school. Thinking and writing about our views about grading and about student behavior can help us become not only aware of them, but can also help us become aware of where our resistance to offering compassion to lots of different kinds of people lies—regardless of who they are and how they might push our buttons. In reflecting on grading and behavior, the point isn't to try and wish our own judgments away about students or overturn basic policies that keep students accountable to learning goals and keep them safe. But these are two areas where it's easy to see how judgments about deservingness show up in our own hearts and minds and probably impact our actions. The following journal reflection might be a place to start.

Journal Reflection: Reflecting on Our Ideas about Deservingness

In this activity, you'll reflect on your ideas about what behaviors "push your buttons," your inferences about the people who do, and what comes to your heart and mind when you think about what it would look like to extend compassion to that person. By extending compassion, we mean arousing empathic care for that person, framing a wish that they be free of suffering that might be linked to the behavior that's "pushing your buttons" and setting an intention to do something to alleviate that suffering. This activity is intended to take no more than 15 minutes, but you can repeat the steps below to explore further how deservingness shapes your actions when people push your buttons:

1. Choose one of two areas where students sometimes push your buttons: (a) meeting your expectations for earning a high grade in your class; or (b) meeting your expectations regarding showing respect for others, perhaps including yourself and other educators.
2. Write down a list of behaviors that regularly push your buttons, that is, examples of instances when students fail to meet your expectations of them.
3. For each of the behaviors you list, write down, "When a student does this, I think they ... ," and describe what you believe their intentions are. When writing these down, don't be afraid to write down your true thoughts in the moment when your buttons are being pushed. You don't have to share what you write down with anyone.
4. For each of the behaviors you list, next write down, "When a student does this, a student deserves to ..."

5. After writing these responses down, pause to reflect: How are your ideas about what they deserve related to your ideas about their intentions? What other implicit biases or explicit rules and expectations lie behind your ideas about what students deserve?

6. Last, for each of the behaviors you write down, describe something that might help you to generate empathic care for the student, and write down something you might do that would be a compassionate response to the behavior, the next time it occurs. Be honest with yourself and also honor your own and others' needs for both accountability and safety.

There is another barrier to offering compassion to others who push our buttons, and that is the fact that some of these people have caused real harm to us in the past, and some may even have perpetrated acts of violence against us. It can be especially hard to generate compassion for such people, and we don't advise starting the process of widening the circle of compassion to such people. It is far better to try to work with "difficult people" who push our buttons but for whom it is possible to generate empathic care with some effort for suffering they might be experiencing. In our courses, we emphasize that it's never the case that even if we can get to the point of extending compassion to such people in our own minds and hearts that we need to be in actual relationship to them, especially if they have hurt us and could hurt us again. When educators hear that, it is often a big relief, and this also gives people the courage to try and widen their circle of compassion just a little farther, through the meditation practice we offer for offering compassion to neutral and difficult beings (see the "Formal Practice: Extending the Circle of Compassion" section later in this chapter).

We can hold boundaries for ourselves and others, and this can be an important part of addressing suffering. Prentis Hemphill (2021), a therapist, organizer, and founder of The Embodiment Institute, describes boundaries as "the distance at which I could love you and me simultaneously". Sometimes that distance is small, but sometimes that distance is quite large and we determine that the most compassionate and loving course of action is to discontinue a relationship. Writer, activist, speaker, and facilitator adrienne maree brown (2021) explains, "boundaries give us the space to do the work of loving ourselves ... They also give us the space to love and witness others as they are, even though they have hurt us" (p. 41). Thus, in such instances, boundaries allow us to attend to our own well-being and give us the space to wish others well, even when they have caused us harm. And in brown's description of boundaries, we are still somehow related or connected to the other person.

As educators and leaders, we can also set clear and firm boundaries that help people act with compassion for all others in the school community. Such boundaries can guide and remind people of the dignity inherent in all members of the school community. Boundaries communicate compassionate behavior and action by signaling what we will do in specific instances. For example, you might set a boundary with a colleague who often speaks negatively about students, letting your colleague know that you are willing to brainstorm strategies to support students in being successful, but that you will not participate in a conversation that focuses on a student's deficits.

One of the teachers in our program, Sarah, wrote about a challenging interaction she had with a colleague in her building, Joe. Joe was in his classroom, shouting at students and throwing students' folders against the floor. Sarah went into the class, and when Joe saw her, he said in a loud voice, "I hate it, I don't want to be here, I want to quit." She looked at him and said, "I will cover your class right now," signaling to Joe that his actions were not okay and at the same time offering to help him and his students. After some resistance, Joe left, and Sarah put on some soothing music for the students.

Setting a boundary with colleagues, as Sarah did with Joe, who was upsetting his students and causing harm, is not easy. Sarah confided to a close colleague that she was shaken by the incident and also concerned for the students who were impacted. Sarah noted that Joe was often a difficult person for her, and that she quickly jumped to judgment of Joe, reflecting that judging him "is out of alignment with my intention of bringing compassion to members of the school community." At the same time, she celebrated that she noticed Joe's suffering in that moment and moved "naturally into action" and that she had the "motivation to improve Joe's and the students' well-being and acted upon it without thinking."

After that incident, Sarah further dedicated herself to her intention to act compassionately, especially when it was challenging to do so:

> When I practice setting intentions in the mornings, I intend to be present with others, be open, and seek to understand. My intention is to continue this practice and especially notice how I show up with Joe in the future. A hope is to notice when I am comparing or being judgmental with Joe and go back to my intention setting. My wish is that I respond as I did in that split second moment with Joe. I noticed suffering, and I acted out of the motivation to relieve the suffering for both him and the students without any other considerations or pauses. My wish is to continue to act out of love and compassion naturally.

Sarah's example highlights the complexities of acting with compassion in challenging situations, and the ways that her compassion practice supported her in simultaneously setting boundaries and in holding both Joe and his students with compassion. Acting with compassion sometimes means observing limits and stepping in to disrupt harm that is being done. Sarah reminds us that we can set boundaries with someone who is causing suffering without demonizing or dehumanizing them. Through her compassion practice, Sarah was able to see Joe was someone who was suffering and felt motivated to act to help him. She set a boundary that established safety for students, while also staying in relationship with Joe, in the way that adrienne maree brown discusses boundaries as "giving space" to love ourselves and others, while also keeping people safe.

Formal Practice: Extending the Circle of Compassion

In Extending the Circle of Compassion, adapted from Jinpa (2015) and CCT™, you'll cultivate compassion toward others, eventually extending the circle to ideally include all beings. Just like in the Embracing Common Humanity practice from Chapter 9, you'll call to mind a loved one, a neutral person, and someone you have trouble relating to or with whom you have difficulty. Next, you will imagine the three people together. You'll then expand the circle of compassion in stages to include those in your school community, your town, your state or region, your country, the continent, and the entire world. You may find the image of expanding the circle of compassion below useful as you begin this practice (see Figure 10.1).

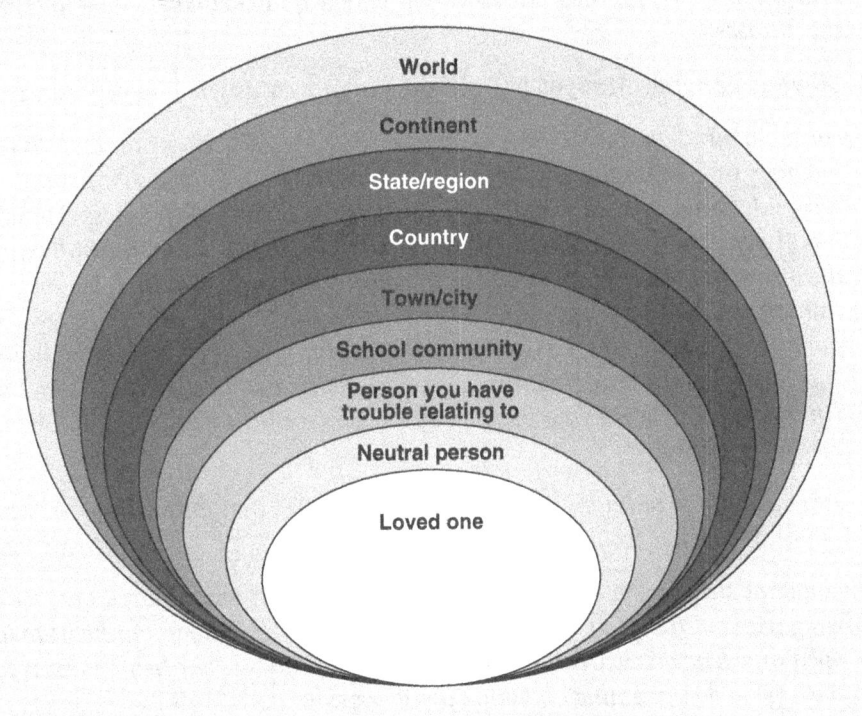

Figure 10.1   Expanding the Circle of Compassion

(continued)

(continued)

At each stage of extending the circle of compassion, there are four key parts. First, you'll picture the person in your mind. Second, you'll think of some suffering, pain, or adversity that person has experienced. Third, you'll wish the person free of suffering, pain, and adversity. Finally, you'll feel this wish with your heart and mind.

You may find that at first it is challenging to cultivate compassion for all beings in the world, but that in setting the intention and continuing to practice Extending Compassion for Others, your experience shifts over time.

Imagine a student or colleague you find it easy to care about and love or feel connected with. Notice how it feels to call to mind this student or colleague. Imagine being with this person. See how easy it is for you to recognize that like you, they wish to be happy.

Now think of a time when this person was going through a hard time. Notice how you may feel a sense of concern or tenderness toward this person. Notice how you may feel for their pain and you may want to help them. Silently recite the phrases:

May you be happy. May you be free from suffering. May you find peace and joy.

Now bring to mind another person, such as a student, a student's parent or family member, or a colleague, whom you recognize but do not have significant contact with, someone with whom you have no special sense of closeness. Think of a real person you see quite often, perhaps someone you see in the hallway or the office, in the cafeteria, at recess, or before or after school. Imagine them in front of you.

Although you do not know this person well, just like you, they wish to be happy. Just like you, they have dreams, hopes, and fears. Just like you, they seek love. On this basis, just like you, this person lives their life as best they can. Silently recite this phrase:

Just as I wish to be happy and do not want to suffer, they also wish to be happy and to be free from suffering.

Now imagine this person is faced with pain, in a conflict with a loved one, struggling with a difficult situation, suffering from sadness. Allow your heart to feel open and tender toward this person. If possible, allow your heart to even feel the urge to do something about it. Silently repeat:

May you be free from this suffering. May you know peace and joy.

Notice how saying these phrases feels in your heart. When thinking about this person's suffering, do you feel connected with them? Do you feel open, receptive, and tender toward this person? Does a feeling of concern for their needs arise? Do you wish to see this person be relieved from that suffering?

Next, bring to mind a student or colleague with whom you may have some difficulty, perhaps someone who irritates you or annoys you, someone who may have done you harm, or who pushes your buttons. Picture this person in front of you here and now.

Although you may have negative feelings about this person, just like you, they are loved by someone. They are a child, a sibling, a parent, a spouse, or a dear friend to someone. Just like you, they seek love and happiness. Silently recite this phrase:

> *Just as I wish to be happy and do not want to suffer, they also wish to be happy and to be free from suffering.*

Now imagine this person is faced with pain, in a conflict with a loved one, struggling with a difficult situation, suffering from sadness. Allow your heart to open toward this person. If possible, allow your heart to even feel the urge to do something about it. Silently repeat:

> *May you be free from this suffering. May you know peace and joy.*

Notice how it feels in your heart when you say these phrases. When thinking about this person's suffering, do you feel connected with them? Do you feel open, receptive, and tender toward this person? Do you feel a sense of concern for their needs? Do you feel a wish to see this person be relieved from that suffering?

Finally, picture all three people together in front of you, and remember that they all equally share the basic desire to be happy and to be free from suffering. On this level, there is no difference among these three people. Silently say the phrases:

> *May you all be free from suffering. May you all know peace and joy.*

Now, in stages, expand your awareness from these three people to those in your school community, from students, to staff, to students' families, to school volunteers.

Then expand your awareness to include all the people in your town and then to all the people in your state.

Expand your awareness again to include all the people in your country, on the continent, and to the entire world.

(continued)

(continued)

The wish for happiness and the wish to overcome pain and adversity are what connect us with all these human beings. Just as you wish to be happy and do not want to suffer, so too do all people in the world. Silently repeat these phrases:

May all people be free from suffering.
May all people be free from pain and sorrow.
May all people be free from fear and anxiety.
May all people know peace and joy.

Allow this feeling of compassion to fill your heart completely and embrace the open-hearted wish to see the easing of others' suffering. Welcome the peace, happiness, and compassion this wish brings to your heart and mind.

Views That Support Widening the Circle of Compassion

We've focused so far on what can get in the way of extending compassion to neutral and difficult beings, but there are also views and attitudes that can help us. Our thinking minds are not just barriers and sources of bias; we can be inspired by the words and actions of others to open our hearts to the suffering of those far away, as well as to those who cause harm to others. Indeed, this is what some of the great leaders of nonviolent movements for social change have done, from Gandhi to King. We don't have to be leaders of social movements, though, to be inspired to act as accomplices to change efforts to bring about more compassionate schools. We just need some thoughts or phrases to help us remember on the spot to stay open-hearted and act from a place of benevolence and with a wish to avoid adding to harm that may have taken place through our own words and actions.

Below are a few phrases that could help, which are modeled after a set of slogans in the Tibetan Buddhist tradition called the *lojong* slogans that come from Atisha, a Buddhist teacher from the tenth and eleventh centuries. The *lojong* slogans are, according to a system widely known today, a set of 59 different sayings, organized into groups, for training the heart in compassion. They are intended to help cultivate views and attitudes that lead us to open our hearts and keep them open, even when—or especially when—we want to shut down.

We all need help sometimes. One reason we get stuck on deservingness is that we value everyone being able to stand on their own two feet. But every one of us at some point depended on a loving adult for our very survival, as His Holiness the Dalai Lama reminds us regularly. Whether or not that was our mother or someone else, we could not take care of ourselves for the first years of our lives. And many of us—if we are lucky enough to grow old—will need help at the end of life too. Remembering that we all need help can allow us to see that sometimes behavior that pushes our buttons reflects an unmet need. Or we can think of the person pushing our buttons as a baby or young child needing help or imagine a time when they were suffering in a way that arouses our sympathy because they need the help of others to overcome that suffering. As Rogers (2003) once wrote: "All of us, at some time or other, need help. Whether we're giving or receiving help, each one of us has something valuable to bring to this world. That's one of the things that connects us as neighbors—in our own way, each one of us is a giver and a receiver" (p. 136).

See the systems that perpetuate the suffering. We tend to see individual behavior as just that—individuals' own behavior, driven by their own motives and backgrounds. But have you ever stopped to think about why our education system routinely fails a small percentage of students, and that there's a high probability that the ones who fail come from groups and communities that are far from power, such as racially minoritized students (Varenne & McDermott, 1998)? Do we ever imagine that it's our schooling practices that create disabilities for children—by requiring them to sit still, be interested in a narrow range of subjects, and show what they know and can do on a regular basis by performing without the aid of any tools whatsoever, even though an intelligent novice in any domain would lean on resources and others for help? A helpful corrective to seeing individual behavior as explained by the motive or background of the person who is pushing our buttons is to see how the systems, structures, rules, and expectations not only reproduce that behavior, but also our own reactions to it, including the complex behavior management systems we put in place, complicated grading schemes we instill, and rules for running a teacher professional learning community we generate to keep everyone "on task" and "in line." Seeing systems as sources of problems is a way to turn the mind toward expanding the circle of compassion, and in the last section of this book, we'll introduce tools and activities to help people "see the system" (Bryk et al., 2015) that is reproducing inequitable social suffering every day in schools.

When someone pushes your buttons, take heart. Smiling, feeling a sense of gratitude, or responding with kindness is probably the opposite of what we are most likely to think to do in a situation when someone pushes our buttons. But when we start to pay attention to our reactions, it's an incredible opportunity to pause and see just how we are getting in the way of enacting a compassionate response to a difficult person, as His Holiness the Dalai Lama said to Ben. And when we do start to see that, we can take heart. Taking heart creates a pause or space for us to fashion a response that doesn't actually reinforce behavior that is problematic in others or that leads to us shutting down either. Our reactions to people who push our buttons often reinforce behavior that pushed our buttons in the first place; the difficult person starts to see that others react to them negatively—seeing them as difficult—and continues to act that way, often justifying their own actions in light of our reactions to them, and we get caught in a self-perpetuating cycle of interpersonal suffering. This phrase is like the *lojong* slogan sometimes rendered as, "Don't make everything so painful," which is really an instruction not to respond to someone being difficult by giving the response that might be expected or logical. Doing so only will make the situation worse, and responding differently can sometimes provoke a surprising response or disrupt the problematic behavior. At the very least, we ourselves can learn to approach difficult situations and people differently with this approach. So instead of getting angry, smile, because you caught yourself being upset by something someone else did.

Use others' words and actions as compost for compassion. When others praise us, it warms our heart, and we are grateful. But it's harder to be grateful when someone is blaming us for the failure of their child or calling us out for forgetting to fulfill an expectation. Still, we can treat the actions and words that push our buttons as opportunities for us to grow—maybe to respond differently from what's expected (taking heart, as in the slogan above), or to consider the ways our own actions might have contributed to the situation at hand. Barbara, an elementary teacher from the television show *Abbott Elementary*, expresses the attitude behind this phrase beautifully: "People have thrown dirt on my name, and others have given flowers. It's all a garden to me." In the garden of our hearts, hurtful words and actions of others can fester inside and start to stink. But with a little anaerobic respiration—in the form of contemplative practice especially—we can turn them into compost. There's a lot of similarity between this phrase and the *lojong* slogan, "Be grateful to everyone," a puzzling slogan about the need for us to develop an attitude of gratitude toward even those who push our buttons.

You can always begin again with generating compassion. Each moment gives us a fresh opportunity to respond differently to a situation, and sometimes we need that encouragement—just to say, all is not lost when we react like we always do to someone who has pushed our buttons. But this phrase can also remind us that we started not with neutral and difficult beings, but with close friends and loved ones, including our animal companions. We did so for a reason, and that is that it's easy to open our hearts to these people. And we need open hearts to be able to expand the circle of compassion. If we start with the neutral and difficult beings, it may be hard for us to remember what it's like to feel empathic care for someone, and to set an intention to act to help in whatever way we can to relieve their suffering. It will not feel the same, when we turn to neutral and difficult beings, of course. We can also be purposeful about working with difficult people in the different role groups we encounter in schools: students, colleagues, family members, leaders. Maybe we find it harder to work with difficult colleagues than with students, or maybe it's the other way around for us. In fact, the differences help us see once again where our own limits and opportunities for growth are. We don't need to judge that in ourselves but approach our own limitations for expressing compassion with friendliness.

The easy can become difficult, and difficult can become easy. The more we practice expanding the circle of compassion, we will discover that our feelings change for particular people. Someone we befriended because of an easy connection becomes more complicated once we get to know them. We have a fight with a close colleague, and we start to see their faults in every interaction we have with them. After practicing with a neutral being, we strike up a conversation with them spontaneously, and suddenly we know more about their lives. And after practicing for a month using a person as a difficult being, we notice our interactions with them have shifted, and they're not really our most difficult person any more. By being aware that our own views can shift about people, we start to see the truth of the idea that a difficult person is someone who is difficult *for us*—and even then, this is true for a time. There's nothing permanent or fixed about a person's identity for us as easy, neutral, or difficult. When we start to see that, we're ready for an even more challenging practice to widen the circle of our compassion.

Tonglen, the Practice of Sending and Taking

One of the other practices that Atisha brought from the ancient kingdom of Bengal, where he was born, to Tibet, is called *tonglen*. Tonglen means "sending and receiving," which seems simple enough, except that in this practice, we work against the grain of our natural inclination to seek out good feelings and pleasure and to push away or avoid pain. In tonglen, we imagine a suffering person in front of us, and we breathe in their suffering, and as we breathe out, we send out love to them, a wish that they be happy. In other words, we're taking in the kinds of pain that neither the other person nor we want and opening our hearts to that. As we take it in, this pain doesn't destroy us—even though we might believe it could, or we worry that we are not maintaining good boundaries. Instead, we see the power of our hearts to transform that pain into light. It doesn't hurt us at all but becomes "compost" for our own compassionate wishes for others. We can practice tonglen for anyone—an easy being, a neutral being, a difficult being, or ourselves. In fact, we can practice it first for ourselves. This is a lot like what we are doing when we stop and practice self-compassion. We don't "breathe it in," but we acknowledge that suffering is here—in our bodies, right now—and really stay with it. So, if we've practiced self-compassion, we're ready for this next step, to breathe in suffering of ourselves or another, and breathe out healing light. The following practice provides a detailed method for practicing tonglen.

Formal Practice: Tonglen

Sit in a comfortable position, either on a chair or on the floor in a position that allows you to feel both alert and at ease.

Place your hands gently on your lap or knees, close your eyes, and take a few deep breaths to settle into the present moment.

Begin by setting a positive intention for your practice. You might think, "May this practice help me to grow in my compassion." Allow your heart to feel whatever love and joy are present to you.

Take a few moments to focus on your breath. Notice the natural rhythm of your inhalation and exhalation, allowing yourself to relax with each breath.

(continued)

(continued)

Now consider someone you care about deeply; it could be a student or colleague, a parent or family member in the school who is facing some challenge or difficulty. It could be a moment of stress, frustration, or sadness. Imagine the suffering as a dark, heavy cloud surrounding them or yourself.

As you inhale, imagine breathing in this dark cloud. Bring it into your heart with the intention to transform it.

As your breath transitions from in-breath to out-breath, for a brief moment, allow the darkness to be transformed by the warmth and light of compassion within your heart.

Then as you exhale, imagine breathing out a bright, warm light—representing kindness, understanding, relief, perhaps even joy or lightness—back to the person or yourself. You can offer the phrases silently to yourself as you do:

May you be free from suffering. May you find peace and joy.

Continue this practice, each time taking in this loved one's suffering as a dark cloud, transforming it in your heart into a warm light and sending it back to this loved one. Each time offering the wish that they be free of suffering and find peace and joy.

Continue to breathe in suffering and breathe out compassion, gradually expanding your focus to include others: your entire class, your colleagues, or even the wider school community.

With each cycle of breath, expand your visualization to include more people. You can begin with those in your immediate environment, wherever you happen to be, and expand the light outward. Imagine sending compassion and relief to all those who may be suffering, even those beyond your immediate surroundings. Repeat the phrases:

May all beings be free from suffering.
May all beings be free from fear and anger.
May all beings find peace and joy.

And as you breathe in, as before, imagine taking away all their suffering, fear, and confusion.

And as you breathe out, imagine offering peace, joy, comfort, and strength.

After several minutes, release the visualization and return your focus to your breath. Take a few deep breaths and allow yourself to feel the warmth and compassion you have generated.

When you are ready, gently open your eyes. Take a moment to reflect on how this practice might influence your day and your interactions with others.

Western psychologists have begun to study tonglen and its effects. In one study (Wallmark et al., 2013), a group of 22 adults were randomly assigned to learn and practice *tonglen,* while another 20 adults were randomly assigned to a control group that would later get the training in *tonglen.* The study found that the adults who practiced tonglen tended to be more likely to engage in perspective taking—that is, seeing other people's points of view—and to report higher levels of self-compassion and mindfulness. There was a shift in their altruistic orientation, too, a shift that was correlated with how much people practiced *tonglen.*

What *tonglen* does is something Chödrön (2001) describes as "ventilation," breathing air into pain and helping us to expand our own views. She writes that "it ventilates our very limited personal reference point, the closed-mindedness that is the source of so much pain" (p. 58) and "ventilate[s] our prejudices and introduce us to a more tender and open-minded world" (p. 60). In other words, tonglen is a good way of working with those views we hold that limit who we think deserves our compassion. It helps us, too, learn to stay with difficult emotions, to "experience discomfort" in the ways that are part of the Courageous Conversations protocol for discussions of race (Singleton & Hays, 2008; see Chapter 8). Brittany, an elementary teacher, explained that she felt better prepared to "navigate the emotions of others ... knowing that I can breathe in those dark clouds and have the strength for them to not affect me, just to recognize them and let them pass. That's been huge for my intra/interpersonal relationships." Tonglen prepares us to feel like whatever comes our way, we can be there for it. It is a powerful practice for cultivating compassion.

Key Ideas from the Chapter

- It's possible, with practice, to widen your circle of compassion to people in your school community who push your buttons and to people you don't know well.
- We may experience obstacles to widening the circle of compassion: we may not see people's suffering, we may feel that some people don't deserve compassion, or these people may have caused real harm.
- We can set clear and firm boundaries that help people act with compassion for all others in the school community.
- We can cultivate views and attitudes that help to open our minds and hearts to extending compassion, even when it's challenging to do so.
- Tonglen is a powerful practice where we send and receive compassion to those who are suffering. This practice reminds us that we have the capacity to help.

Part 4

Creating Compassionate Schools

Chapter 11
Humanizing School Environments

As people flourish, the meaning of learning itself evolves alongside the proliferation of human possibilities.
—Manuel Espinoza & Shirin Vossoughi, "Perceiving Learning Anew:
Social Interaction, Dignity, and Educational Rights"

No doubt as you have been reading this book and engaging with the practices and exercises offered, you have been bringing more compassion into your daily life. Like many of the educators we've worked with, you might have noticed that you are more patient with your own family members, that you are better able to meet your students' needs because you are more aware of their suffering, or that you are learning to talk to yourself as you would a friend. These shifts in your daily interactions are something to celebrate! You can build on these individual shifts to invite others into collective, compassionate action to make change and alleviate suffering at the community level. This is what compassionate leadership is all about.

Leading and sustaining change to alleviate suffering and promote well-being in your community is an "inside-out" job, one that requires the inner resources strengthened by contemplative practice and the practical tools for seeing the system. While we shift the focus to planning and action in the fourth section of this book, we encourage you to continue engaging with the contemplative practices offered in the previous chapters, including the formal and on-the-spot practices. You may even find it beneficial to try out these practices or discuss your experiences of the practices with colleagues and collaborators in your school community.

Forms of Suffering in Schools

For many students and adults, schools can be sites with many pain triggers throughout the day. Being a student can mean being continually evaluated by teachers and peers. Many years ago, a pair of anthropologists of education wrote:

> We are increasingly overwhelmed with the importance of those times in every day when each child is put on the line, times when each child is asked to perform some difficult task with the consequence of being called either competent/incompetent or smart/dumb. A good part of any teacher's day can be understood in terms of occasioning such scenes and even worrying about their timing for different children so as not to put them on a line in ways that either underchallenge or embarrass them. (McDermott & Hood, 1982, p. 236)

The processes of evaluating students may be so ubiquitous that we don't even notice them, nor pause to consider the consequences, in terms of the suffering that calling on students to be knowledgeable about something or another all day can cause. The meaning of assessment as "sitting beside" a student—from the Latin word *assidere*—seems so far from the practices we use every day to evaluate what students know, whether when we ask them questions, test them, or assign a grade to a performance. What might it even mean to think of assessment as a caring practice that can bring us closer to our students (cf., National Academies of Sciences Engineering and Medicine, 2022), rather than one that puts distance between us and our students?

For many of our students, their identities put them at risk for other forms of suffering that exist independent of and intersect with the pain of evaluation, including discrimination and exclusion. For example, for Black students, schools can be primary sites of suffering, places where the ways that Black children are treated outside the school—where they may be viewed as threats or as "miniature adults" rather than as children—are mirrored within schools' disciplinary practices and within the everyday interactions that happen in classrooms. Educational policy researcher Michael Dumas (2014) writes that attention to this form of suffering is necessary to understand how the policies that shape educational practice are actually lived, and how such policies leave an impression on "flesh, bone and soul" (p. 2). He argues that while we may read about different forms of Black suffering—in the past, or in the present—there has been less attention given to what it is to live the experience of having a full array of society's institutions against you, or to live with the sense that one could always be taken back to a place of trauma and pain or subject to violence. Pausing to contemplate and attend to these forms of suffering can provoke a wide range of emotions—from fear to outrage to numbness—depending on who we are, our circumstances, and our capacity to be present to this suffering.

For young people who live in the fear of experiencing day-to-day racialized suffering, their own awareness of it shapes how they engage with school in ways that can provoke in us a sense of urgency to relieve their suffering. Christopher Wright et al. (2018) offer an insightful case study involving a small group of Black elementary-age girls that illustrates the consequences of racism in schools and the impact of racism on students having to worry about being brought back to places of pain and suffering. They provide a vivid vignette of three Black girls participating in an engineering design challenge developed collaboratively by Wright's research team and a classroom teacher. The researchers observed that, rather than debating and deciding on a design based on evidence, data, criteria, or tradeoffs as was intended in the engineering curriculum, the girls opted to combine their ideas. One girl shared their reasoning, explaining that her group can get a little excited and loud when they are discussing ideas. If the teacher thought they were too loud, she'd think they were arguing and they would get sent to the office and administration might think it was a fight. They could get suspended and then get in trouble at home. So, for that, they weren't going to debate their engineering designs (Wright et al., p. 194).

In our own certificate program, educators have reported a wide range of forms of suffering in their field notes. Teachers have borne witness to a student's pain after being hit with an instrument by another student in music class. Teachers have described talking with parents of a transgender student who wanted their child to participate in a school team sport, knowing that the student did not feel comfortable playing on the school-assigned team. Teachers have discussed with a special education coordinator about the limited support available to two of the educator's special education students for meeting goals in their Individualized Education Plan (IEP).

How can we understand such suffering and learn to stay present to it? And what orientation might we take to addressing that suffering, from a place of deeper understanding of its sources? Here, we turn to scholars in the field of health sociology for guidance both in defining this kind of suffering and orienting us to alleviating it.

Defining Social Suffering

We use the term *social suffering* throughout this book to name the kind of suffering we seek to help educators address in schools. Accounts of social suffering in the social sciences focus on people's lived experiences of pain, damage, injury, deprivation, and loss, understood as shaped by wider social, political, economic, and cultural forces (Kleinman et al., 1997; Wilkinson, 2005, 2012). Such accounts understand that how we experience pain and distress are deeply rooted in historical and sociocultural contexts, contexts that are themselves shaped by different forms of oppression—such as discrimination and misrecognition. All suffering is rooted in larger social systems—both our own and that of others—and some is even the result of policies and programs designed specifically to alleviate suffering (Kuah-Pearce et al., 2014).

Social suffering is also about the everyday ways that people experience pain, the things we take for granted and may even think of as "normal" or that we expect to face in an inequitable society. Social suffering includes damage to one's sense of dignity and self-worth when one's dreams and sense of possibilities are thwarted by the sense that everyday life is a slog, limited in its possibilities for freedom, well-being, and happiness (Bourdieu, 2000). When we pay attention to the social suffering around us, we start to notice the way that many of the policies, routines, and practices in organizations like schools are dehumanizing, to the extent that they contribute to this feeling that participation in these practices is meaningless and dignity-denying, rather than dignity-affirming (Espinoza et al., 2020). To be sure, it takes both skill in noticing and a willingness to sit in deep discomfort to look clearly at these everyday forms of suffering.

Attending to social suffering doesn't end with noticing it and sitting with it. Rather, we also pay attention to the humanity of those who suffer, who manage in the face of difficulty and pain, and who find meaning in life despite the many forms of suffering. Accounts of social suffering are not just stories of damaged people in damaged communities (cf., Tuck, 2009); attention to social suffering demands we pay attention to how people maintain their basic humanity when faced with immense pain (Wilkinson, 2005) and how people make meaning of their suffering in everyday life, including the moral tensions and political tensions they feel (Wilkinson, 2012). It means making room for discussions of social suffering experienced by young people in our classrooms, that is, making present the ethical and political tensions they encounter in everyday life, a notion that education researchers Calabrese Barton and Tan (2020) refer to as *rightful presence*. Making room in the classroom for students to express both their current struggles and a desire for a different future involves pushing ourselves as educators to think of equity beyond simply providing access to what we are teaching now in our classrooms. It invites us to sit beside young people in their suffering and to make room to dream together about possible futures for themselves, their families, and communities. From the standpoint of rightful presence, our compassionate wish is to work side-by-side with youth toward a more just future. Ultimately, attending to social suffering has the potential to guide us both ethically and politically in the world, to become advocates for and collaborators with children and youth and their families in our schools.

Because it is often difficult to see social suffering, we encourage educators to think of it as requiring attention to different aspects of the experience of social suffering. While social suffering can be thought of as a name for something big, complex, and difficult to describe if easy to sense, it can help to explore its intrapersonal, interpersonal, and community aspects specifically. Focusing on these aspects has been helpful for educators in our programs to "see" dimensions of social suffering in their schools they had not before. Two aspects are most readily visible to educators, namely the ways that we experience suffering in our emotional and thinking lives (intrapersonal) and how suffering shows up within our individual relationships with others (interpersonal). It is often harder to see within our intrapersonal and interpersonal suffering the community aspects of suffering, that is, the ways in which our suffering arises from policies, routines, and practices in our school and how that suffering is related to ideologies and views held in our community, or state, and country. This is so in part because the community aspect of suffering is in some ways the water we are always swimming in, and so it is difficult to see. But our culture also orients us to and reinforces seeing suffering primarily as arising from "bad" intentions or behavior, psychological "deficits," and personality conflicts, rather than as arising from larger systemic or community-level processes.

To make visible these three different aspects of suffering—the intrapersonal, interpersonal, and community level—consider the vignette earlier in the chapter from Christopher Wright and colleagues' study. Wright et al. (2018) noticed something unexpected about the girls' engagement with the engineering task: rather than discuss with each other about the pros and cons of different designs, they avoided any potential for disagreement by combining their ideas. On the one hand, these girls were "getting along," but what makes this an instance of suffering is that they were trying to avoid engaging in argument from evidence. And so, the interpersonal aspect of suffering here might be called "avoidance." Wright's team also documented the intrapersonal aspect of suffering here—namely fear that was leading the girls to avoid engaging in argument with one another. And in interpreting the event later, Wright's team located the source of fear and avoidance within larger community-based patterns in which Black girls are treated with suspicion when they raise their voices or express their ideas in classrooms, as if they are always "talking back" to the teacher. In this vignette, we can see how making sense of the interaction requires all three lenses on social suffering.

We can ask: if the community aspects of suffering are so hard to see—and perhaps even harder to change—why focus on them at all? One reason is that to many children, youth, and adults whose identities are marginalized in schools and communities, the community aspects *are* visible and are necessary lenses to make sense of social suffering. Thus, to the extent social suffering focuses on experience, the community aspects of social suffering are integral to understanding them. A second reason is that a failure to see community aspects can lead to less skillful responses to suffering, which in turn can lead to more suffering. One response to the girls in Christopher Wright's engineering program, might be, "Don't be afraid, there's no real risk to you, just engage in argument to come up with a better design." But such an intervention would miss the web of interpersonal relationships that matter to the girls (i.e., their relationship to their parents), as well as the historical legacies and larger system of practices that lead the girls to wonder where the next threat to their safety and well-being will come from in the school. Telling the girls "don't be afraid" would also dismiss the girls' fears (the intrapersonal aspect of suffering) as invalid and unimportant, diminishing the girls' experiences and denying their dignity. Third, focusing only on the intrapersonal and interpersonal aspects of social suffering is likely to lead away from interpreting others' actions generously (see "Activity: Interpreting Others' Actions Generously"), and toward deficit framings of others, assumptions of poor intent, and blame. For instance, from one narrow perspective, the girls could be viewed as "bad" at engineering, based solely on their observable behavior, without any deeper inquiry into the context or history. In other words, it is likely to lead us away from a compassionate response, because we are holding tight to views that interfere with seeing others as deserving of our care and compassion.

Activity: Interpreting Others' Actions Generously

Worline and Dutton (2017) study compassionate organizations and have found that when people within organizations, such as schools, *generously interpret* others' actions, it opens possibilities for compassion to arise. When we interpret actions generously, we give people the benefit of the doubt and we avoid jumping to conclusions, making assumptions, or casting judgment. We can interpret actions generously through adopting a stance of curiosity and withholding blame. When a student doesn't turn in an assignment, we can ask ourselves, is it possible that this student is suffering in some way? Doing so allows us to begin to notice suffering that may be present, including intrapersonal, interpersonal, and community aspects of suffering. Engaging with the student with curiosity means we can use kind and direct inquiry to learn more about the student's experience and to determine a skillful and compassionate response. Interpreting people's actions generously requires that we see them as worthy of compassion and that we affirm their dignity. This involves honoring people's experiences and feelings, especially as they relate to how they experience suffering. A skillful response is one that involves "withholding blame and engaging in compassionate conversations that allow for generous interpretations about what's happening, while still setting high standards and holding people accountable for consequences" (Worline & Dutton, 2017, p. 47).

In many instances, interpreting one's actions generously is counter-cultural and complex, especially when we are not always aware of the forms of suffering someone may be experiencing. It requires us to be brave, to step outside of the typical ways of seeing someone's behavior, and to recognize our own capacity for meeting suffering when it arises. There are times when we can't do anything to change the fact that our students are suffering, but we can meet their suffering with care and with our presence. As Hanh (1997) said, "The most precious gift we can offer others is our presence. When mindfulness embraces those we love, they will bloom like flowers."

In this activity, you are invited to generously reinterpret a recent interaction. Call to mind a difficult conversation you had with someone at school—perhaps it was a student, a colleague, or a student's family member—where you initially jumped to a conclusion or made an assumption about something they said or did.

- How can you interpret their words or actions generously?
- How might this person be suffering? Consider intrapersonal, interpersonal, and community aspects of suffering.
- What might you say or do to learn more about their experiences of suffering? How might you affirm their dignity and cultivate presence?
- Set an intention for generously interpreting others' actions within your school community.

To truly understand why some students suffer in schools, we need to look beyond individual behaviors and interactions. We can ask ourselves: What kinds of suffering happen often in schools? Who is most affected, and why? How are systemic racism and oppression in society reflected in the suffering we see in our schools? The injustices and violence that Black, Indigenous, and People of Color (BIPOC) face in the larger society are repeated and even intensified in schools, making them places of intense suffering. While schools can be places of hope and success, they also often perpetuate inequity, in a process that can be described as "successful failure" (Varenne & McDermott, 1998), whereby for generation after generation of students, we always fail a certain percentage of students. To effectively and compassionately respond to this suffering, we need to understand systemic inequities and take actions that acknowledge and work to change these harmful patterns.

In our certificate program, we ask educators to identify a form of social suffering that they want to address in their schools, and we invite them to consider all three aspects—the intrapersonal, interpersonal, and community—in framing an intention about alleviating this form of suffering in their school community. Within this activity, our educators have highlighted the ways that shame, perfectionism, and comparing themselves to others are intrapersonal aspects of suffering they experience and that interfere with compassion. With respect to interpersonal aspects of suffering, educators have highlighted distrust and resentment caused by prior actions of others—whether they be students, colleagues, parents, or administrators. At the community level, educators have pointed out that challenging aspects of social suffering include conflicts in cultural values, specifically in connection to compassion and care, institutionalized racism and oppression, and grading and evaluation practices. When people in the school community don't share these values, people suffer, and some groups suffer more than others. We offer the journal reflection, Social Suffering in My School, as a first step toward creating a more compassionate school.

Journal Reflection: Social Suffering in My School

Reflect on how you interpret the idea of social suffering:

- What is social suffering?
- What social suffering are you aware of in your school?
- What social suffering exists in your school that might be visible to some people, but not others?

Next, complete the following table to identify how the different aspects of social suffering show up in your school and for whom, as well as the intrapersonal, interpersonal, and community barriers to responding compassionately to this form of social suffering. As best as possible, identify groups of people in your school community who are most impacted by this form of suffering, as well as the varied ways that each aspect manifests within these groups' experience. Avoid making assumptions, such every member of the group experiences suffering in the same way. You are likely not aware of all forms of suffering in your school, nor are you likely privy to the ways in which the suffering impacts each person. In doing this activity, you might realize that you don't fully know the experience of the group who is suffering, and you can note this in the table. Alternatively, you may be more aware of some forms of suffering because of your own identity and positionality or because others with similar identities confide in you.

	How does the suffering show up in my school?	Who is suffering?	What are possible barriers to compassion?
Intrapersonal Aspects of Suffering			
Interpersonal Aspects of Suffering			
Community Aspects of Suffering			

Refining Our Intentions: Creating Humanizing School Environments

Creating compassionate schools begins by recognizing where the school environment could be made more *humanizing*, that is, one where the dignity of each person is honored and affirmed. Humanizing means recognizing the full humanity of people as social, historical, thinking, and creative individuals who engage with the world (del Carmen Salazar, 2013). A humanizing environment fosters a sense of belonging and acknowledges the complexity of what it means to show up as fully human in a space, making room for the full range of emotions that people experience when engaged in social activity. Educational environments are humanizing when they support mutual care and help students and educators take up questions about educational, social, and cultural justice (Camangian & Cariaga, 2022; Paris & Winn, 2014). Humanizing schools allow for the people within them to flourish, for "as people flourish the meaning of learning itself evolves alongside the proliferation of human possibilities" (Espinoza & Vossoughi, 2014, p. 288).

The word humanizing takes its full meaning from considering its opposite, *dehumanizing*. Brazilian educator and philosopher Paolo Freire (1970/2002) wrote, "Concern for humanization leads at once to the recognition of dehumanization" (p. 43). By this he marks the fact that much of education—particularly the education of people living in poverty and people living in colonized lands—is oriented toward controlling students and teaching them concepts and ideas that contribute to maintaining control over them, and not to their freedom. Indeed, the concept of humanization that comes from Freire and others inspired by his work emphasizes the importance of what it means to be free to explore the full range of one's individual and collective potential within a world that is actively hostile to such a pursuit.

Creating humanizing environments in schools, then, requires an awareness of how interpersonal acts that show care to others are potentially more than simple acts of kindness. Those acts of care are humanizing when they push against efforts to control students and instead support their self-determination, when they honor the ways of knowing and being that students bring to class as valued and necessary resources for learning, and when they bring students together in ways that help them recognize what they have in common with others who are working toward freedom (Camangian & Cariaga, 2022). They are humanizing when we move from being allies of our students, to being "co-conspirators" with them, as Love (2019) writes, that is, when acts of care are also acts of resistance to treating children and youth as bodies to be controlled. Acts are dehumanizing when they are in the service of controlling or managing students, when they invite students to discount their own funds of knowledge in service of learning "proper English" or canonical content, and when they fail to help students in building meaningful community in the classroom. Valenzuela (1999) refers to "aesthetic care," which reflects an adherence to the values of schooling and traditional curriculum over valuing children and youth's humanity first. To create compassionate schools, we need what Valenzuela (1999) calls "authentic care," that is, care that both reflects awareness of and seeks to change the conditions that threaten students' well-being in the first place (see, also, Ginwright, 2015).

Caring relationships that are humanizing matter in our relationships with other educators as well. All too often, teachers are expected to put aside their own needs and limits in the service of schools' requirements. We and other teams of scholars (e.g., Allen et al., 2022) have found that it is possible—even necessary—to create humanizing learning spaces with teachers to support their growth and our collective work to create more compassionate schools. For example, we co-designed most of our certificate program with educators during the COVID-19 pandemic, and when we shifted online, we immediately sensed a need to prioritize creating a caring space for educators who were facing immense pressures and stress in the shift to remote teaching. We re-structured the co-design process to make room for open sharing of challenges they were facing and discussion of how compassion practices might help. In studying the process, we found educators highly valued this approach; moreover, they began to apply compassion not only in the settings of remote teaching but among friends and family because they saw them as potentially beneficial for their personal relationships (Potvin et al., 2024). As one of our co-design teachers, Adrienne, shared:

> One big takeaway from the co-design process was a strong sense of community. I can feel isolated sometimes in my job and it was amazing to work with so many people who have the common goal of bringing more compassion into the world. Especially in this time where there are so many things to be depressed about, this really restored my faith in humanity and helped me realize what is important in life and in my job. It helped to hear that others struggle with very similar situations in the educational world. I saw immediate impacts in my day-to-day life and my work. It has helped me bring a sense of compassion to every interaction with parents, students, and even my own family. (Potvin et al., 2024, p. 19)

Holding Space for Possibility

So far in this chapter, we have emphasized attention to suffering, even as we discussed the need for more humanizing environments in education. Clear seeing of suffering is indeed the first step toward a skillful compassionate response to suffering. At the same time, dwelling in the vastness of suffering caused by systems of oppression that are so much bigger than us can lead to a sense of hopelessness, which is yet another form of suffering. It is critical, then, in working toward more compassionate schools, that we hold space for possibilities for being in communities of learning that we might not have ever dreamed of—or allowed ourselves to dream of. Holding spaces for dreaming together about what our schools could be is a critical step in the humanization of schools.

Dreaming together about possible futures—sometimes called *social dreaming* (Espinoza, 2008)—is critical for another reason. Many of the challenges facing schools today—particularly considering the multiple, overlapping crises we confront related to how to live sustainably on the planet—simply require us to speculate about how to bring about desirable futures for schools that go beyond what we have created. We will, no doubt, need to rely on many of the ideas and infrastructures for how to support learning that support us well, but we need to think far beyond existing disciplinary knowledge and connect to sources of wisdom about how to live on the planet sustainably, so that we can thrive as human communities on this planet (National Academies of Sciences Engineering and Medicine, 2024).

In our certificate program, we include a practice that is intended to help people first dream individually about possible future communities and schools, and then to share their visions with others, as one step toward building more compassionate schools. It is also a concrete way to hold space—through active visualization—for possibilities for humanizing environments that do not yet exist in schools today.

Formal Practice: Imagining a Flourishing School Community

Imagining a Flourishing School Community is adapted from Ekman (n.d.), who developed this practice to support adults in imagining both flourishing and kindness. We have adapted it to focus on supporting educators in imagining new, flourishing forms of communities and then using that as a departure point for imagining new kinds of schools.

For this practice, find a comfortable seated position, and begin by noticing your sensations in your body, as they are right now. As you pay attention to these sensations, notice how they shift and change, notice if they feel pleasant, unpleasant, or neutral. Bring attention to any part of the body where you feel tension and invite a feeling of relaxation or ease.

Once you have settled in and become more aware of the sensations of your body, imagine how you might feel if you were part of a community that is truly flourishing, a community where people feel deep well-being and happiness. Perhaps a memory surfaces, or an image or idea comes to mind. Consider what this feels like to be in such a community. What would it feel like to be part of such a community?

Using your breath, take this memory, this image, this idea, or imagination and turn it into an intention. As you inhale, draw in this idea of collective flourishing and contentment. And when you exhale, send out the wish for this joy,

(continued)

(continued)

this contentment, this happiness—here and now. Inhale, drawing in. Exhale, extending a wish that the joy and flourishing you are imagining increases within and among the community. Repeat this a couple of times with the rhythm of your own breath, drawing in this heartfelt aspiration for collective flourishing—and extending it out to your wider community.

Recognize that there are factors that support this collective flourishing and well-being, including situations and circumstances, people, resources. Call to mind that which would most support a community in sustaining well-being and flourishing. Some of these things may already be present and others may be needed.

Consider what it is that you need from your school community to sustain this flourishing and well-being. What qualities would you need to cultivate? What would most support your school community in sustaining flourishing? Some of these qualities you may already have and others you may need to strengthen.

Inhale, drawing in that which is needed to support you. Exhale, "May we cultivate the qualities we need to support our flourishing and well-being." Inhale, drawing in. Exhale, extending out this wish for collective well-being, "May we meet one another in our wish for flourishing and sustain this vision of collective well-being." Repeat twice more on the rhythm of your own breath, drawing in this aspiration to cultivate strengths we need for our collective well-being.

And now shift your attention toward how you would most like to be present in your interactions with others in your school community. What are the qualities you would like to bring to your interactions and exchanges? How would you like to be of service as educators in this world? Reflect and consider: What are the ways in which I really can show up wholeheartedly? Maybe there's a memory or image of what this is like—through your interactions with others—colleagues, students, family members, or friends. Use your breath to draw in this image of yourself as you aspire to be with others. And exhale, "May I be of service. May I be wholehearted in my presence. May I cultivate the qualities most needed to be of service to others." Inhale, drawing in this aspiration. And exhale, extending out.

Release all thoughts, memories, and images. Notice how the body, mind, and heart feel right now. Close with three long inhales and three long exhales.

Jot down your reflections of this practice, including the images that came up for you. If reading this book with others, share your images and discuss what resources and practices already exist for building a flourishing community in your school, as well as what resources and practices are needed. How might you bring or build new resources and practices that flow from your dreaming?

Key Ideas from the Chapter

- All suffering is rooted in larger social systems, and some suffering is the result of policies and programs designed specifically to alleviate suffering.
- Addressing social suffering has the potential to guide us both ethically and politically, to become advocates for and collaborators with children and youth and their families.
- We can consider the intrapersonal, interpersonal, and community aspects of suffering to help make suffering in our schools more visible and can allow for more skillful responses.
- We need to understand systemic inequities and take skillful actions that acknowledge and work to change these harmful patterns.
- Creating compassionate schools begins by recognizing where the environment could be made more humanizing, and by holding space for dreaming together about what our schools could be.

Chapter 12
Building a Shared Commitment to Compassionate Action

Nothing can stop the power of a committed and determined people to make a difference in our society. Why? Because human beings are the most dynamic link to the divine on this planet.
  —*Hon. John Lewis,* Across That Bridge: Life Lessons and a Vision for Change

In the last chapter, we introduced lenses for helping to think about social suffering at three different levels: the intrapersonal, the interpersonal, and the community. Drawing upon the previous practices, resources, and ideas in this book, including the lenses for thinking about social suffering, we now turn to helping you create a compassionate action plan that you can implement in your school with a team. The broad purpose of this plan will be to change policies, practices, routines, and expectations to address a form of social suffering that is persistent and inequitable.

To help you develop this plan, we introduce tools to sharpen your thinking about changes that might be needed at the community level in your school to make it more compassionate. The sequence and content have been informed by our work with educators in the certificate program. Trying out the tools in the order they are presented will support you and your team in creating collective, compassionate change in your school community. We provide examples, too, of how educators in our program used these tools to set intentions for change and to grow a collective commitment to those changes by developing a deeper understanding of the values shared among members of a team and the school community.

In this chapter, we provide guidance for setting intentions regarding the change you would like to see in your school, present a framework for organizing more compassionate schools, and describe an activity to help build a shared commitment within a team and across a school for expanding compassion across the organization. Before we do so, we need to describe what an educator team is, its role, and why we try to work with teams of educators to create school change.

The remainder of the chapters in this section will help you build out your compassionate action plan. In the next chapter, we focus on tools that help you to see your school as a system and you will craft an aim statement that aligns to your intention and guides your compassionate action plan. Then, in Chapter 14, we introduce tools for enacting compassionate collective change in your school and for evaluating the effectiveness of the change you implement.

There are three key assumptions behind the tools and practices presented in this chapter. First, to create more compassionate change, we need to be clear about our intentions. Our intentions set a compass for our collective action. Second, to clarify the scope of possibilities for achieving our intention, we need some research-based tools to help us think about what compassion can look like in an organization. Many of us work in places where suffering is more common than compassionate action, and so we need some guidance just to get started. Third, school change happens best when we work together from a place where we can find common ground, in terms of the values that guide us. We need to know not just our personal "why" but also our collective "why," that is, what motivates us to want to work together to create more compassionate schools.

Establishing an Educator Team

When educators apply to be part of our certificate program, we encourage them to form a team with others in their school of three to four people. Initially, these teams tend to be made up of educators from the same grade level or department, but occasionally teams are made up of a mix of educators in different roles, such as classroom teachers, librarians, counselors, and administrators. And some teachers join our certificate program solo, but they may also have leadership roles where they have the authority to implement the plans they devise in our program. They can also include families and young people as full partners, though their inclusion requires extra care and sensitivity to dynamics of power that can undermine their sense of having a say in a schoolwide effort at change.

The plans that we feature in this chapter and in the next two chapters represent a diversity of teams and individuals like this. The four educators on the elementary school team played different roles in their school. Sarah is a third-grade language teacher,

Stephanie a physical education teacher, Emma a music teacher, and Taryn a first-grade teacher. A second team, the high school team, works in a rural high school in Colorado. Madison from the team is an English Language Development (ELD) Coach, Gricel a Spanish teacher, and Samila a school counselor. Meaghan and NB both took part in our certificate program as individuals. When Meaghan was part of the program, she was a member of the leadership team at her middle school, serving as an assistant principal and an instructional coach, after having been a mathematics teacher for several years. NB is also an assistant principal for an elementary school, where she plays a variety of roles as an operations manager, instructional coach, and family engagement coordinator.

Why build a team or be concerned about the power and authority of school community members to make changes in their schools? For one, community-level aspects of suffering are always the consequences of decisions—decisions made by educators, administrators, students, and family members every day. But the decisions made by those with power and authority often have consequences that ripple out to impact many people, and those effects can last when they impact policies and routine practices of schools. Decisions, then, impact multiple people in different ways; moreover, they are rarely made by individuals, either, but by groups of people working together. Thus, teams are an important place for initiating change. A second reason to build a team is that working closely with others can help strengthen our commitment and resolve to change. When we give voice to our personal intentions to colleagues, to students, and to family members, it helps them become a stronger driver of our own action. When we have others whom we know share our intentions, it helps us stay motivated and answerable to others when we face obstacles. A third reason is that we know that for schools to change, there needs to be a shared commitment to the endeavor. Our own experience and scores of research studies (e.g., Coburn, 2003; Datnow & Stringfield, 2000; Mehan et al., 2010) tell us that when people don't endorse a change effort, it is difficult for it to succeed. A team can help us establish a commitment to a shared vision for change.

If you are putting together your team, it can be helpful to consider the kinds of roles that would be important to have represented on your team, as well as the power and authority of people on the team. Perhaps you already have a team that is responsible for directing school-wide change, such as a school site council or a team dedicated to well-being. These teams could be the focal group for developing an action plan to create a more compassionate school. Alternately, grade-level or department teams could be tasked with coming up with plans around a common aim, and so a team could include representatives from every grade-level or department. A team could be based in an existing committee or group, such as a parent-teacher council. Not all existing teams, though, include key interest holders—that is, representation of people who will be most impacted by whatever plan is put into place. We recommend using a four-square template like the one shown in Figure 12.1 to purposefully select members of a team to represent those with more or less interest and say in the school, so that your team is inclusive.

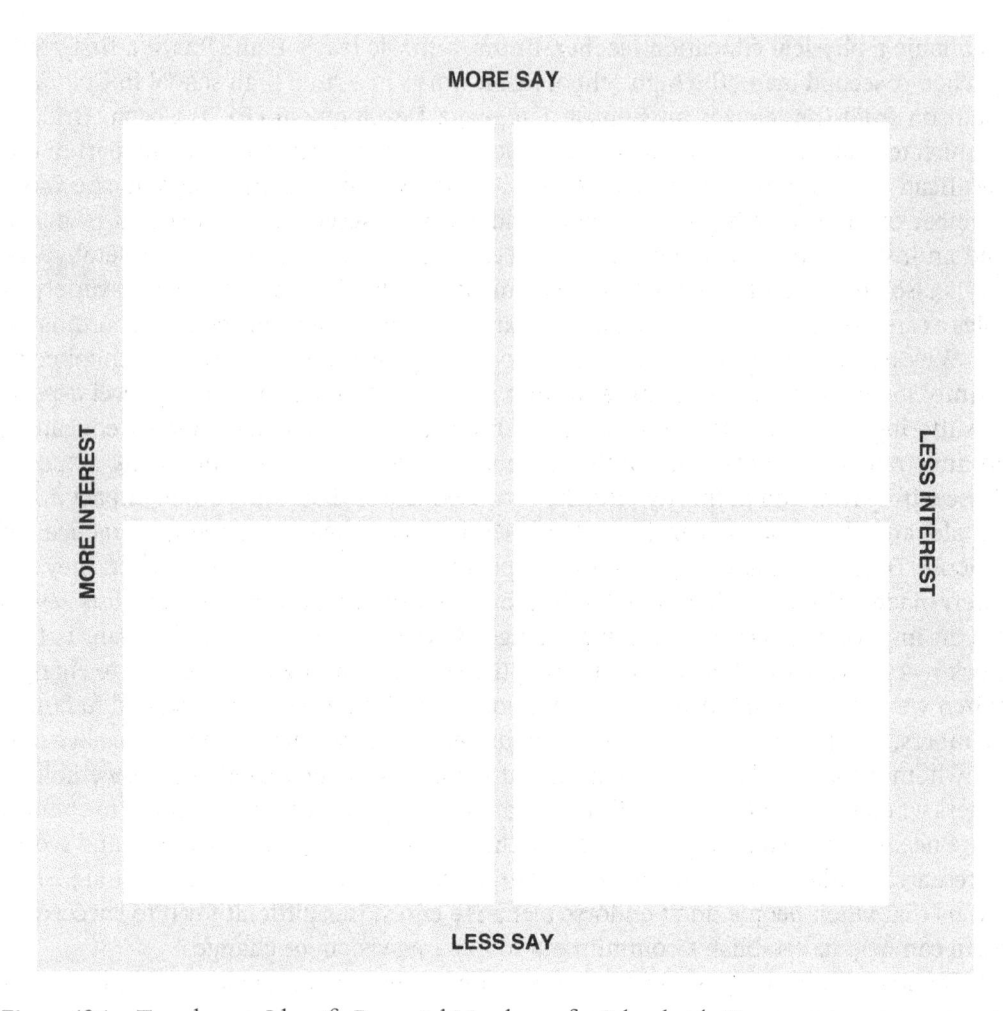

Figure 12.1 Template to Identify Potential Members of a Schoolwide Team
SOURCE: Team Composition Protocol (Adapted from the Advancing Coherent and Equitable Systems of Science Education Project)

In thinking about who does and doesn't have a say typically in matters regarding school policies and practices, the distinction between *power and authority* on the one hand and *status* on the other are important. As we define it here, power and authority have to do with the capacity to act that derives from having some formal role in a school—as a member of a school site council, a principal, counselor, or teacher. Each of us in a school has *some* power and authority, which might be reflected in our job descriptions or contracts, but it's always bounded by other people's power and authority. Status can overlap with power and authority, when someone is highly regarded who also has a position of authority. But sometimes people without power and authority are regarded highly for their expertise, their leadership, their connections, or their capacity to act with or without formal power. Those "high status" people are critical to any school change endeavor, but their "say" in matters may not be so visible, even when it is great. Their opinions about a particular endeavor matter as to whether others will see it as worth their time and commitment.

It's not enough to invite new people to a decision-making table; we need to set the table differently, if our goal is to shift power and authority dynamics in a school to make it more compassionate. We need to pause and ask: who is left out and how can we invite them to the table with care? We need to think about the lived experiences and knowledge that are relevant to our plans and how we will elicit, welcome, and hold those with care on our team. We need to identify roles that team members could play, roles that might go beyond those that are already on an established team. Changing organizations requires many different kinds of leaders, from people who are visionaries to implementers to those who are "front line responders" (Iyer, 2020). We need to consider the networks of people who are connected to those we invite, and how those we invite in might be sources of input as we engage in our ongoing work. We also need a set of working agreements that we make together and keep alive through regular reflection and by having processes in place to address harms when agreements are broken.

Activity: Composing a Team

Below are steps to composing a team that is inclusive and that has people who can work together to implement an action plan to bring about a more compassionate school.

1. Identify key people who might be potentially impacted by your compassionate action plan.

    People who may be impacted, that is, key interest holders, need representation and power on the collaborative team. Try to think beyond immediate interest holders. For example, in education, interest holders are often thought of as students, teachers, and families. Consider the people who will be immediately impacted as well as more distal interest holders, like people whose jobs may be impacted at the district level or in the community, when you implement your plan.

2. Map the relative power of each of your interest holder groups to set terms of discussion about what is important with regards to the plan.

    It is important for equity to begin with a recognition that people do not arrive at a team with the same amount of power. Power includes the ability to

(continued)

(continued)

allocate or direct resources to support a particular initiative or program that comes from one's position. But power also relates to people's social identity, such as their race. One way to think about power in the context of educational transformation is that it involves both having a say, and more than that, having a seat at the table and to set the terms of discussion, that is, what the conversation is about.

Map the interest holders you listed in the previous step onto the grid shown above then return to the reflective questions below:

- Which interest holders currently have the most and least say as to the terms of the focus and activities of your compassionate action plan?
- For each group with the least say, identify at least 1–2 people who are leaders you might bring into a team, and take note of types of groups where you don't know anyone. Who might you know that could help you connect to this group?
- For groups with the most say, identify at least 1–2 people who are leaders who must be at the table for any change effort to be effective, because of the power they hold. Who would be a good participant on a team, who is also a good listener, who makes room for multiple voices to be heard?

3. Identify relevant lived experiences that are critical to be reflected and incorporated into the plan.

   Lived experiences may include categories such as geographic experience, experience as a part of a religious, linguistic, or ethnic group, experience in a profession, experience in a discipline, or experience as a parent, for example. As a group consider both the categories and the domains within those categories that may be relevant for your plan.

   Once you've identified these, discuss with your team:
   - What lived experiences do you bring to the team?
   - Which experiences are you learning about for the first time today?
   - How might the relevant elements of your experience shift in terms of how they matter, depending on the context?
   - Are there some experiences needed on the team that aren't represented, given the focus of your plan?

4. Identify the roles that team members could fill and skills they will need.

   You may wish to consult tools like this one to help inspire you: https://buildingmovement.org/our-work/movement-building/social-change-ecosystem-map/

5. Map potential team members' influence on the system and relationships to each other.

   Use the matrix shown in Figure 12.2 to review and organize your thinking from steps 1–4 for each potential team member. Then, think about each potential team members' network of influence and relationships with other potential members and capture your notes in the last three columns of the matrix. If all members of a team have a shared sphere of influence, or are already well connected to each other, you might consider reaching beyond your existing network.

6. Synthesize and consider next steps.
   - Who are some people who could be good for the team?
   - What more do you need to learn about organizations or people, to make sure the team is better prepared to address equity and justice?

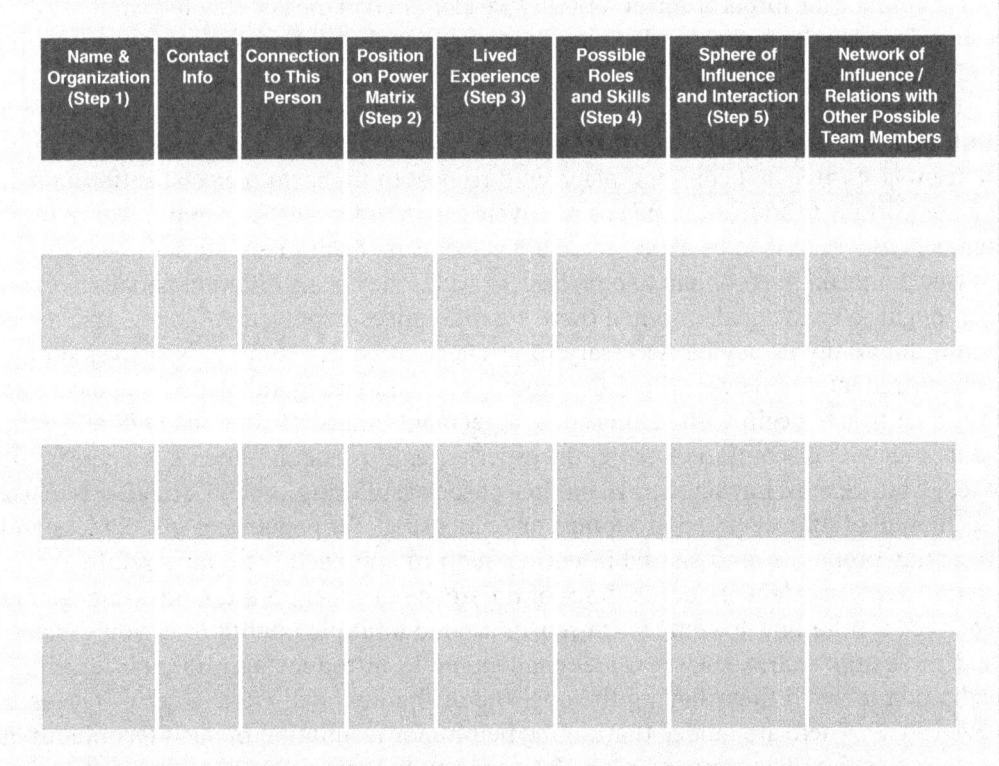

Name & Organization (Step 1)	Contact Info	Connection to This Person	Position on Power Matrix (Step 2)	Lived Experience (Step 3)	Possible Roles and Skills (Step 4)	Sphere of Influence and Interaction (Step 5)	Network of Influence / Relations with Other Possible Team Members

Figure 12.2 Matrix to Map Potential Team Members' Influence and Relationships

Setting a Common Intention

As the Honorable John Lewis (2012) wrote, "nothing can stop the power of a committed and determined people to make a difference in our society" (p. 7). Articulating a shared commitment through a common intention is a powerful practice as you embark on making a difference together in your school community. We've presented intention setting already in this book as a personal practice, something we can do at the beginning of our day or before an important meeting to get clear on our own wishes for how we want to be present and to benefit others. A common intention can function much in the same way, except it's for a team initially, and ideally, it's something that everyone in the school can get behind. In addition, instead of setting an intention for a day, our intention might motivate our action for a month, semester, or a year or more. We might even set an intention that is ambitious enough that it would take a lifetime to accomplish. An intention in this respect can work as a compass for us to keep going for a very long time. Imagine what it would be like if we could eliminate the forms of social suffering we identified in the last chapter: wouldn't that be amazing? Think of what kind of place our school might be. It might even approach the kind of school we dreamed about in the final exercise of the last chapter.

One way of arriving at a shared intention among members of a team is to use a think-pair-share format before starting to integrate intentions into a collective one. If the team is starting at a common place with respect to the form of social suffering that you are working to address, it may be relatively easy to integrate the perspectives of team members. But if, as is to be expected on a diverse team, team members start with different viewpoints on the problem to be solved, or when they bring different perspectives on what ought to be the goal, or when there are differences in power, authority, and status within the group, it may be necessary to privilege or center some perspectives on the problem and intention over others. One strategy for addressing imbalances in power and positionality is to begin with setting some agreements ahead of time that will allow the group to sit with discomfort or center the experiences of particular interest holders in the school who are most impacted by the source of social suffering at hand. Another is to use a technique of affinity-based groupings or "caucusing" for generating initial ideas and presenting proposals for a shared intention. A third approach is to purposefully create groups where people work across lines of difference to generate initial ideas or even to generate ideas for how to come to consensus around multiple intentions. If you've never tried these approaches, they can feel challenging to introduce and do require skillful facilitation to avoid them having the opposite of the intended effect (Curry-Stevens & Jarvis, 2022). There are guides that can be helpful for facilitation of such techniques in small groups (e.g., Landreman, 2013; National Equity Project, 2013), as well as training available from different groups in how to use such strategies (e.g., the National Equity Project and the Institute for Cultural Affairs International). We mention them here, because using these tools helps to address an important aspect of "setting the table" when people come to the table with unequal status, power, and authority. This is so, because these strategies can be helpful in providing a sense of belonging and solidarity to participants in teams with less formal power and authority, and they can also reduce the dominance of voices that tend to dominate in groups, particularly those of people with more race- and gender-based privilege. Key considerations to keep in mind as you build consensus in groups is considering what social risks people are navigating in speaking up and speaking out, and building ways to reduce that risk as best you can as a facilitator.

Just as sources of social suffering can be focused on a single group or on multiple groups in a school, so can intentions for alleviating suffering. In the past, teams and individuals in our certificate program have focused on specific groups of students, on teachers, or on multiple groups. Here are the intentions from three of the educator teams and individuals we'll be following over the next three chapters, where we will present aspects of their action plans for creating more compassionate schools:

High School Team: May our staff feel supported, safe, loved, and valued so that they may flourish in our school community and better support students and other staff.

Meaghan: May our school community (staff, students, and families) be free of the suffering caused by lack of trust and inconsistency with leadership.

NB: May our newcomer families who don't yet have cultural or systemic context be free from suffering due to the inequitable access to community resources, support and understanding.

We had not yet supported the practice of intention setting when the Elementary School Team was part of the program, and so their intention is not included here. We developed this practice, because we realized that the process of setting goals for compassion might benefit from going through an iterative process, beginning with bringing together individual intentions, and then following up with activities to help expand the sense of possibilities for how schools might become more compassionate organizations.

Activity: Setting a Common Intention

We invite you to set a common intention with members of your team.

1. Determine your process for setting a common intention (e.g., think-pair-share, setting agreements, caucusing, creating groups for working across lines of difference).

2. Review your journal entry from the previous chapter on social suffering in your school. If you could eliminate or change one or more policies, programs, or practices in your school that cause many people suffering, that could help

(continued)

(continued)

the people in your school community flourish, what would that be? Of these situations, which ones impact groups that are already marginalized the most?

3. Share your ideas with your group and together begin to articulate the form of social suffering you wish to alleviate in your school community.

4. Together, develop a common intention. You may find it helpful to use the sentence frame: "May X be free of Y form of suffering and the causes of this suffering."

Expanding Possibilities: Introducing the Compassion Organizing Framework

Most programs that focus on developing educators' inner capacities for care and compassion support, as we do, educators' skills in meeting their own suffering with mindfulness and curiosity, as well in addressing suffering that can arise in interactions with others. But our program goes further to help educators imagine and plan responses to suffering at the organizational level. For many of our educators, this is unfamiliar territory. Some of them have little experience with being in schools where compassion is a guiding value. Still others have a hard time imagining what compassion at the community level could look like.

We invite educators to engage with a framework from organizational research, the compassion organizing framework as developed by Dutton et al. (2006) and expanded by Worline and Dutton (2017). This framework suggests that the first step in building more compassionate organizations is to establish practices that help people within them notice, interpret, and respond to suffering among the members of the organization. It's not just about individual responses to observed pain; organizations need adequate resources and a supportive community network to effectively care for those in distress. To adapt this framework for our purposes, we incorporated a focus on equity and justice into the framework. Structural inequalities often contribute to the suffering experienced by students and staff, making it crucial to address these root causes. We wanted educators to recognize and respond to social suffering in ways that honor the ingenuity, agency, dignity, and self-determination of those affected.

The compassion organizing framework is grounded in case studies of how organizations have responded to suffering in compassionate ways. It includes many different examples of things that people can do—as individuals, as groups, within and outside formal channels—to alleviate suffering. As such, it provides educators with a lot of different initial ideas for how they can realize their intentions—many more, in fact, than a small group could possibly undertake on their own. But having more ideas is a great place to begin to formulate more specific aims and action steps to accomplish those aims, which we discuss in the chapters that follow. We provide the following table to educator teams to complete to help them imagine possible activities. As it illustrates, there are many categories of action that can be undertaken at different levels—the personal, interpersonal, and community level. We suggest that you use the Compassionate Action Brainstorming Tool to brainstorm possible activities with your team for making compassionate change in your school.

Activity: Brainstorming Compassionate Actions

Compassionate Action Category	Intrapersonal Actions	Interpersonal Actions	Community Level Actions
Make people aware of how pain and suffering is experienced differently by different groups			
Improvise or change routines and policies to make it possible to help alleviate suffering			
Eliminate barriers or reduce bureaucratic stumbling blocks to helping			
Create flexibility with tasks so people can work/learn/live in ways that match their preferences and what they are able to do			
Offer reassurance and safety when people may feel vulnerable/ worried about how their situation might put them at risk within the school/district			

(continued)

Compassionate Action Category	Intrapersonal Actions	Interpersonal Actions	Community Level Actions
Generate or gather resources to assist			
Intervene to reduce pain associated with tasks			
Monitor and regularly check in on the situation			
Create rituals that bring people together around common pain			
Communicate ways that the community is helping			

It is often the case that ideas for community-level actions are harder for educator teams to generate initially, because we tend to focus on the intrapersonal and interpersonal levels more. We share the actions imagined by our one of the teams and one of the individuals that they generated at the community level as examples to help you and your team imagine what might be possible.

Compassionate Actions Brainstormed by Focal Teams and Educators

Compassionate Action Category	Elementary School Team	NB
Make people aware of how pain and suffering is experienced differently by different groups	Show part of "Breaking the Silence" (2013) video that presents experiences of LGBTQIA+ students. Have teachers identify their own gender identity biases.	Put together a resource drive for items that newcomer families need most. Distribute resources on an as-needed basis. Invite everyone I know.

Compassionate Action Category	Elementary School Team	NB
Improvise or change routines and policies to make it possible to help alleviate suffering	Use the toolkit developed by the district to guide our process.	Create a fund of used uniforms and sweatshirts. Offer them to incoming students before requesting that they purchase anything. Provide all school supplies for all students. Hire parents part-time on campus.
Eliminate barriers or reduce bureaucratic stumbling blocks to helping	Use the toolkit, showing the district support.	Apply for a grant to fund initiative to support newcomer families. Set up a community board for people to promote their services and skills and help each other out.
Create flexibility with tasks so people can work/learn/live in ways that match their preferences and what they are able to do		Ensure that the dress code for school events is flexible enough to never have to go and buy clothing. Host monthly "birthday parties" for all kids for a shared celebration. Set conscious discipline practices.
Offer reassurance and safety when people may feel vulnerable/worried about how their situation might put them at risk within the school/district		Create a school culture of acceptance, compassion, and vulnerability through strong professional development efforts. Never let the police onto the school campus if they are coming for immigration reasons.

(continued)

Compassionate Action Category	Elementary School Team	NB
Generate or gather resources to assist	Start with resources found in the certificate. Be on the lookout for age-appropriate books/readings.	Get in touch with community organizations to see about centralizing support resources for families. Apply for all the grants that we qualify for. Allocate the money honestly.
Intervene to reduce pain associated with tasks	Cultivate presence—nothing to do, focus on being, listening. Withhold blame of others, if not on board, and of ourselves if it is not going the way we want.	Volunteer to be a peer-mentor to help connect vulnerable families to things that they need.
Monitor and regularly check in on the situation	See if we can do professional development on a monthly basis. Add information into weekly blog.	Check in with organizations to see how they view the changing needs of community members.
Create rituals that bring people together around common pain	Create a group for students.	Put together a "farmers market" once a month on campus to provide goods, music, food, community, and resources. Build a cultural fair where each family showcases parts of their culture for collective appreciation.
Communicate ways that the community is helping	Bring in speakers and advocates (local PFLAG chapter).	

Uncovering Our Collective Why

In our certificate program, once a team has set an intention and brainstormed some possible actions, they pause to consider again *why* specific actions might actually alleviate suffering. The "Five Whys" activity, which we adapted from organizational change work, is typically used to help identify root causes of problems (Serrat, 2017). We use it instead to encourage educator teams to uncover their deep beliefs about why particular changes they might try could alleviate the inequitably experienced form of social suffering they are targeting in their action plans.

For our version of the Five Whys activity, teams begin with choosing an action they could take to change a rule, routine, policy, or practice to alleviate suffering in their school (see the following table). Then, they ask and discuss the first "why": Why do we think changing this rule/routine/policy/or practice could make our school more compassionate? The team writes down the answers they discuss, and then asks the second "why" question, using their answer to the first "why" question as the starting point: And why would *this* help our school become more compassionate? The team continues until they have answered "why" five times.

Activity: Writing Your Five Whys

1. What <u>rules</u>, <u>routines</u>, <u>policies</u>, or <u>practices</u> (school environment) would make it possible for us to become a more compassionate school?

2. Why would [Answer to 1] help us become a more compassionate school?

3. Why would [Answer to 2] help us become a more compassionate school?

4. Why would [Answer to 3] help us become a more compassionate school?

5. Why would [Answer to 4] help us become a more compassionate school?

6. Why would [Answer to 5] help us become a more compassionate school?

The process almost always yields some root values or beliefs that diverse groups of people can agree on for building a compassionate school. Some of the answers to the fifth "why" question from the teams we are following include:

High School Team: ALL of our students will start flourishing, feel safer, and be supported for their unique circumstances and experiences. This will also be due to staff viewing others holistically and compassionately.

Meaghan: Recognizing suffering and giving space for compassion would help us become a more compassionate school because collective effort would be given to sources of suffering and trust would be developed through that vulnerability.

NB: If families have a better chance at success in school and in life, we are not only promoting compassion for our students and their futures, but also for their families and ultimately our communities.

Using the Five Whys can help to build a shared understanding of what motivates different people to work toward creating more compassionate schools. While after five questions, what the group arrives at may feel abstract and lofty, it can be helpful to return to this "why" when the team gets going and needs a boost of energy. After all, this represents our deepest beliefs and thinking about why what we are doing matters.

Key Ideas from the Chapter

- This chapter introduces the first steps of developing a compassionate action plan to create community-level change to address a form of social suffering that is experienced inequitably by a group of people.
- When establishing a team, consider the kinds of roles that should be represented, the power and authority of the people on the team, and who is missing and how to include them.
- Setting a common intention with your team helps you to be clear on your wishes for your school and can motivate action at the community level.
- The compassion organizing framework can guide you in creating a more compassionate school through establishing practices that help people in your school notice, interpret, and respond to suffering.
- Once you've set a common intention and brainstormed possible actions, it's beneficial to consider why you think those actions could alleviate an inequitably experienced form of social suffering.

Chapter 13
Preparing for Collective Compassionate Action by Seeing the System

[Equity] requires us to think hard about the role of systems and structures in our lives, our communities, and our society and to find a way to make the invisible visible. Mostly, it requires us to dig deep into our internal desire for fairness and summon the courage to do hard things, like redesign entire organizations.
—*Minal Bopaiah,* Equity: How to Design Organizations Where Everyone Thrives

Compassionate leaders can hold any role within the school community—not just formal positions—and you have the capacity to be a compassionate leader. To understand what it means to lead with compassion, we draw on a distributed theory of leadership (Spillane et al., 2001). This theory is premised on the idea that all educators have the capacity to exercise leadership through attuning to the social suffering that exists within the school community, and to respond skillfully, flexibly, and creatively to alleviate or disrupt the cycles of suffering through collaborative, skillful action. Our decisions matter, regardless of the formal power we hold (National Academies of Sciences, Engineering, and Medicine, 2024).

In this chapter, we invite you to return to your intentions for alleviating social suffering in your school and to plan for compassionate action, building upon the thinking and work you've already done in the previous chapter. We introduce tools to help you see your school as a *system* of components made up of people, processes, policies, routines and interactions, to look for possibilities within the system to make compassionate change, and to focus on what compassionate change can look like in your community. We encourage you to hold your dream for a compassionate school close as you take steps to bring that vision to life.

Seeing Your School as a System

Schools are systems made up of policies, practices, people, routines, rules, and expectations. Systems never change fast or easily; resistance to change is embedded in enduring institutions or organizations, such as schools. This doesn't mean that organizations can't change or that we shouldn't work to make them more compassionate. What it does mean is that we need to set realistic expectations for how and when the change can occur, and to sustain hope that change is possible. You can be an important and powerful advocate for compassionate change.

A key assumption we bring to our work with educators is that to change a school, we need to see the school as a system as it is now functioning to produce the dynamics and outcomes we experience every day in our hearts, minds, and bodies (the intrapersonal) and in our interactions (the interpersonal), an idea we introduced in Chapter 10. Currently, your school as a system is producing—likely again and again—a form of social suffering that you would like to see diminished or eliminated. But just as it has the potential to produce suffering, schools as systems can encourage and facilitate compassionate action. For that to occur, though, we need a way to see our schools as systems composed of key parts, interactions, and drivers that move them in some directions, but not others. In short, we need to first "diagnose" our schools, so that we can direct our actions skillfully toward changing our schools.

However, it's not always easy to diagnose our schools, as some of the components within a system may be obvious to us (e.g., the principal, rules about discipline), while others may be less visible or hidden (e.g., unstated expectations, such as only tenured teachers can speak up in staff meetings). And many of us aren't in the habit of seeing our schools as systems—as a set of interrelated components that produce particular outcomes. In her book, *Equity: How to Design Organizations Where Everyone Thrives*, Minal Bopaiah (2021) asserts,

> [Equity] requires us to think hard about the role of systems and structures in our lives, our communities, and our society and to find a way to make the invisible visible. Mostly, it requires us to dig deep into our internal desire for fairness and summon the courage to do hard things, like redesign entire organizations. (p.120)

To see the system, to make the invisible visible, requires a shift in our focus, moving away from a focus on individual actions or personalities toward understanding how policies, practices, people, routines, rules, and expectations work in concert to produce the outcomes we observe and feel. We can analyze our school systems to understand how they can be at times compassionate and inclusive, while at other times lead to suffering and marginalization.

Two Metaphors for Schools That Help Us See Them More Clearly

Several metaphors for systems have been proposed to help leaders see their schools more clearly, and here we introduce two that have helped educators understand their schools better. The first of these is to understand schools as composed of *layered infrastructures,* that is, sets of procedures and processes, rules and expectations, and routines that are intended to guide people's actions (Penuel, 2019). The layers of infrastructure that make up the school as an organization impact students' experiences of schooling and educators experiences of the workplace. Class schedules direct teachers' and students' time and attention. Routines for passing in the hallway direct students' bodies. Policies related to dress code detail what students can wear. Discipline policies and practices outline expectations for student behavior as well as guidance for how educators should enforce the expectations. Curricula, textbooks, and pacing guides influence what concepts, skills, and topics teachers will teach and when, as well as what students will learn. You can probably think of many other components of your school that guide people's actions, such as academic standards, decision-making processes, structures for professional learning and collaboration, and extra-curricular activities available to students, to name a few.

To make compassionate change that takes hold and is sustained requires that we look at the alignment and coherence of the components of the system that matter. Seeing the school as a system of layered infrastructure allows us to begin to recognize how these components work together to impact the full experience of school for members in the community. For instance, to create a sense of belonging and safety within her school for newcomer families, NB leveraged her school's pre-existing routine of home visits to families to learn more about their needs and experiences and refined the existing enrichment programming to include parents. We can also begin to see how these layers may contribute to meaningful and even joyful experiences, while some may contribute to suffering. Seeing the system in this way helps us to identify possibilities for greater connection, care, and compassion and to plan for sustaining the changes we make.

The second metaphor is to see schools as *complex ecosystems,* which helps us to see how the dynamics of people's interactions lead to outcomes we might not predict or hope for.

This metaphor helps us to think about how people's interactions with one another, as well as the ways in which they interact with policies, routines, and procedures influence what happens in school communities. Schools are webs of social connections, and the people within our schools are interdependent. As we've discussed in previous chapters, our well-being is connected to and dependent upon many others, and the actions of a person or group impact all others in the community. When one group of people in our school community suffers, it impacts all of us. The ways that we interact with and treat one another matter, and the metaphor of schools as ecosystems helps to see that even small interactions matter in big ways.

We can identify elements of the ecosystem that bring people together to carry out certain actions according to specific goals. For instance, your school might have common planning time for grade-level teachers to collaborate on lessons, design assessments, and discuss student progress. We can also begin to recognize the many factors that influence the nature of these interactions. For instance, whether or not you had a say in developing a policy or routine might impact your level of commitment, how you interpret the policy, or the extent to which you prioritize a routine.

These metaphors can help us see more clearly the ways in which our schools operate and the ways in which the people and elements interact that lead to the outcomes we observe. It also helps us to identify interactions and elements at play that may have been invisible to us upon first look. Practices such as Appreciating Others (Chapter 9) and Extending the Circle of Compassion (Chapter 10) can also help us see, contemplate, and appreciate the ways we are dependent upon and connected with all others in our school community. Once we make the parts of the system visible, we can begin to plan intentionally for skillful compassionate change that can be sustained. We can avoid quick fixes or responses that might lead to additional harm or other unintended consequences. When we see the system clearly, we are much more likely to act skillfully to address suffering. It can be helpful to employ some tools to help us see the system and to sharpen our focus.

Seeing the System through Actor Network Maps

An actor network map is one tool that can help you see the school as a system. By "actor" we refer not just to individuals and groups, but also to other components within the system such as policies, planning documents, frameworks, routines, digital resources, and physical space or materials (Bell et al., 2021). Actor network maps are used to map the current landscape of your school, allowing you to understand how seemingly disparate actors contribute to particular outcomes or effects. Actor network maps can help you to better understand the people, policies, and practices that support or hinder your progress toward developing a compassionate school. This information can be used to mobilize resources to support your intention for alleviating suffering and to bring about compassionate action at the organizational level.

You can use an actor network map to create a visual representation of the actors, or components, of the system that contribute to or hinder collective compassionate action within schools. An actor network map allows you to characterize the particular influence each component has over efforts for compassion within your school. The map also allows you to identify which components align with your vision and intention for compassion and which are not aligned, and to see the relationships between components within the system. Before creating your own actor network map, we encourage you to take a look at the maps created by Meaghan and the High School Team, to whom we introduced you in the previous chapter.

Recall that Meaghan's intention was to alleviate the suffering in her community caused by lack of trust and inconsistency with leadership. In her analysis, she identified two actors that aligned with her intention, including the student experience survey and her principal (Figure 13.1). She identified several actors as neutral: the principal manager, the leadership team, and the grade-level chairs. Meaghan also identified actions not aligned with her intention, such as the school performance framework and daily morning meetings of staff. After analyzing the ways in which actors were connected or not, Meaghan realized that she could leverage the connection between

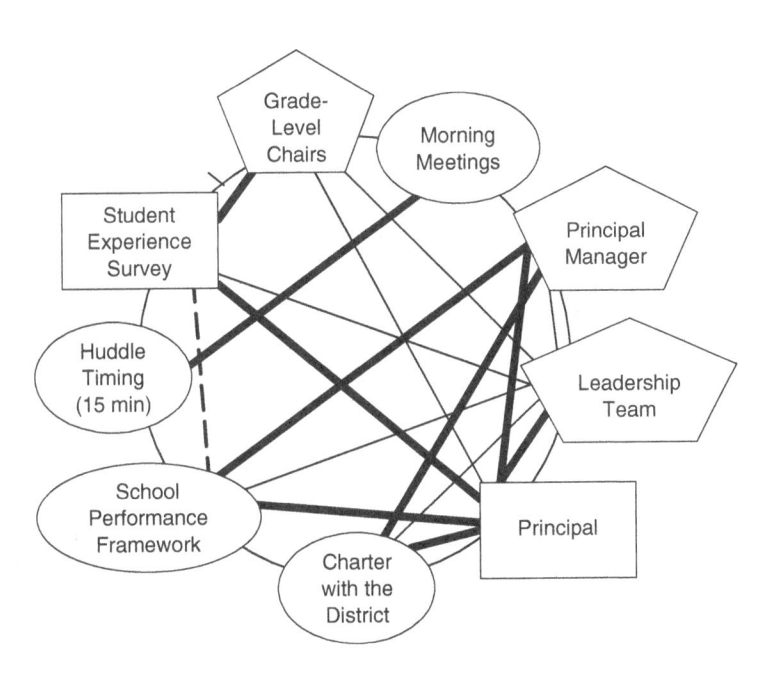

Figure 13.1   Meaghan's Actor Network Map

the principal and principal manager to ensure that the principal manager supported her compassionate action plan "because of the impact it could have on the well-being of the principal, her leadership team, and the school community as a whole." She also realized that she could activate another node in her actor network, the student experience survey, a measurement tool already used in her school, to learn more about the suffering of students in her school community. Creating her actor network map also helped Meaghan to realize that it was "really important that we start to see trust and cohesion-building early in the process."

The High School Team's intention was that their staff feel supported, safe, loved, and valued so that they may flourish in their school community and better support students and other staff. They identified a number of actors that aligned with their intention, such as school administrators and the parent-teacher organization (Figure 13.2). In creating their map, the team realized just how much support they already had for their compassionate action plan, but that many of the actors had not yet been asked to help. They reflected that creating the actor network map and analyzing their school as a system,

> helped us recognize how many people are in positions and already set up to support potentially. It also helped us realize that maybe we've just never asked for support, so we don't know how people will respond. It's not that our school community DOESN'T want to, but they might not be fully aware.

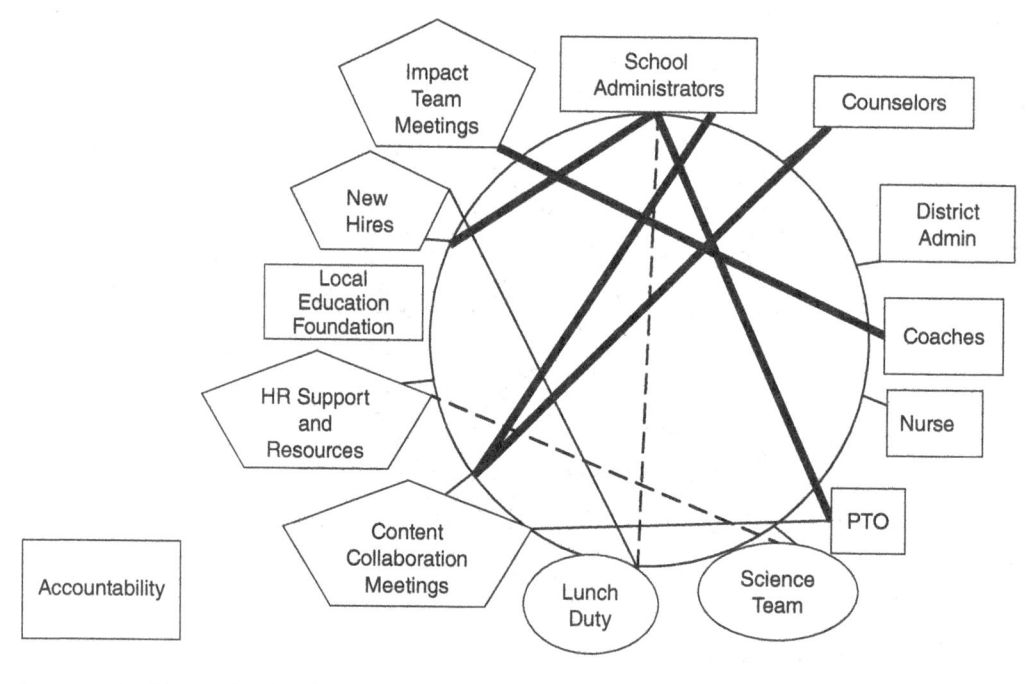

Figure 13.2 The High School Team's Actor Network Map

Creating Your Own Actor Network Map to See Your System

Now, it's your turn to create an actor network map of your school as a system. We recommend that you begin by returning to the common intention you articulated in the previous chapter. Next, brainstorm a list of the actors—policies, practices, and people—that could either support or hinder you in bringing this intention into action. Focus on the policies, practices, rules, and people that your team can either directly or indirectly influence, rather than things that are completely outside of your control. You may also consider actors that aren't immediately obvious to you—perhaps local advocacy groups or curriculum companies. Remember, actors can include specific people, school or district policies, planning documents, established routines, digital resources, and physical materials or space. From your brainstormed list of actors, select 10 that you think are the most important and relevant to your common intention, regardless of whether they are supportive or not.

You can use the diagram shown in Figure 13.3 to create the map by adding the 10 actors you selected. Use a rectangle to represent the actors that are aligned to your intention, a pentagon for actors that you feel are neutral, and an oval for actors that are opposed. Try to avoid using large groups of people on the map who are composed of a mix of supportive, neutral, and opposed individuals (e.g., teachers), but rather identify specific individuals or subgroups (e.g., science teachers), since it's hard to know how to proceed when the group is made up of so many different kinds of actors (Riedy et al., 2018). That doesn't mean you don't include parents or teachers, but that you get specific about the groups or individuals that are likely to influence whether or not your plan is successful.

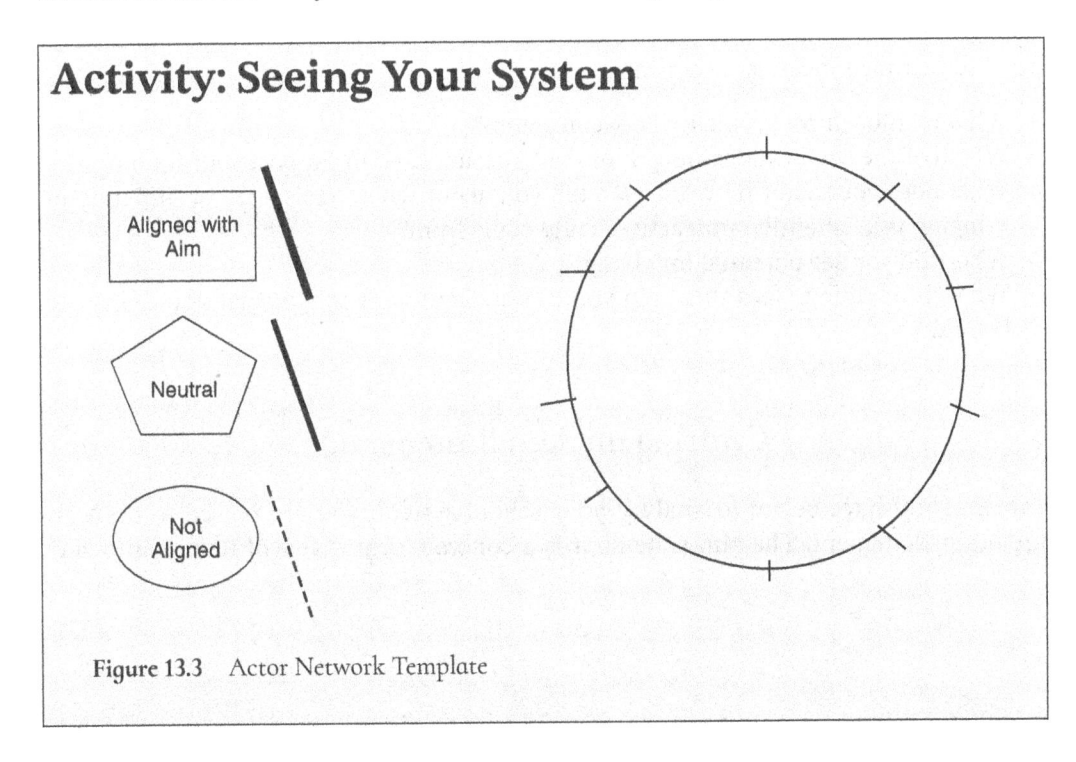

Activity: Seeing Your System

Aligned with Aim

Neutral

Not Aligned

Figure 13.3   Actor Network Template

Next, analyze the relationships between components, noting which components are allied or connected to one another, such that they could not be separated, and which components have a connection that is weak and changeable. You can use a thick line to connect components that are allied or connected. In Meaghan's example earlier in this chapter, the principal and principal manager were closely connected, so she used a thick line to connect them. You can use a dotted line to connect components where the connection is weak.

While your actor network map is a reflection of the current landscape of your school, you can use this tool to identify ways to reorganize or catalyze actors or to introduce a new actor into the system to produce the compassionate change you are hoping to see. The actors you identified as aligning with your intention (rectangles) can be activated as resources and allies to help you bring your intention into reality. You may consider persuading (in the case of people) or revising or adjusting (in the case of materials, policies, or practices) neutral actors (pentagons) to support your intention. There may be some actors not aligned to your intention (ovals) whom you wish to persuade, while for others you decide not to spend time and energy lingering on that part of the system. This may take skillful discernment, to determine where to focus your time and energy and to decide if and how you can move forward with your plan, even if these people or groups are resistant. For some of the individuals and groups you put into ovals, you may try to allay their fears and worries. We will address how to talk to different groups of people about your compassionate change ideas in the next chapter. For now, spend some time analyzing your school system in relation to your intention for alleviating suffering by considering the questions below. If possible, discuss your responses with members of your team or other allies. If it's not possible to talk with someone else, you can instead spend some time reflecting in writing.

- What relationships do you see between actors?
- Which of the actors and connections could be activated to support your intention?
- What does your actor network map tell you about where resistance or difficulty in bringing your intention into action could come from?
- Where do you see potential for change?
- What, if anything, does this help you to see about your school that you didn't see before?

Crafting an Aim Statement

Now that you have begun to analyze your school system, you are poised to draft an initial aim statement. The aim statement is a concrete goal that will help you to stay oriented to the compassionate change you wish to see in your school community. Aim statements are similar to other kinds of goals you likely have set in the past, such as "SMART" goals, in that they are measurable and time-bound. Aim statements also specify who is responsible for contributing to meeting your aim. The people you've included in your actor network map are likely some of the people who will contribute to meeting your aim.

As you work to craft your aim statement, return to both the intention you set and the brainstorming you did in the Compassionate Action Brainstorming Tool in the previous chapter. Consider which of the actions that you brainstormed at the community-level would support more of the interpersonal and intrapersonal compassionate actions you wish to see. Consider where you (and your team members) have agency, authority, and energy to make change. Think about how the actions you might pursue support your intention and how the actions would help alleviate suffering for those most directly and acutely impacted by it. The key is to select a focus for your compassionate change that closely aligns to your intention for alleviating social suffering and where you, with support from others, have agency and authority to move the needle. Remember, too, that social suffering is a form of suffering that is experienced *inequitably,* that is, where those who are impacted are people who feel the impact more and have less power themselves to address the sources of suffering. This is an important step in preparing for compassionate action at the school level.

We suggest spending the time now in reflection and discussion with your team members about the focus of your aim statement. Consider together: How big is the cause of suffering? Are other people suffering, besides the group identified in your intention? Are there other ways of thinking about the cause of suffering before moving forward? To answer these questions, you may choose to collect and analyze some baseline data to learn more about the experience of suffering that you notice. Perhaps your school or district already collects this information through surveys or feedback forms. Or perhaps you need to collect your own data, which could include talking with people you believe are impacted by the form of suffering identified or even sending out a brief survey to learn more. In the next chapter, we'll talk specifically about how to evaluate your progress toward your aim using practical measures.

As you develop your aim statement, it can be valuable to focus on where there is collective energy and willingness to grow within your community. You can use your actor network map analysis to identify people and resources that are needed to make progress in alleviating social suffering. In the aim statement, you will get concrete by specifying a target for improvement. This target will be linked to a measure, so that you can understand if your efforts are alleviating suffering.

Here are the aim statements that the four educator teams and individuals we introduced you to in the previous chapter crafted to guide their work.

The Elementary School Team: By the end of the 2022–23 school year, staff will begin to recognize how we can create a safe, affirming school culture that includes creating space for gender-diverse students. Staff will recognize and discuss their own implicit bias around gender identity and the impacts they hold. Staff will have an opportunity to bring compassion to all students by practicing the use of different gender-related language. Staff will also use their learning to take action by evaluating upcoming lessons or their own actions to incorporate or explore different gender identities in lessons.

The High School Team: By the end of the 2024–2025 school year, a small group of educators will develop a Care Team for the staff to strengthen relationships, their well-being, and foster more intra and interpersonal compassion through positive and meaningful interactions and team building activities. This will lead to growth in being able to have more generous interpretations of suffering toward themselves, coworkers, and extending to students, it will be known through results from the Panorama survey and feedback.

Meaghan: By Winter Break, our Leadership Team will be invested in and eager to participate in a daily ritual/routine during our morning huddle in which we work to collectively build trust, cohesion, and compassion within our school community. This ritual/routine will include setting intentions, building self-awareness, practicing mindfulness, and asking for help so that we center our work each day on the collective well-being of and trust within our team and school community.

NB: By the end of the 2024–2025 school year, our team will acquire the funding to restructure our programming and offer work opportunities to families in need. We will partner with local organizations to ensure our families have opportunities for after school care and enrichment, immigration support, and additional needed resources. This will bring our newcomer families a sense of security, safety, and belonging, which shall ease their suffering. Success will be evidenced by: higher attendance rates, higher employment rates, higher housing rates, positive survey data.

We encourage you, if possible, to draft an aim statement with your team or other allies. Aim statements include the following elements: what you hope to accomplish and for whom, what actors and what strategies are needed to accomplish the aim, and by when and how much. You can use the following chart to jot down ideas. We encourage you to see your aim statement as iterative; to return to it from time to time and revise it as you get input from key actors and as you learn more about the qualities of the suffering you are hoping to alleviate. In the next chapter, we'll provide tools for expanding upon the ideas in your aim statement, including identifying action steps and measures to track your progress toward making compassionate action within your school.

Activity: Crafting Your Aim Statement

	Notes/Ideas
What do you hope to change and for **whom**?	
What will the change **look like** in practice?	
What **actors** and what **strategies** are needed?	
By **when** do you hope to accomplish it?	
How will the change alleviate social suffering in your school?	
How will you know **it worked**?	
Using your notes from the rows above, draft your **aim statement**.	

Key Ideas from the Chapter

- Schools can be understood as systems made up of policies, practices, people, routines, rules, and expectations.
- To change a school, we need to see the school as a system as it is now functioning to produce the dynamics and outcomes we experience every day.
- An actor network map is a picture showing the components and interactions and their alignment in the school system, and it can help you identify leverage points for change in your school.
- An aim statement can give focus to your action plan when it articulates what you hope to change, for whom, by when, and who needs to be involved in making the change. It also requires a goal that is measurable and a strategy that is well-suited to meet that goal.

Chapter 14
Leading for Compassionate Change

It is important to take action and to realize that we can make a difference, and this will encourage others to take action and then we realize we are not alone and our cumulative actions truly make an even greater difference. This is how we spread the Light. And this, of course, makes us all even more hopeful.

—Jane Goodall

Compassionate leadership takes both courage and wisdom, and it's a collective effort. It takes courage to face suffering and to help others attune to suffering, especially when that suffering is caused by or perpetuated by everyday school procedures. It is no easy task to lead efforts that call for disrupting or rethinking rules, routines, or policies that are deeply embedded in the way schools are organized. At times, it may feel like complex, challenging, or slow work, but it's also urgent and necessary for addressing everyday suffering in schools. As such, it's important to know if efforts to enact compassionate change are effective and in alignment with our intentions for creating a more compassionate school environment. As Jane Goodall reminds us,

> It is important to take action and to realize that we can make a difference, and this will encourage others to take action and then we realize we are not alone and our cumulative actions truly make an even greater difference.

But how do we figure out what kind of action to take, and how do we encourage others to take action? In this chapter, we'll introduce tools for enacting compassionate collective change, evaluating the effectiveness of school-level change and compassionate action, and persuading and inspiring others to action.

Theory of Compassionate Change

In our work with educators, we've found that articulating a theory of compassionate change helps them to determine the actions they need take to accomplish their aims. A theory of compassionate change is a visual representation and summary of how and why you expect compassionate change to happen in your school context. Developing a theory of compassionate change not only helps you and your team to identify next steps, but it is a useful tool for communicating your ideas to others in your school community. It also helps you to identify key early indicators of successes and problems in implementation and to determine an evaluation plan to help you track those indicators.

Change does not just come from top-down actions, but rather you will find that you need a broad base of support to bring your compassionate change ideas to life to accomplish your aim of alleviating social suffering. To begin, we invite you to consider initial actions that can encourage a broad base of support and that can be catalysts for change to policies or practices in your community. Take a moment to review NB's example theory of compassionate change (Figure 14.1). To work toward her aim of alleviating suffering for newcomer students and families, NB identified initial actions for securing support for her plan from families, staff, and community organizations, including: applying for grant funding to support new programs, restructuring current school programs, making home visits to learn more about families' needs, and developing a plan to forge partnerships

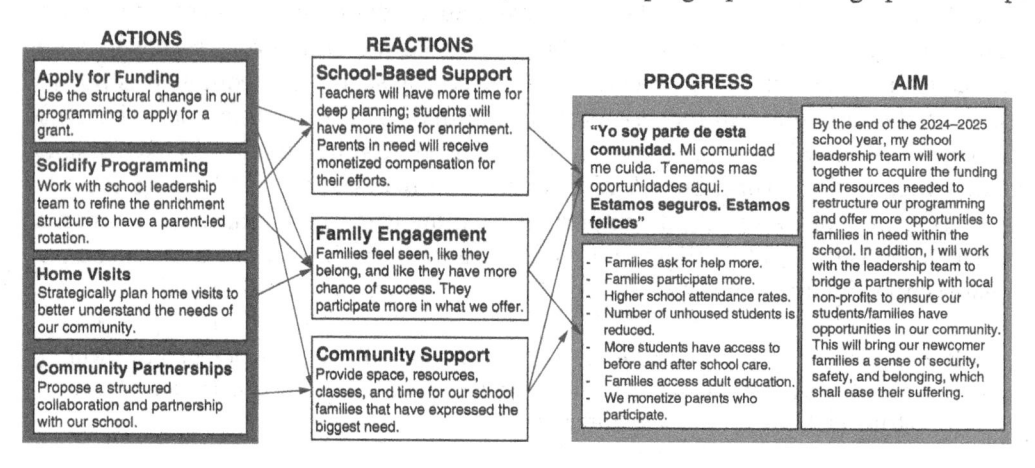

Figure 14.1   NB's Theory of Compassionate Change

with local community organizations. She then considered how people might respond to these initial actions. These responses served as a set of early indicators that she might (or might not) be on her way to accomplishing her aim. If your aim involves implementing a new policy or program like NB's, you will need buy-in and support from key actors in your community and it is helpful to plan for this before you take action.

To work toward their aim of developing a Care Team for staff to strengthen the community, the High School Team identified concrete actions such as introducing the idea of the Care Team at a faculty meeting, hosting community events, and offering support to staff members experiencing difficulties (see Figure 14.2). They theorized that staff would respond positively and would support and engage with the Care Team efforts and treat one another more compassionately. Regardless of the change you are hoping to make, you'll need to inspire a sense that the change is possible and that those in your school community, with collective effort, can make it happen.

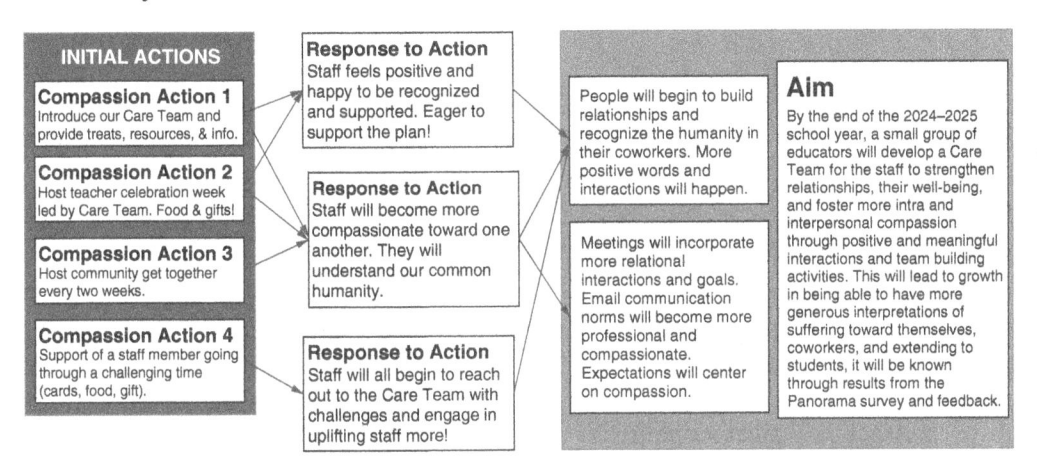

Figure 14.2 The High School Team's Theory of Compassionate Change

Drafting Your Theory of Compassionate Change

You can use the blank template provided (Figure 14.3) to draft with your team your theory of compassionate change. You will need the planning tools you've completed in previous chapters to reference in this activity, including your intention (Chapter 12), Compassionate Action Brainstorming Tool (Chapter 12), actor network map (Chapter 13), and aim statement (Chapter 13). The provided template is meant as a base to get you started, but feel free to adapt it to your unique situation and context.

We suggest doing some backward planning to articulate your theory of compassionate change. You can begin by placing your aim statement in the box on the far right and then work your way from right to left. Consider the things that people will say or do

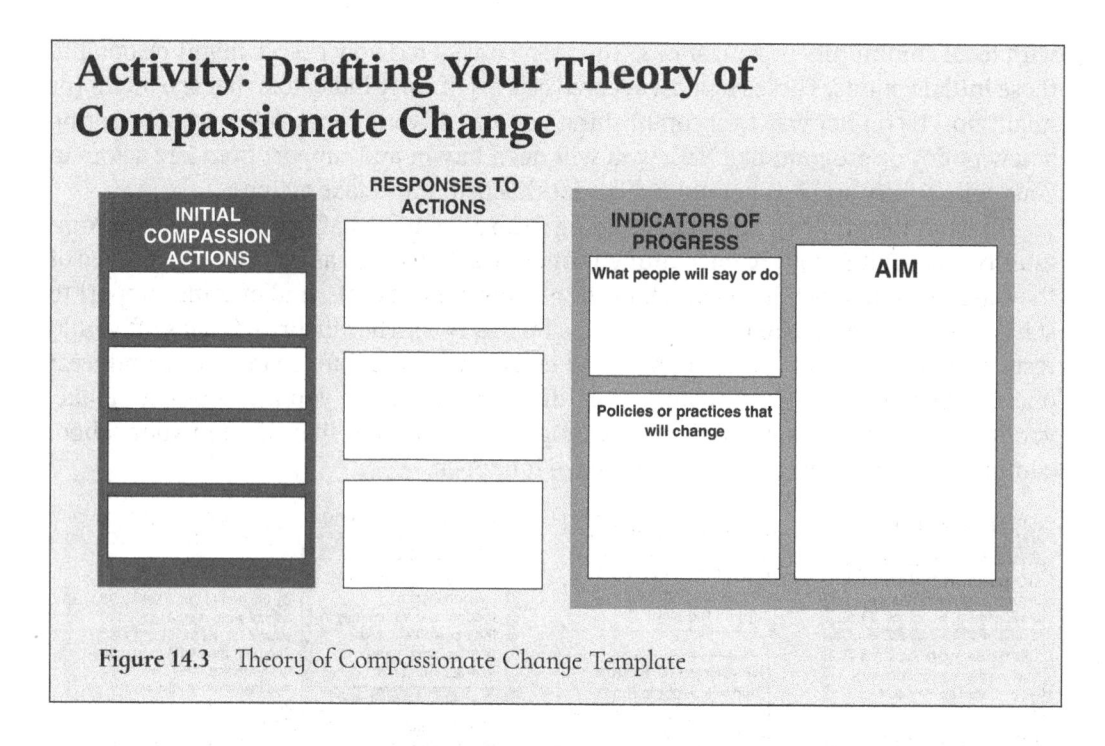

Figure 14.3   Theory of Compassionate Change Template

if you make progress toward your aim and identify the policies and practices that will change if you make progress. Think about some initial actions that will catalyze this change. It may be helpful to review your ideas in the Compassionate Action Brainstorming Tool and prioritize those that you think will most support your aim.

Then you can consider responses to the actions you've identified. This is where your actor network map comes into play. Consider how the actors you identified as allies, neutral people, and opponents might respond to your initial actions and contribute to your aim. Theorizing what happens in the middle—between the initial actions and the accomplishment of the aim—is the most critical step as there is always a lot that happens in the middle that shapes if your plan will be a success. For this reason, we suggest taking the time to anticipate how the key actors will respond to the compassionate actions you have planned. In some cases, their responses may necessitate adding another column of actions before you can arrive at indicators of progress: the things people will do or say or policies and practices that will change. A theory of change that fully articulates the small steps and processes involved in realizing an aim can help you and your team keep track of the progress you are making toward an aim.

Now, connect the initial compassionate actions with responses to action, and then connect responses to actions to indicators of progress using arrows. As a final step, we invite you to return to the intention you wrote for alleviating suffering in your school community to ensure your theory of compassionate change addresses the suffering you hope to alleviate in your school community.

Your ultimate aim may require bold action and significant changes to policies and practices, changes that will take trust and buy-in from many actors in the school to accomplish. You may realize that you need to take a step back and begin with trust-building activities. If some of these initial actions feel small in size and scope, that's okay. As we've seen in previous chapters, opening hearts to suffering that exists in our communities is vulnerable work and can take time. Bigger actions will require more people working together, and that means taking initial steps to gather those people together, steps that can be small and incremental. We've found that spending time up front to put relationships over tasks is worthwhile for building the kinds of caring and inclusive communities we envision.

Planning for Compassionate Action

Now that you've articulated your theory of compassionate change, it's time to begin planning out your action steps in more detail and creating a timeline. We suggest beginning with the initial compassionate actions from your theory of compassionate change, breaking them into discrete steps so that they become a "to-do" list that you can ask others for help to accomplish. For instance, an initial action that NB identified in her theory of compassionate change was to "apply for funding." In her plan, she broke this action into smaller steps, including "attend a grant writing workshop" and make "a list of other grants that we may qualify for." See if you can identify a list of action steps that is more than you can do alone. NB planned to enlist the help of district grant writing specialists and her school leaders for these smaller steps. For each step, plan when you will take the step and who will be involved. Then, consider what it will look like, sound like, or feel like to make progress at each step. You can use the following blank chart to help you plan the steps you will take to alleviate social suffering in your school community and add rows as needed. Remember, you will likely adjust your plan as you engage school community members and gather more information.

Activity: Planning for Compassionate Action

Step (What will you do and how?)	Timing (When will you take this step?)	People (Who will be involved in this step?)	Indicator of Progress (What does "progress" look, sound, and/or feel like?)

Evaluating Progress Toward Your Aim

You've made your plans for alleviating a form of social suffering in your school that impacts people inequitably. But now you might be wondering: Once we start to take action, how will we know if what we are doing is better than what was done before? It can be valuable to evaluate your progress along the way, so that you can determine if your actions are alleviating suffering or if they are having unintended effects that lead to more suffering. You may decide to use existing school measures or data such as student discipline data, student attendance, or a family engagement survey or you may need to create your own measures.

In our certificate program, we support educators in developing their own "practical measure" that is tied to their specific aim and intention. Practical measures can help you gather information about how your compassionate change is working in your school community. Practical measures are short instruments that can be given as part of an activity and are easy to administer and analyze (LeMahieu & Cobb, 2025; Yeager et al., 2013). Practical measures are neither for research nor for accountability, but rather they are for improvement, in this case for tracking intermediate steps and progress toward your aim of addressing suffering. Practical measures could include a brief student or staff survey, an observation checklist, a two- or three-question interview, or even a creative prompt with a rubric where students represent their ideas through art. Practical measures can be given repeatedly, at key moments throughout your compassionate change project, to track your progress over time. The information that you gather can help you make adjustments to your plan. You may also find that it's necessary to revise your aim as you gather more information and learn more from people who are impacted.

The key to successful practical measure development is to create items, or questions, that are tied to your theory of compassionate change. We suggest developing a survey with no more than six items, so that it is easy for people to complete quickly. Before you create your survey, decide who will take the survey. We encourage you to really think about whose voice it's important for you to listen to—and you may actually need to give your survey to different groups of people or create two different versions of the survey. For instance, Meaghan instituted a change to her Leadership Team's morning routine to improve trust and community across her school. She developed a survey to give to her Leadership Team and another survey to give to teachers to monitor if her compassionate change was having an impact on these two groups.

Revisiting your "indicators of progress" column in your theory of compassionate change—the things that people will do, say, feel that will make progress toward the aim—can help you choose what to include on your survey and who should complete it. Pay attention to the group of people you identified here—this is likely the group that you will want to survey. For instance, NB's indicator of progress was that families felt that they were part of the community, so she planned a survey to give to families several times throughout the year as she implemented her compassionate change ideas.

As a next step, we suggest reviewing surveys that already exist that are close to your topic, to get an idea of the kinds of questions you might include on your own survey. For example, you might review the Panorama Education (`https://www.panoramaed.com/`) surveys for students, families, and educators focused on school climate or the Tripod Education (`https://www.tripoded.com/`) surveys on student and teacher well-being as well as systems and practices within the school. We also recommend visiting the EdInstruments website that includes an extensive list of surveys searchable by topic (`https://edinstruments.org/`). We've included some example items from educators' surveys below, where they asked respondents to agree or disagree with the following statements.

NB's survey items administered to families:

- My family belongs to this community.
- We have what we need to feel secure.

The High School Team's survey items administered to staff:

- Staff in this school trust each other.
- Staff in this school care for one another.

The Elementary School Team's survey items administered to teachers:

- I build a safe, affirming classroom environment for all gender diverse students.
- I changed lessons to include a gender diverse curriculum.

Meaghan's survey items
  Administered to the Leadership Team:

- The opening routine of our Leadership Team meetings helps me feel more connected to the team.
- The opening routine of our Leadership Team meetings helps me show up in a more caring and thoughtful way throughout the day.

Administered to teachers:

- My school leaders model the behavior they hope to see in the school community.
- The Leadership Team sees me as a person.

Once you've decided to whom you will give the survey, you can begin drafting your questions using the indicators of progress that you've identified. For instance, the High School Team identified as an indicator of progress that staff "begin to build relationships and recognize the humanity in their coworkers." In their practical measure survey, they included items such as: "Staff in this school care for each other" and "I express feelings of support, helpfulness, and encouragement to other staff members."

You can use the Practical Measure Survey Planning Tool to develop a survey that can help you understand your progress toward your aim. Decide how often and when you will administer the survey. Remember, it can be valuable to administer the survey and review responses several times over the course of implementing your compassionate change so that you can adjust your plan as needed.

Activity: Developing a Survey to Track Your Progress

Who will take the survey?

Brainstorm at least 10 possible questions or items to measure progress toward your aim.

Compare your brainstormed list to your theory of compassionate change. Which of the actions have the potential to **change** (improve) how people respond to the questions?

Which items could people answer multiple times over the course of your project, including before it begins?

Do items need to be modified, so as to not be an additional cause of suffering for people, especially those experiencing social suffering? If some need to be modified, write the revised version here.

What are you hoping to learn from people's responses?

When will you give the survey? Identify multiple time points when you can give the survey.

When and how will you look at survey responses?

How will you use the data?

Evaluating efforts to bring about compassionate change in schools can be an emotionally laden experience (Potvin, 2021). It can be challenging, for instance, to look at data that signals that despite best efforts to alleviate suffering, students are still experiencing pain or that colleagues are resistant to new ideas. Caring for oneself and for allies in this work is important, especially when things don't go as planned. We encourage you to hold your intention for alleviating suffering in your school community and to return to the tools and resources for cultivating compassion for yourself (see Chapters 6–8).

When considering how to evaluate your plan, you may choose to add measures that you do not collect, but that would be good indicators of the success of your plan. For example, if your team's aim pertains to expanding restorative practices in the school for establishing and maintaining a respectful community, you might expect to see fewer suspensions in the school. With any evaluation, it's best to have more than one indicator to gauge the success of an initiative.

Persuading and Inspiring

Compassionate leadership also requires persuading and inspiring others to join your efforts to alleviate inequitable suffering. We introduce one more tool in this chapter to invite you to consider the needs and concerns of specific people on your actor network maps, to envision ways to mobilize them to act in support of a more compassionate school. Specifically, you can consider how to activate an ally, bring on board a neutral person, and allay the concerns of a potential opponent. Understanding where each person is coming from and framing conversations with various actors is an important component of leadership that inspires compassionate action. In planning for these conversations, you may realize that you need to learn more about someone, and that your first step is to engage with them with care and to listen. You may also realize a skillful approach to talking with them, especially if you think they might be resistant to your idea.

For the final tool, we introduce an adapted version of a persona tool. Personas are often used by designers to represent fictional people based on data gathered about users of a product. Rather than focus on fictional people, the Compassionate Persona Template invites you to focus on key actors relevant to accomplishing your aim. Using the Compassionate Persona Template is meant to encourage you to recognize the dignity of each person and hold them with compassion, and to consider the most effective way to engage with them about your compassionate change ideas. You may find it helpful to review the neutral person persona created by the High School Team shown in the following table before you create your own.

The High School Team's Persona

Neutral Person: Principal

What is this person's role in your school community?	Principal
What status, power, authority do they hold?	Leads school, makes key decisions
Describe, as best you can, this person's identity and consider the multiple facets of their identity. How does their identity impact what they notice and care about?	She is our principal and most of the time she's willing to be neutral and pays attention to what can be beneficial/negative for our school/staff. She has a strong will and does not give up easily. She's very strategic, engaging, and caring. She is not afraid of going against the flow if needed.
Where does this person tend to put their time and energy in school? You can also consider out-of-school, if it is relevant to your project.	Most of her time and energy goes to solving students' issues, dealing with parents, and data analysis, but she is also concerned about the staff, students' well-being, and community involvement.
What excites this person?	Basically everything, but she enjoys working with staff. She also loves math and making sure she shines on students' day.
What tends to scare this person or what tends to make them feel trepidation?	Data and making sure our school is meeting expectations and hitting our goals.
What else do you want to know about this person as it relates to your project?	Would she be interested in having a Care Team at our school? What resources can she get, if any, for our project? Would she like to be a member of the Care Team?
What do you hope for in terms of their involvement with your project?	That she will provide time for our Care Team to work with staff and create more spaces during events to address relationships, connections, and social and emotional learning.

You can begin by selecting one ally, one neutral person, and one opponent from your actor network map. The Compassionate Persona Template shown next can help you to develop a persona for each person; you can copy the template if you plan to develop a persona for each person. Consider each prompt in the template as it relates to your aim statement and action plan. Use your knowledge and relationship with the person, along with a generous interpretation to craft each persona. Creating the compassionate persona can help you to: (1) see your colleagues and other members of your school community as people; (2) engage with their unique concerns, to either enlist their support or allay their concerns; (3) do as a good leader does, in communicating to people in ways that inspire them to positive action.

Activity: Developing Compassionate Personas

Ally, Neutral Person, or Opponent? _____

What is this person's role in your school community?

What status, power, authority do they hold?

Describe, as best you can, this person's identity and consider the multiple facets of their identity. How does their identity impact what they notice and care about?

Where does this person tend to put their time and energy in school? You can also consider out-of-school, if it is relevant to your project.

What excites this person?

What tends to scare this person or what tends to make them feel trepidation?

What else do you want to know about this person as it relates to your project?

What do you hope for in terms of their involvement with your project?

Rehearsing Conversations

Now that you've developed your compassionate personas, you can rehearse the conversations you might have with each person. While this activity can feel vulnerable and even challenging, educators in our program have found this process to be invaluable. You will need a partner for this activity. In this activity, you can rehearse pitching your compassionate change idea and aim to one of your personas, played by your partner. If you are rehearsing with an ally, you can make a specific ask of them to do something to support your plan. If you are rehearsing with a neutral person, invite their involvement or support. If you are rehearsing with an opponent, address their concerns.

Before you begin, prepare yourself by reminding yourself of your intentions for the conversation and offering compassion phrases silently to the ally, neutral person, or opponent (e.g., _May you be well_). You can then tell your partner about the person you have selected for this rehearsal. We suggest sharing what you've written in your Compassionate Persona Template so that your partner can play-act the person. Then, initiate the conversation about your intention and aim to address some form of social suffering in your school community.

Your partner can respond the way the person might be expected to respond. Your partner can invent something that might make it difficult to say "yes" to helping you out at first (e.g., "I'm not sure I have time in my busy schedule to take on another initiative.").

We offer some sentence frames that you can use to help you rehearse your conversation. These are not meant to be prescriptive but rather provide guidance if you aren't sure how to begin. We encourage you to adapt them to fit your context and your persona so that they feel authentic to you.

- *We/I have noticed that _____ (specific group of people) seem to be hurting/suffering/ struggling at school because of _____.*
- *Now that we/I see the hurting/suffering/struggling, we/I feel moved to do something about it. We/I have a plan for addressing their suffering at the school-level through compassion, and one that will require our collective efforts.*
- *Our aim is to _____ (share aim statement). We/I think this will benefit the entire school community because _____.*

For the ally, make a specific ask:

- *Given your interest in/experience/role with _____, we'd love for you to help with _____.*
- *Would you be willing to _____?*

For the neutral person, invite support:

- *Together, we could make meaningful change to help _____.*
- *We'd love for you to support it by _____.*
- *If you'd like to be more involved, we welcome that too.*

For the opponent, allay their concerns:

- *You might be worried about _____. We thought about that in our planning, and we believe we addressed it by _____.*
- *Do you have any other concerns we should consider?*
- *It's also okay if you don't want to be involved, but we did want to let you know about this change/idea.*

Following the conversation, you can debrief with your partner. How did it feel to rehearse that conversation? What went well? What would you like to change when you have this conversation with the actual person? You might even realize that something about your compassionate action plan needs to change; rehearsals can help you to see how you can improve upon your plans. Personas help you remember the humanity of the people involved, and that allies, neutral people, and opponents all have real needs and concerns you can address. Through focusing on different kinds of people, you can appreciate how you need to tailor your messages to different people, to gain their support or allay their concerns. We often don't plan for difficult conversations and may even avoid having them; rehearsal is a powerful way to plan for such conversations that we might otherwise be afraid to undertake.

Acting with Compassion

We began this chapter by asserting that compassionate leadership takes wisdom and courage. Setting an intention and offering compassionate wishes are important leadership resources to prepare for courageous or difficult conversations. When used in concert with the tools in this chapter, your team has the potential to develop a plan that can result in real change that holds the humanity of the people in the school community at the center.

Some educators from our certificate program have shared with us about the impact of their compassionate action plans in their school communities. One high school team shared that they "led compassionate mindfulness practices during staff meetings throughout the year" to address the pain and isolation their colleagues felt, and "encouraged coworkers to consider one another's experiences more compassionately." Another high school team who created supports for improving communication shared that their compassionate plan "had an impact on the way staff related to one another and the students as well." We hope that you feel inspired and ready to inspire and prepare others in your school community to recognize dignity, to attune to needs and concerns, and to approach one another with an attitude of compassion and humility so that your school can be a welcoming, caring, and safe environment for all who enter its doors.

We also know that things in schools don't always go as planned. You have a new principal who sets different priorities from the previous principal. The district implements a policy that has consequences for how teachers' and students' time is structured. A colleague whom you counted on as an ally changes schools. Tragedy strikes your community. If you, too, find that an unexpected event threatens to undermine or derail your compassionate action plan, take heart knowing that you are not alone and that your planning is not in vain. Many educators in our compassion certificate who we have supported in the summer to develop a collective action plan have returned to school in the fall to discover that they need to make adjustments to meet their new current reality.

As an example, the Elementary School Team found themselves in such a position, when a new administrative team took over leadership of their school. The new principal shifted the school's priority and focus away from the social and emotional well-being of students and to improving student academic outcomes. Emma, a member of the team, said that the new school year was "a bit of a rough start," and that the school-wide launch of their compassion change project was pushed back. Rather than lose hope, Emma shared, "I have used compassion to try to understand our new administration's point of view and give grace and understanding as they are learning the ropes. I have also used compassion to support some of my close teacher friends who have really struggled with the change."

After working on his change plan with us during the summer, Ben moved states and took a new teaching position. Rather than abandon his commitment to making school an inclusive environment for students, Ben drew on what he learned in the compassion certificate program to attune to suffering in his new school and take action at the community level to address it. Ben explained, "I recognized some places where students had interests and weren't having them met by the existing school structure." As a result, he started several clubs for students, including the Asian Community Diversity Club and sought out grants to secure funding for these extracurricular activities. He also found ways to "protect ... some kids who were getting bullied," including students who identified as transgender and students on the autism spectrum.

You may find that like Emma and Ben, you need to adjust your plans based on unanticipated changes, roadblocks, or resistance. Indeed, the more you seek to address inequitable forms of suffering, the more likely it is you will tap into deeper forms of resistance. It's important to anticipate this and not be surprised by it. Leading this kind of compassionate change often requires iterative cycles of planning, acting, and evaluating based on what you learn along the way. You may find it necessary to return to the tools in this section and update your initial ideas.

We also encourage you to rely on the foundation you've built through cultivating compassion to care for yourself and others, and to approach your leadership efforts with courage, open-heartedness, friendliness, and curiosity. The formal and on-the-spot compassion and dignity practices can support you as you bring your plans to life, especially when you encounter roadblocks or resistance. We also suggest returning to the journal reflection, Offering Care and Presence to Another, in Chapter 5. You may find a new pathway forward, recognize where in the system you have capacity and agency to make change, identify new allies, or recognize that despite some resistance, it's possible to move forward with your efforts to alleviate social suffering.

Like Emma, Ben, and many of our other educators, your planning has helped you to see systems differently, to see clearly the social suffering that exists and is perpetuated within your school, to articulate your intention for alleviating social suffering, and to determine what you can do to help. You have gained skills and resources to adapt to changing circumstances and maintain your sense of agency, creativity, courage, hope, and possibility for a compassionate school. You, your students, their families, and your colleagues will most certainly benefit from your efforts to act with compassion, affirm their dignity, and to provide skillful leadership in the face of suffering.

Key Ideas from the Chapter

- A theory of change articulates visually what you hope to accomplish, the strategies you plan to test, and people's expected responses to your strategic action.
- Practical measures can help you know whether your strategies are making progress toward your aim.
- Preparing and rehearsing for conversations with potential allies, neutral people, and opponents of your plan can help build support for your plan.
- The plan is a first step toward change: it may need to be revised in light of changing circumstances in your own life and in your school.

Conclusion

To me, compassion has meant finding hope in places I thought were hopeless.
—Colleen, Middle School Science Teacher

Leading action aimed at creating more compassionate schools is often slow and hard work. It simultaneously requires self-compassion and putting oneself at the edge of one's own knowledge and comfort level. It calls for courage in dwelling in uncertainty and in cultivating skillful means for responding to the suffering that exists and persists through policies, routines, and practices within schools. It requires patience: when acting for change we don't often see big changes immediately. The kinds of compassionate action we advocate for and describe in this book are often about changing the very foundations of many of our schools today. It also requires working with others. In some ways this is welcome, because leadership can be lonely work; in other ways, working with others is hard because relational and collective work can be messy, slow, and complicated. None of us can alone make changes to our schools without the support and engagement of others.

School Change Is an Inside-Out Job

We've organized this book from the perspective that school change is an "inside-out" job, and that change is possible. As NB put it:

> The opportunity to formally engage in work of this nature has been so impactful and, dare I say, life-changing for me. I know that I have been impacted in positive ways and it has changed the lens that I use to see myself, my peers, my colleagues, my city and the greater world. Adding this perspective has been a welcomed change.

Just as we introduced contemplative practices to support inside-out changes in the certificate program NB experienced, we've introduced contemplative practices in this book in order to support and resource you while you work to make your school more compassionate. We also intend that you integrate mindfulness and compassion for self and others into the actual work of changing your school with others. We hope that integration happens in two ways. First, while this is not a book that is focused on teaching mindfulness or compassion practices to students or to colleagues, by cultivating your own mind and heart, you can make yourself and your environment into a refuge for your students and your colleagues. You can respond to students, colleagues, parents, and others in your school community with openness, curiosity, and friendliness, listening to and attuning to their unique perspectives, experiences, and needs.

There's a second way we hope you will integrate your practices into your work as a team to create a more compassionate school. The lenses of mindfulness, curiosity, and compassion are valuable for each step you take in implementing your action plan. In that sense, our path is also our destination. You can create a more compassionate school by embodying it in every step. We invite you to return again and again to the inner contemplative practices and interactive practices introduced in this book as resources and tools for sustaining your work, especially when challenges arise. One of our educators, Stephanie, described our certificate program as having

> ... given me tools to act more compassionately toward my students, my colleagues, and our broader community. The course has also given me confidence to discuss concepts of compassion, self-care and the necessity for them. I have also become an advocate for more self-compassion and mental health work in our schools.

Mindfulness, curiosity, care, and compassion all have an external component that is essential to their development, which can take the form of advocacy as it did for Stephanie. This book is therefore different from other self-help books for supporting teachers dealing with stress and burnout. We have emphasized throughout the book the importance of noticing pain and suffering in our schools and the centrality of cultivating compassion in our interpersonal relationships. As we pay attention with mindfulness, curiosity, and kindness to the people before us, to how we are interacting with colleagues, family members, and students, we are actively cultivating this external component of compassion. Educators who have gone through our certificate program say over and over again that it has improved the quality of their relationships with others and with themselves, having taken part in the practices and learning activities. The impacts don't just stop for them when they leave the school building: educators say that the practices benefit their relationships with friends and family (Potvin et al., 2024). Because caring relationships are core to our well-being, this is an important benefit of cultivating compassion within our interactions with others. But these, too, can serve another purpose, in modeling and becoming the kind of school we want to be, moment-to-moment, by how we treat one another. Just as our commitment to cultivating our own mindfulness and kind hearts can be a foundation for changing our schools, so can enhancing our intra- and interpersonal relationships.

A Call for Wise Hope

We are moved by the words of Colleen, a middle school science teacher, who told us, "To me, compassion has meant finding hope in places I thought were hopeless" and it is our wish that you, too, carry hope with you. At the heart of this book is a call for audacious and wise hope for healing schools—hope that our schools can be better places for children, families, and communities that suffer now from harmful policies and practices. We have an important role to play in making our schools better places. And together, we can do what it takes to alleviate—and even end—some forms of suffering in our schools. Cultivating that kind of hope requires us to turn again and again back to our practice and to find strength within communities. Both are necessary to realize the promise of school change from the inside out.

Aimee, a high school teacher at an alternative school, taught us about cultivating hope and supporting her colleagues "to maintain their joy, creativity and love," even when it seems "impossible due to the oppressive systems within education." At the end of the compassion certificate, she reflected that she learned "how to make this work sustainable by starting with ourselves, making the inner work outer and the outer work inner. We do have a huge impact on our world through our students and through our interpersonal relations at school." Aimee powerfully asked, *"How can I, through my inner work, bring that joy and compassion into all aspects I touch in education? And what could the potential reverberations be throughout society?* It's hopeful." As you take what you've learned from engaging with this book and your colleagues, we invite you to pause and contemplate your own responses to Aimee's questions and the ways you might carry hope, compassion, and joy into your school community.

Working Together to Envision and Create
Compassionate Schools

In the last section of this book, we provided guidance for forming a team at your school to help make it a more compassionate community for everyone—and for the specific groups in your school community that experience inequitable social suffering. We know that even for a team, it is possible to become discouraged. An administrator changes or changes their mind about the school's priority. A valued colleague is skeptical of the plan and voices that skepticism to others, turning more against your efforts. The plan is implemented, but it doesn't have the desired effect. All of these things can and do happen every day with school change initiatives. But those challenges don't have to put an end to your effort. They invite us to say to ourselves, "Well, perhaps not *yet*, but who knows?" and "Let's think of another way we can try." Returning to an open mind and heart of possibility, we are reminded that one of the powers of meditation practice is to help us begin again, over and over again. We have a hard time getting and staying concentrated on the breath, or saying phrases of loving kindness, but we can *always* begin again. And meditation builds our muscle for remembering that.

Our hope and our capacity to begin again will be stronger if we join together with other educators who are—just like us—committed to bringing about compassionate change in their schools, recognizing the dignity of the members of the school community and promoting efforts aimed at healing. This network of educators may include colleagues within schools or districts, but it may also include the community of educators we have cultivated through our programs and research. Strengthening and tapping into networks is an important resource for sustaining change efforts because this work is complex and often requires coordinated action, and because people within networks can offer one another care and compassion. It takes all of us to do this work, and often in a school it takes courage to get the ball rolling, to organize and persuade and inspire others to join us. Taryn, an elementary teacher who had been advocating for increased services for her special education students, realized that she was part of a larger network and could offer her care to the special education teacher who was overwhelmed, reflecting, "We are all arriving at school with our own hopes and needs and those needs are often ignored because we are governed by the curriculum, structure, roles and responsibilities, and systems put into place. This helped me to respond in a way where I asked her how we could help. What did she need from us to take some of the load off?"

In our own work, we bring together educators regularly. Some come to our monthly meetings of members and graduates of our certificate program. Others join in our Compassion Cultivation Training for Educators that we offer each semester. Still others join us for special events for educators we hold. We invite everyone reading this book to join our community at the Renée Crown Wellness Institute, to be part of something bigger and to connect with like-minded educators. For more information and to join our mailing list, you can visit our website at https://www.colorado.edu/crowninstitute/.

Dedication and Gratitude Practice

At the conclusion of the book, we want to remind you of the power of dedicating your activities—at the close of a day, week, month, or semester, or after implementing your action plan. A dedication is not only a form of closure; it is also a way to remind ourselves that we undertook these activities not just to seek relief from our own pain or to gain pleasure or power for ourselves. Instead, dedication involves the idea that our efforts are more than for ourselves, that our intentions and actions ripple out, often in ways that we can't anticipate or may never know. Through the dedication practice, we return to our intentions, check in on them, and perhaps even adjust them. And as always, we rejoice in whatever good actions we have taken to benefit others and in the actions others in our school have taken that have made our school a more compassionate place to learn and be. As a closing exercise, we invite you to recognize people in your networks, past and present, who have helped you in your journey toward becoming compassionate leaders and change agents. Reflect in your journal on the ways in which these people have helped you on your journey and then offer them gratitude and generosity. Perhaps you write a letter or email to someone who has helped you on your journey, or call them on the phone, to let them know how you feel about their efforts. Finally, consider how you want your reading and engagement with this book to bring benefit and reflect on a wish you have for yourself, for these people, and/or your hopes for the wider world. This practice can strengthen both the internal and external components of gratitude and care for others.

A dedication reminds us, too, to celebrate our own good qualities. If you have made it through this book and tried even a small percentage of the activities on your own or with others, you can celebrate that. It is time well-spent that you have given to cultivate your own good heart and equanimity of mind. Take time to acknowledge this and to celebrate this accomplishment, however modest or grand it might feel, to have engaged with this material.

Last, we wish to close with our own dedication. We hope that whatever benefit engaging with this book has had for you, your relationships, and your school, that it may ripple out to benefit all beings. Consider all the dozens of educators, including you, who have engaged in compassion practices, reflected on how to realize compassionate intentions through their interactions, and are taking action to transform their schools. We hope that the book has contributed in a small way—but continues to do as it moves into the world—to alleviating suffering and creating more compassionate schools everywhere. We hope this book, by supporting such work, also helps to bring about a more just and sustainable world of the kind we all want to live in and flourish.

References

Alasiri, E., Bast, D., & Kolts, R. L. (2019). Using the implicit relational assessment procedure (IRAP) to explore common humanity as a dimension of self-compassion. *Journal of Contextual Behavioral Science, 14*, 65–72. https://doi.org/10.1016/j.jcbs.2019.09.004

Allen, A. B., & Leary, M. R. (2010). Self-compassion, stress, and coping. *Social and Personality Psychology Compass, 4*(2), 107–118. https://doi.org/10.1111/j.1751-9004.2009.00246.x

Allen, K. M., Nash, K. T., Thomas, K., & Everett, S. (2022). "An oasis in the Sahara": Humanizing professional learning during the pandemic and beyond. *Language Arts, 100*(1), 8–20. https://doi.org/10.58680/la202232008

Amrein-Beardsley, A., & Holloway, J. (2019). Value-added models for teacher evaluation and accountability: Commonsense assumptions. *Educational Policy, 33*(3), 516–542. https://doi.org/10.1177/0895904817719519

Annamma, S. A., Anyon, Y., Joseph, N. M., Downing, B., & Simmons, J. (2019). Black girls and school discipline: The complexities of being overrepresented and under studied. *Urban Education, 54*(2), 211–242. https://doi.org/10.1177/0042085916646610

Argrys, C. (1990). *Overcoming organizational defenses: Facilitating organizational learning*. Pearson.

Ashar, Y. K., Andrews-Hanna, J. R., Yarkoni, T., Sills, J., Halifax, J., Dimidjian, S., & Wager, T. D. (2016). Effects of compassion meditation on a psychological model of charitable donation. *Emotion, 16*(5), 691–705. https://doi.org/10.1037/emo0000119

Ashar, Y. K., Andrews-Hanna, J. R., Dimidjian, S., Wager, T. D. (2017). Empathic care and distress: Predictive brain markers and dissociable brain systems. *Neuron, 94*(6), 1263–1273. https://doi.org/10.1016/j.neuron.2017.05.014

Atlas, L. Y., & Wager, T. D. (2012). How expectations shape pain. *Neuroscience Letters, 520*(2), 149–148. https://doi.org/10.1016/j.neulet.2012.03.039

Bandura, A. (1999). Moral disengagement in the perpetration of inhumanities. *Personality and Social Psychology Review, 3*(3), 193–209. https://doi.org/10.1207/s15327957pspr0303_3

Batson, C. D. (2009a). These things called empathy: Eight related but distinct phenomena. In J. Decety & W. Ickes (Eds.), *The social neuroscience of empathy* (pp. 3–15). Boston Review. https://doi.org/10.7551/mitpress/9780262012973.003.0002

Batson, C. D. (2009b). Two forms of perspective taking: Imagining how another feels and imagining how you would feel. In K. D. Markman, W. M. P. Klein, & J. A. Suhr (Eds.), *Handbook of imagination and mental stimulation* (pp. 267–279). Psychology Press.

Batson, C. D., Fultz, J., & Schoenrade, P. A. (1987). Distress and empathy: Two qualitatively distinct vicarious emotions with different motivational consequences. *Journal of Personality, 55*(1), 19–39. https://doi.org/10.1111/j.1467-6494.1987.tb00426.x

Batson, C. D., Lishner, D. A., Carpenter, A., Dulin, L., Harjusola-Webb, S., Stocks, E. L., Gale, S., Hassan, O., & Sampat, B. (2003). "... As you would have them do unto you": Does imagining yourself in the other's place stimulate moral action? *Personality and Social Psychology Bulletin, 29*(9), 1190–1201. https://doi.org/10.1177/0146167203254600

Bell, P., Riedy, R., Penuel, W. R., Neill, T. (2021 November). Organizing for educational transformation using Actor-Network Theory. https://stemteachingtools.org/brief/81

Bishop, S. R., Lau, M., Shapiro, S., Carlson, L., Anderson, N. D., Carmody, J., Segal, Z. V., Abbey, S., Speca, M., Velting, D., & Devins, G. (2004). Mindfulness: A proposed operational definition. *Clinical Psychology: Science and Practice, 11*(3), 230–241.

Bohannon, A. X. (2023). Attending to school leadership attention Northwestern University. Evanston, IL. https://www.proquest.com/docview/2903739309

Bopaiah, M. (2021). *Equity: How to design organizations where everyone thrives.* Berrett-Koehler Publishers.

Bourdieu, P. (2000). *The weight of the world: Social suffering in contemporary society.* Stanford University Press.

Boyle, G. (2010). *Tattoos on the heart: The power of boundless compassion.* Free Press.

Breines, J. G., Thoma, M. V., Gianferante, D., Hanlin, L., Chen, X., & Rohleder, N. (2014). Self compassion as a predictor of interleukin-6 response to acute psychosocial stress. *Brain, Behavior, and Immunity, 37*, 109–114. https://doi.org/10.1016/j.bbi.2013.11.006

Brous, S. (2024, January 19). Train yourself to always show up. *The New York Times.* https://www.nytimes.com/2024/01/19/opinion/religion-ancient-text-judaism.html

Brown, B. (2018). *Dare to lead: Brave work. Tough conversations. Whole hearts.* Random House.

brown, a. m. (2019). *Pleasure activism: The politics of feeling good.* AK Press.

brown, a. m. (2021). *Holding change: The way of emergent strategy facilitation and mediation.* AK Press.

Bryk, A. S., Gomez, L. M., Grunow, A., & LeMahieu, P. G. (2015). *Learning to improve: How America's schools can get better at getting better.* Harvard University Press.

Calabrese Barton, A., & Tan, E. (2020). Beyond equity as inclusion: A framework of "rightful presence" for guiding justice-oriented studies in teaching and learning. *Educational Researcher, 49*(6), 433–440. https://doi.org/10.3102/0013189X20927363

Camangian, P., & Cariaga, S. (2022). Social and emotional learning is hegemonic miseducation: Students deserve humanization instead. *Race Ethnicity and Education, 25*(7), 901–921. https://doi.org/10.1080/13613324.2020.1798374

del Carmen Salazar, M. (2013). A humanizing pedagogy: Reinventing the principles and practice of education as a journey toward liberation. *Review of Research in Education, 37*(1), 121–148. https://doi.org/10.3102/0091732X12464032

Chödrön, P. (1997). *When things fall apart: Heart advice for difficult times*. Shambhala.

Chödrön, P. (2001). *The places that scare you: A guide to fearlessness in difficult times*. Shambhala.

Chödrön, P. (2009, Winter). Unlimited friendliness: Three steps to genuine compassion. *Tricycle*. https://tricycle.org/magazine/unlimited-friendliness.

Chödrön, P. (2013, Summer). Meditating with emotions: Drop the story and find the feeling. *Tricycle*. https://tricycle.org/magazine/meditating-emotions/

Coburn, C. E. (2003). Rethinking scale: Moving beyond numbers to deep and lasting change. *Educational Researcher, 32*(6), 3–12. https://doi.org/10.3102/0013189X032006003

Cohen, D. K. (2011). *Teaching and its predicaments*. Harvard University Press.

Condon, P., Desbordes, G., Miller, W. B., & DeSteno, D. (2013). Meditation increases compassionate responses to suffering. *Psychological Science, 24*(10), 2125–2127. https://doi.org/10.1177/0956797613485603

Cosley, B. J., McCoy, S. K., Saslow, L. R., & Epel, E. S. (2010). Is compassion for others stress buffering? Consequences of compassion and social support for physiological reactivity to stress. *Journal of Experimental Social Psychology, 46*(5), 816–823. http://dx.doi.org/10.1016/j.jesp.2010.04.008.

Curry-Stevens, A., & Jarvis, R. (2022). Caucusing updated: Innovations to build belonging and empowerment. *Journal of Transformative Education, 21*(3), 332–353. https://doi.org/10.1177/15413446221129860

Datnow, A., & Stringfield, S. (2000). Working together for reliable school reform. *Journal of Education for Students Placed at Risk (JESPAR), 5*(1–2), 183–204. https://doi.org/10.1080/10824669.2000.9671386

Dawkins, R. (1976/2016). *The selfish gene*. Oxford Landmark Science.

Dowling, E. (2021). *The care crisis: What caused it and how can we end it?* Verso.

Dreisoerner, A., Junker, N. M., & van Dick, R. (2021). The relationship among the components of self-compassion: A pilot study using a compassionate writing intervention to enhance self-kindness, common humanity, and mindfulness. *Journal of Happiness Studies, 22*, 21–47. https://doi.org/10.1007/s10902-019-00217-4

Duckworth, E. (2006). *"The having of wonderful ideas" and other essays on teaching and learning*. Teachers College Press.

Dumas, M. J. (2014). "Losing an arm": Schooling as a site of black suffering. *Race Ethnicity and Education, 17*(1), 1–29. https://doi.org/10.1080/13613324.2013.850412

Duncan-Andrade, J. M. R. (2009). Note to educators: Hope required when growing roses in concrete. *Harvard Educational Review, 79*(2), 181–194.

Dutton, J. E., Worline, M. C., Frost, P. J., & Lilius, J. (2006). Explaining compassion organizing. *Administrative Science Quarterly, 51*(1), 59–96. https://doi.org/10.2189/asqu.51.1.59

Eaton, A., & Warner, L. R. (2021). Social justice burnout: Engaging in self-care while doing diversity work. In M. E. Kite, K. A. Case, & W. R. Williams (Eds.), *Navigating difficult moments in teaching diversity and social justice* (pp. 31–43). American Psychological Association. https://doi.org/10.1037/0000216-003

Eisenberg, N., Cumberland, A., & Spinrad, T. L. (1998). Parental socialization of emotion. *Psychological Inquiry, 9*(4), 241–273. https://doi.org/10.1207/s15327965pli0904_1

Ekman, E. (n.d.). Imagining flourishing and kindness: A mindfulness practice for adults. *Greater Good in Education.* https://ggie.berkeley.edu/practice/imagining-flourishing-and-kindness-a-mindfulness-practice-for-adults/?_ga=2.74386768.392200593.1585311098-1079093703.1576252924#tab__2

Engel, S. (2013). The case for curiosity. *ASCD, 70*(5).

Engen, H. G., & Singer, T. (2015). Compassion-based emotion regulation up-regulates experienced positive affect and associated neural networks. *Social Cognitive and Affective Neuroscience, 10*(9), 1291–1301. https://doi.org/10.1093/scan/nsv008

Erickson, F. (2011). On noticing teacher noticing. In M. Sherin, V. Jacobs, & R. Philip (Eds.), *Mathematics teacher noticing: Seeing through teachers' eyes*, 17–34. Routledge.

Espinoza, M. L. (2008). *Humanization and social dreaming: A case study of changing social relations in a summer migrant educational program*, University of California Los Angeles. Los Angeles, CA.

Espinoza, M., & Vossoughi, S. (2014). Perceiving learning anew: Social interaction, dignity, and educational rights. *Harvard Educational Review, 84*(3), 285–313. https://doi.org/10.17763/haer.84.3.y4011442g71250q2

Espinoza, M. L., Vossoughi, S., Rose, M., & Poza, L. E. (2020). Matters of participation: Notes on the study of dignity and learning. *Mind, Culture, and Activity, 27*(4), 325–347. https://doi.org/10.1080/10749039.2020.1779304

Ewert, C., Vater, A., & Schröder-Abé, M. (2021). Self-compassion and coping: A meta-analysis. *Mindfulness, 12*(5), 1063–1077. https://doi.org/10.1007/s12671-020-01563-8

Farley, J., Risko, E. F., & Kingstone, A. (2013). Everyday attention and lecture retention: The effects of time, fidgeting, and mind wandering. *Frontiers in Psychology, 4*(619), 1–9. https://doi.org/10.3389/fpsyg.2013.00619

Fischer, N. (2013). *Training in compassion: Zen teachings on the practice of lojong.* Shambhala

Fiske, S. T. (1980). Attention and weight in person perception: The impact of negative and extreme behavior. *Journal of Personality and Social Psychology, 38*(6), 890906. https://doi.org/10.1037/0022-3514.38.6.889

Fredrickson, B. L., Cohn, M. A., Coffey, K. A., Pek, J., & Finkel, S. M. (2008). Open hearts build lives: Positive emotions, induced through loving-kindness meditation, build consequential personal resources. *Journal of Personality and Social Psychology, 95*(5), 1045–1062. https://doi.org/10.1037/a0013262.

Freire, P. (1970/2002). *Pedagogy of the oppressed.* Continuum.

Fronsdal, G. (2020, June 12). Refuge (5 of 5): Being a refuge to others. *AudioDharma Talks.* https://irc.audiodharma.org/talks/11544.

Frost, P. J. (2003). *Toxic emotions at work: How compassionate managers handle pain and conflict.* Harvard Business School Press.

Gade, C. B. N. (2012). What is Ubuntu? Different interpretations among South Africans of African descent. *South African Journal of Philosophy*, *31*(3), 484–502. https://doi.org/10.1080/02580136.2012.10751789

Garcia, A. (2019). A call for healing teachers: Loss, ideological unraveling, and the healing gap. *Schools: Studies in Education*, *16*(1), 64–83. https://doi.org/10.1086/702839

Gardiner, W., Hinman, T. B., Tondreau, A., Degener, S., Dussling, T. M., Stevens, E. Y., Wilson, N. S., & White, K. (2023). When 'nice' isn't: Confronting niceness and whiteness to center equity in teacher education. *Action in Teacher Education,* 45(2), 90–106. https://doi.org/10.1080/01626620.2022.2158390.

Gerber, Z., & Anaki, D. (2021). The role of self-compassion, concern for others, and basic psychological needs in the reduction of caregiving burnout. *Mindfulness*, *12*(3), 741–750. https://doi.org/10.1007/s12671-020-01540-1

Gibson, A. (2018, Dec. 27). "Boomerang Valentine [Video]." YouTube. https://www.youtube.com/watch?v=0HWQ08XAYbY

Gilbert, P. (2017). Compassion as a social mentality: An evolutionary approach. In P. Gilbert (Ed.), *Compassion: Concepts, research, and applications* (pp. 31–68). Routledge.

Gilbert, P., McEwan, K., Matos, M., & Rivis, A. (2011). Fears of compassion: Development of three self-report measures. *Psychology and psychotherapy: Theory, research and practice*, *84*(3), 239–255.

Ginwright, S. A. (2015). Radically healing Black lives: A Love note to justice. *New Directions for Student Leadership*, *2015*(148), 33–44. https://doi.org/10.1002/yd.20151

Ginwright, S. A. (2018, May 31). The future of healing: Shifting from trauma informed care to healing centered engagement. *Medium.* https://medium.com/@ginwright/the-future-of-healing-shifting-from-trauma-informed-cRe-to-healing-centered-engagement-634f557ce69c

Goetz, J. L., & Simon-Thomas, E. (2017). The landscape of compassion: Definitions and scientific approaches. In Seppälä, E. M., E. Simon-Thomas, S. L. Brown, M. C. Worline, C. D. Cameron, & J. R. Doty (Eds.), *The Oxford handbook of compassion science* (pp. 1–16). Oxford University Press.

Goetz, J. L., Keltner, D., & Simon-Thomas, E. (2010). Compassion: An evolutionary analysis and empirical review. *Psychological Bulletin,* *136*(3), 351–374. https://doi.org/10.1037/a0018807

Goldin, P.R., & Jazaieri, H. (2017). The Compassion Cultivation Training (CCT) Program. In Seppälä, E. M., E. Simon-Thomas, S. L. Brown, M. C. Worline, C. D. Cameron, & J. R. Doty (Eds.), *The Oxford handbook of compassion science* (pp. 237–246). Oxford University Press.

Gross, K., & Wronski, J. (2021). Helping the homeless: The role of empathy, race and deservingness in motivating policy support and charitable giving. *Political Behavior*, *43*, 585–613. https://doi.org/10.1007/s11109-019-09562-9

Gustin, L. W., & Wagner, L. (2013). The butterfly effect of caring – clinical nursing teachers' understanding of self-compassion as a source to compassionate care. *Scandinavian Journal of Caring Sciences*, *27*(1), 175–183. https://doi.org/10.1111/j.1471-6712.2012.01033.x

Halifax, J. (2009). *Being with dying: Cultivating compassion and fearlessness in the presence of death*. Shambhala.

Halifax, J. (2018). *Standing at the edge: Finding freedom where fear and courage meet.* Flatiron Books.

Halifax, J. (2021, September 28). Understanding wise hope [blog post]. Upaya Zen Center. https://www.upaya.org/2021/09/understanding-wise-hope/

Hanh, T. N. (1997). *Living Buddha, living Christ.* Riverhead Trade.

Hanh, T. N. (2017). *The art of living.* HarperOne.

Hanh, T. N., & Weare, K. (2017). *Happy teachers change the world: A guide for cultivating mindfulness in education.* Parallax Press.

Hanson, R. (2011). *Just one thing: Developing a Buddha brain one simple practice at a time.* New Harbinger Publications, Inc.

Harris, L. T., & Fiske, S. T. (2006). Dehumanizing the lowest of the low: Neuroimaging responses to extreme out-groups. *Psychological Science, 17*(10), 847–853. https://doi.org/10.1111/j.1467-9280.2006.01793.x

Hasenkamp, W. (Host). (2020, June 10). john powell — othering & belonging [Audio podcast episode]. In Mind & Life podcast. Mind & Life Institute. https://podcast.mindandlife.org/john-powell/

Hashem, Z., & Zeinoun, P. (2020). Self-compassion explains less burnout among healthcare professionals. *Mindfulness, 11*(11), 2542–2551. https://doi.org/10.1007/s12671-020-01469-5

Hemphill, P. (2021, April 5). Instagram post [quote image]. https://www.instagram.com/p/CNSzFO1A21C/

Hersey, T. (2022). *Rest is resistance: A manifesto.* Little, Brown Spark.

Hirshberg, M. J., Flook, L., Moss, E. M., Enright, R. D., & Davidson, R. J. (2022). Integrating mindfulness and connection practices into preservice teacher education results in durable automatic race bias reduction. *Journal of School Psychology, 91,* 50–64. https://doi.org/10.1016/j.jsp.2021.12.002

His Holiness the Dalai Lama. (2019). *Be angry.* Hampton Roads Publishing.

hooks, b. (1996). *Killing rage: Ending racism.* Hold Paperbacks.

Hutcherson, C. A., Seppälä, E. M., & Gross, J. J. (2008). Loving-kindness meditation increases social connectedness. *Emotion, 8*(5), 720–724. https://doi.org/10.1037/a0013237

Iyer, D. (2020). *The social change ecosystem map: Definition of roles.* Building Movement Project. https://buildingmovement.org/wp-content/uploads/2020/10/Ecosystem-Roles-2020.pdf

James, A., Jenks, C., & Prout, A. (1998). Theorizing childhood. In C. Jenks (Ed.), *Childhood: Critical concepts in sociology* (pp. 195–218). Polity Press.

Jarymowicz, M. (1992). Self, we, and other(s): Schemata, distinctiveness, and altruism. In P. M. Oliner, S. P. Oliner, L. Baron, L. A. Blum, D. L. Krebs, & M. Z. Smolenska (Eds.), *Embracing the other: Philosophical, psychological, and historical perspectives on altruism* (pp. 194–212). New York University Press. https://doi.org/10.18574/nyu/9780814762622.003.0016

Jazaieri, H., & Rock, M. L. (2021). Putting compassion to work: Compassion as a tool for navigating challenging workplace relationships. *Mindfulness, 12,* 2552–2558. https://doi.org/10.1007/s12671-021-01695-5

Jazaieri, H., McGonigal, K., Lee, I., Jinpa, T., Doty, J., Gross, J. & Goldin, P. (2017) Altering the trajectory of affect and affect regulation: The impact of compassion training. *Mindfulness,* (9), 283–293. https://doi.org/10.1007/s12671-017-0773-3

Jefferson, R., Barreto, M., Verity, L., & Qualter, P. (2023). Loneliness during the school years: How it affects learning and how schools can help. *Journal of School Health, 93*(5), 428–435.

Jennings, P. A., & DeMauro, A. A. (2017). Promoting the ethics of care in a mindfulness-based program for teachers. In L. Monteiro, J. Compson, & F. Musten (Eds.), *Practitioner's guide to ethics and mindfulness-based interventions* (pp. 229–251). Springer. https://doi.org/10.1007/978-3-319-64924-5_9

Jennings, P. A., & Greenberg, M. T. (2009). The prosocial classroom: Teacher social and emotional competence in relation to student and classroom outcomes. *Review of Educational Research, 79*(1), 491–525. https://doi.org/10.3102/0034654308325693

Jennings, P. A., Frank, J. L., Doyle, S. L., Oh, Y., Davis, R., Rasheed, D., DeWeese, A., DeMauro, A. A., Cham, H., & Greenberg, M. T. (2017). Impacts of the CARE for Teachers program on teachers' social and emotional competence and classroom interactions. *Journal of Educational Psychology, 109*(7), 1010–1028. https://doi.org/10.1037/edu0000187

Jennings, P. A., Doyle, S. L., Oh, Y., Rasheed, D., Frank, J. L., & Brown, J. L. (2019). Long-term impacts of the CARE program on teachers' self-reported social and emotional competence and well-being. *Journal of School Psychology, 76,* 186–202. https://doi.org/10.1016/j.jsp.2019.07.009

Jha, A. (2021). *Peak mind: Find your focus, own your attention, invest 12 minutes a day.* HarperOne.

Jinpa, T. (2015). *A fearless heart: How the courage to be compassionate can transform our lives.* Avery.

Kabat-Zinn, J. (1990). *Full catastrophe living: Using the wisdom of your mind to face stress, pain and illness.* Dell.

Kanov, J. (2021). Why suffering matters! *Journal of Management Inquiry, 30*(1), 85–90. https://doi.org/10.1177/1056492620929766

Kaufman, P. & Schipper, J. (2018). *Teaching with compassion: An educator's oath to teach from the heart.* Rowman & Littlefield.

Kimmerer, R. W. (2015). *Braiding sweetgrass: Indigenous wisdom, scientific knowledge, and the teachings of plants.* Milkweed Editions.

King Jr., M. L. (2010). *Strength to love: Gift edition.* Fortress Press.

Kirby, J. N. (2017). Compassion interventions: The programmes, the evidence, and implications for research and practice. *Psychology and Psychotherapy: Theory, Research and Practice, 90,* 432–455. https://doi.org/10.1111/papt.12104

Kirschner, H., Kuyken, W., Wright, K., Roberts, H., Brejcha, C., & Karl, A. (2019). Soothing your heart and feeling connected: A new experimental paradigm to study the benefits of self-compassion. *Clinical Psychological Science, 7*(3), 545–565. https://doi.org/10.1177/2167702618812438

Kleinman, A., Das, V., & Lock, M. (1997). *Social suffering.* University of California Press.

Klimecki, O. M., & Singer, T. (2014). Empathy and compassion. *Current Biology, 24*(18), p. 875–878. https://doi.org/10.1016/j.cub.2014.06.054

Klimecki, O. M., & Singer, T. (2015). Compassion. In A. W. Toga (Ed.), *Brain mapping: An encyclopedic reference* (Vol. 3, pp. 195–199). Elsevier.

Kuah-Pearce, K. E., Kleinman, A., & Harrison, E. (2014). Social suffering and the culture of compassion in a morally divided China. *Anthropology & Medicine*, 21(1), 1–7. https://doi.org/10.1080/13648470.2014.880873

Kumashiro, K. (2015). *Against common sense: Teaching and learning toward social justice.* Routledge.

Lalvani, P. (2015). Disability, stigma and otherness: Perspectives of parents and teachers. *International Journal of Disability, Development and Education*, 62(4), 379–393. https://doi.org/10.1080/1034912X.2015.1029877

Lama, D., Tutu, D., & Abrams, D. C. (2016). *The book of joy: Lasting happiness in a changing world.* Penguin.

Lampert, M., Franke, M. L., Kazemi, E., Ghousseini, H., Turrou, A. C., Beasley, H., Cunard, A., & Crowe, K. (2013). Keeping it complex: Using rehearsals to support novice teacher learning of ambitious teaching. *Journal of Teacher Education*, 64(3), 226–243.

Landreman, L. M. (2013). *The art of effective facilitation: Reflections from social justice educators.* Routledge.

Leary, M. R., Tate, E. B., Adams, C. E., Batts Allen, A., & Hancock, J. (2007). Self-compassion and reactions to unpleasant self-relevant events: The implications of treating oneself kindly. *Journal of Personality and Social Psychology*, 92(5), 887–904. https://doi.org/10.1037/0022-3514.92.5.887

LeMahieu, P. G., & Cobb, P. (Eds.). (2025). *Measuring to improve: Practical measurement to support continuous improvement in education.* Harvard Education Press.

Lerner, M. J. (1980). *The belief in a just world: A fundamental delusion.* Plenum Press.

Lewis, J. (2012). *Across that bridge: A vision for change and the future of America.* Hachette Books.

Linehan, M. M. (2014). *DBT skills training manual.* Guilford Press.

Ling, D., Olver, J., & Petrakis, M. (2020). Investigating how viewing common humanity scenarios impacts compassion: A novel approach. *British Journal of Social Work*, 50(6), 1724–1742. https://doi.org/10.1093/bjsw/bcz124

Lingo, K. J. (2021). *We were made for these times: Ten lessons for moving through change, loss, and disruption.* Parallax Press.

Loewenstein, G., & Small, D. A. (2007). The scarecrow and the tin man: The vicissitudes of human sympathy and caring. *Review of General Psychology*, 11(2), 112–126. https://doi.org/10.1037/1089-2680.11.2.112

van Loon, A., Goldberg, A., & Srivastava, S. B. (2024). Imagined otherness fuels blatant dehumanization of outgroups. *Communications Psychology*, 2(39), 1–14. https://doi.org/10.1038/s44271-024-00087-4

Lorde, A. (1988). *A burst of light and other essays.* Dover.

Love, B. L. (2019). *We want to do more than survive: Abolitionist teaching and the pursuit of educational freedom.* Beacon Press.

Magee, R. V. (2019). *The inner work of racial justice: Healing ourselves and transforming our communities through mindfulness.* Penguin.

Mascaro, J. S., Florian, M. P., Ash, M. J., Palmer, P. K., Frazier, T., Condon, P., & Raison, C. (2020). Ways of knowing compassion: How do we come to know, understand, and measure compassion when we see it? *Frontiers in Psychology*, 11, 547241. https://doi.org/10.3389/fpsyg.2020.547241

McDermott, R. P., & Hood, L. (1982). Institutionalized psychology and the ethnography of schooling. In P. Gilmore & A. A. Glatthorn (Eds.), *Children in and out of school: Ethnography and education* (pp. 232–249). Center for Applied Linguistics.

McDonald, M. A., Meckes, S. J., & Lancaster, C. L. (2021). Compassion for oneself and others protects the mental health of first responders. *Mindfulness*, *12*(3), 659–671. https://doi.org/10.1007/s12671-020-01527-y

McLaren, P. (1991). Critical pedagogy: Constructing an arch of social dreaming and a doorway to hope. *Journal of Education*, *173*(1), 9–34.

Mehan, H., Hubbard, L., & Datnow, A. (2010). A co-construction perspective on organizational change and educational reform. *Teachers College Record*, *112*(13), 98–112. https://doi.org/10.1525/ae.1990.17.2.02a00060

Meyer, D. K. (2016). Emotion regulation in classrooms. In K. R. Wentzel & G. Ramani (Eds.), *Handbook of social influences in school contexts: Social-emotional, motivation, and cognitive outcomes* (pp. 192–207). Routledge.

Meyer, E. J., Leonardi, B., & Keenan, H. B. (2022). *Transgender students and policy in K-12 public schools: Acknowledging historical harms and taking steps toward a promising future.* National Education Policy Center.

Miller, P. J., Potts, R., Fung, H., Hoogstra, L., & Mintz, J. (1990). Narrative practices and the social construction of self in childhood. *American Ethnologist, 17* (2), 292–311. https://doi.org/10.1525/ae.1990.17.2.02a00060

Miller, P. J., Wiley, A. R., Fung, H., & Liang, C.-H. (1997). Personal storytelling as a medium of socialization in Chinese and American families. *Child Development, 68*(3), 557–568. https://doi.org/10.1111/j.1467-8624.1997.tb01958.x

Monroe, K. R. (1998). *The heart of altruism: Perceptions of a common humanity.* Princeton University Press.

Mrazek, M. D., Smallwood, J., Franklin, M. S., Chin, J. M., Baird, B., & Schooler, J. W. (2012). The role of mind-wandering in measurements of general aptitude. *Journal of Experimental Psychology: General, 141*(4), 788–798. https://doi.org/10.1037/a0027968

Murthy, V. H. (2020). *Together: The healing power of human connection in a sometimes lonely world.* Harper.

National Academies of Sciences Engineering and Medicine. (2022). *Taking stock of science standards implementation: Proceedings of a virtual summit.* The National Academies Press. https://doi.org/10.17226/26549

National Academies of Sciences Engineering and Medicine. (2024). *Equity in preK-12 STEM education: Framing decisions for the future.* National Academies Press. https://doi.org/10.17226/26859

National Equity Project. (2013). *Community agreements: Implementing, monitoring & repairing.*

Neff, K. D. (2003). Self-compassion: An alternative conceptualization of a healthy attitude toward oneself. *Self and Identity*, *2*(2), 85–101. https://doi.org/10.1080/15298860309032

Neff, K. D., & Pommier, E. (2012). The relationship between self-compassion and other focused concern among college undergraduates, community adults, and practicing meditators. *Self and Identity*, *12*(2), 160–176. https://doi.org/10.1080/15298868.2011.649546

Neff, K. D., Kirkpatrick, K. L., & Rude, S. S. (2007). Self-compassion and adaptive psychological functioning. *Journal of Research in Personality, 41*(1), 139–154. https://doi.org/10.1016/j.jrp.2006.03.004

Neff, K. D., Rude, S. S., & Kirkpatrick, K. L. (2007). An examination of self-compassion in relation to positive psychological functioning and personality traits. *Journal of Research in Personality, 41*(4), 908–916. https://doi.org/10.1016/j.jrp.2006.08.002

Neff, K. D., Toth-Király, I., Knox, M. C., Kuchar, A., & Davidson, O. (2021). The development and validation of the state self-compassion scale (long- and short form). *Mindfulness, 12*, 121–140. https://doi.org/10.1007/s12671-020-01505-4

Neto, R. D. C. A., Golz, N., Polega, M., & Stewart, D. (2022). The impact of curiosity on teacher–student relationships. *Journal of Education, 202*(1), 15–25. https://doi.org/10.1177/0022057420943184

Nussbaum, M. (1999). *Sex and social justice.* Oxford University Press.

Nye, N. S. (1995). *Words under the words: Selected Poems.* The Eighth Mountain Press.

O'Donohue, J. (1997). *Anam cara: A book of Celtic wisdom.* Harper Perennial.

Olendzki, A. (2005). "Sedaka Sutta: The Bamboo Acrobat" (SN 47.19), translated from the Pali by Andrew Olendzki. *Access to Insight (BCBS Edition).* http://www.accesstoinsight.org/tipitaka/sn/sn47/sn47.019.olen.html

Oliver, M. (2009). *Red bird.* Beacon Press.

Otake, K., Shimai, S., Tanaka-Matsumi, J., Otsui, K., & Fredrickson, B. L. (2006). Happy people become happier through kindness: A counting kindnesses intervention. *Journal of Happiness Studies, 7*(3), 361–75. https://doi.org/10.1007/s10902-005-3650-z.

Paris, D., & Winn, M. T. (Eds.). (2014). *Humanizing research: Decolonizing qualitative inquiry with youth and communities.* SAGE.

Pascoe, C. (2023). *Nice Is not enough: Inequality and the limits of kindness at American High.* University of California Press.

Pasquerella, L., McNair, T. B., & Saffold, J. R. (2019). Finding our common humanity amidst "the fierce urgency of now". *Change: The Magazine of Higher Learning, 51*(1), 28–34. https://doi.org/10.1080/00091383.2019.1547076

Peng, J., Chen, Y., Xia, Y., & Ran, Y. (2017). Workplace loneliness, leader-member exchange and creativity: The cross-level moderating role of leader compassion. *Personality and Individual Differences, 104*, 505–515. https://doi.org/10.1016/j.paid.2016.09.020

Penuel, W. R. (2019). Co-design as infrastructuring with attention to power: Building collective capacity for equitable teaching and learning through design-based implementation research. In J. M. Pieters, J. M. Voogt, & N. N. P. Roblin (Eds.), *Collaborative curriculum design for sustainable innovation and teacher learning* (pp. 387–401). Springer. https://doi.org/10.1007/978-3-030-20062-6_21

Penuel, W. R., Potvin, A. S., Dimidjian, S., Jinpa, T. (2024). Leaders cultivate compassion and dignity within themselves and their schools. In K. Lasater and K. N. LaVenia (Eds.), *Compassionate leadership for school improvement and renewal* (pp. 3–26). Information Age Publishing.

Pitts, J. (2020, Sept. 29). Self-care can be social justice. *Learning for Justice Magazine.* https://www.learningforjustice.org/magazine/selfcare-can-be-social-justice

Potos, A. (2021). *Marrow of Summer.* Kelsay Books.

Potvin, A. S. (2021). "Students speaking to you": Teachers listen to student surveys to improve classroom environment. *Learning Environments Research, 24,* 239–252. https://doi.org/10.1007/s10984-020-09330-1

Potvin, A. S., Penuel, W. R., Dimidjian, S., & Jinpa, T. (2023). Cultivating skillful means of care in schools through compassion practice and individual and joint inquiry. *Mindfulness, 14*(10), 2499–2515. https://doi.org/10.1007/s12671-022-01867-x

Potvin, A. S., Teeters, L. P., Penuel, W. R., & Dimidjian, S. (2024). Humanizing co-design through attention to educators' affective and relational experiences. *Journal of the Learning Sciences, 33*(1), 41–79. https://doi.org/10.1080/10508406.2024.2318557

Preckel, K., Kanske, P., & Singer, T. (2018). On the interaction of social affect and cognition: Empathy, compassion and theory of mind. *Behavioral Sciences, 19,* 1–6. https://doi.org/10.1016/j.cobeha.2017.07.010

Presnell, D. (2018). Preventing and treating trauma, building resiliency: The movement toward compassionate schools in Watauga County, *North Carolina. North Carolina Medical Journal, 79*(2), 113–114.

Raab, K. (2014). Mindfulness, self-compassion, and empathy among health care professionals: A review of the literature. *Journal of Health Care Chaplaincy, 20*(3), 95–108. https://doi.org/10.1080/08854726.2014.913876

Raja, S. N., Carr, D. B., Cohen, M., Finnerup, N. B., Flor, H., Gibson, S., Keefe, F. J., Mogil, J. S., Ringkamp, M., Sluka, K. A., Song, X.-J., Stevens, B., Sullivan, M. D., Tutelman, P. R., Ushida, T., & Vader, K. (2020). The revised International Association for the Study of Pain definition of pain: Concepts, challenges, and compromises. *Pain, 161*(9), 1976–1982. https://doi.org/10.1097/j.pain.0000000000001939

Ramahlo, T., Pereira, J., & Ferreira, C. (2021). How compassionate abilities influence the experience of loneliness and quality of life of people with and without chronic physical disease? *The Journal of Psychology: Interdisciplinary and Applied, 155*(8), 679–694. https://doi.org/10.1080/00223980.2021.1952922

Riedy, R., Van Horne, K., Bell, P., Penuel, W. R., Neill, T., & Shaw, S. (2018). Mapping networks to help education leaders gain insights into complex educational systems. In J. Kay & R. Luckin (Eds.), *13th International Conference of the Learning Sciences* (Vol. 1, pp. 656–662). London, UK: International Society of the Learning Sciences.

Rogers, F. (1995). *You are special: Words of wisdom for all ages from a beloved neighbor.* Penguin.

Rogers, F. (2003). *The world according to Mister Rogers: Important things to remember.* Hyperion.

Rosenberg, M. B. (2003). *Nonviolent communication: A language of life.* Puddledancer Press.

Safi, O. (2016, Jan. 14). Widen the circle of love. *On Being.* https://onbeing.org/blog/widen-the-circle-of-love/

Schooler, J. W., Reichle, E. D., & V., H. D. (2004). Zoning out while reading: Evidence for dissociations between experience and metaconsciousness. In D. T. Levin (Ed.), *Thinking and seeing: Visual metacognition in adults and children* (pp. 203–226). MIT Press.

Schussler, D. L., DeWeese, A., Rasheed, D., DeMauro, A. A., Doyle, S. L., Brown, J. L., Greenberg, M. T., & Jennings, P. A. (2019). The relationship between adopting mindfulness practice and reperceiving: A qualitative investigation of CARE for teachers. *Mindfulness, 10,* 2567–2582. https://doi.org/10.1007/s12671-019-01228-1

Schussler, D. L., Harris, A. R., & Greenberg, M. T. (2020). A qualitative investigation of a mindfulness-based yoga program for educators: How program attendance relates to outcomes. *Psychology in the Schools, 57*(7), 1077–1096. https://doi.org/10.1002/pits.22374

Segal, Z. V., Williams, J. M. G., & Teasdale, J. D. (2002). *Mindfulness-based cognitive therapy for depression: A new approach to preventing relapse.* Guildford Press.

Selassie, S. (2020). *You belong: A call for connection.* HarperOne.

Serrat, O. (2017). *Knowledge solutions: Tools, methods, and approaches to drive organizational performance.* Springer-Verlag.

Shamay-Tsoory, S. G., Aharon-Peretz, J., & Perry, D. (2009). Two systems for empathy: A double dissociation between emotional and cognitive empathy in inferior frontal gyrus versus ventromedial prefrontal lesions. *Brain, 132*, 617–627.

Shankar, P., Chung, R., & Frank, D. A. (2017). Association of food insecurity with children's behavioral, emotional, and academic outcomes: A systematic review. *Journal of Developmental & Behavioral Pediatrics, 38*(2), 135–150. https://doi.org/10.1097/DBP.0000000000000383

Sheppard, K. (2015). Compassion fatigue among registered nurses: Connecting theory and research. *Applied Nursing Research, 28*(1), 57–59. https://doi.org/10.1016/j.apnr.2014.10.007

Silk, J. B., & House, B. R. (2011). Evolutionary foundations of human prosocial sentiments. *Proceedings of the National Academy of Sciences, 108,* 10910–10917. https://doi.org/10.1073/pnas.1100305108

Silk, J. B., & House, B. R. (2016). The evolution of altruistic social preferences in human groups. *Philosophical Transaction of the Royal Society B, 371*(1687), 1–9. https://doi.org/10.1098/rstb.2015.0097

Singer, T., & Klimecki, O. M. (2014). Empathy and compassion. *Current Biology, 24*(18), R875.

Singleton, G. E., & Hays, C. (2008). Beginning courageous conversations about race. In M. Pollock (Ed.), *Everyday antiracism: Getting real about race in school* (pp. 18–23). The New Press.

Skiba, R.J., Michael, R.S., Nardo, A.C., & Peterson, R.L. (2002). The color of discipline: Sources of racial and gender disproportionality in school punishment. *The Urban Review 34*, 317–342. https://doi.org/10.1023/A:1021320817372

Slivjak, E. T., Pedersen, E. J., & Arch, J. J. (2022). Evaluating the efficacy of common humanity enhanced exposure for socially anxious young adults. *Journal of Anxiety Disorders, 87*(102542). https://doi.org/10.1016/j.janxdis.2022.102542

Solórzano, D.G. & Ornelas, A. (2002). A critical race analysis of Advanced Placement classes: A case of educational inequality. *Journal of Latinos and Education, 1*(4), 215–229. https://doi.org/10.1207/S1532771XJLE0104_2

Spalding, K. L., Bhardwaj, R. D., Buccholz, B. A., Druid, H., & Frisén, J. (2005). Retrospective birth dating of cells in humans. *Cell, 122*(1), 133–143. https://doi.org/10.1016/j.cell.2005.04.028

Spillane, J. P., Halverson, R., & Diamond, J. B. (2001). Investigating school leadership practice: A distributed perspective. *Educational Researcher, 30*(3), 23–28.

Stevenson, O., & Allen, A. B. (2017). Women's empowerment: Finding strength in self compassion. *Women & Health, 57*(3), 295–310. https://doi.org/10.1080/03630242.2016.1164271

Strauss, C., Taylor, B. L., Gu, J., Kuyken, W., Baer, R., Jones, F., & Cavanagh, K. (2016). What is compassion and how can we measure it? A review of definitions and measures. *Clinical Psychology Review, 47*, 15–27. https://doi.org/10.1016/j.cpr.2016.05.004

Teeters, L. P., Trejo, B., Gleason, E., Zigarelli, J., Shedro, M., Alvarez, A., & Schultz, K. (2022). Circles de confianza: Promoting the well-being of latine youth via multimodal testimonio. *Journal of Latinos and Education, 22*(5), 2151–2163. https://doi.org/10.1080/15348431.2022.2096028

Tomasello, M. (2008, Oct. 30). Ontogenetic origins of human altruism. Tanner Lecture, Stanford University.

Tomasello, M., Carpenter, M., Call, J., Behne, T., & Moll, H. (2005). Understanding and sharing intentions: The origins of cultural cognition. *Behavioral and Brain Sciences, 28*(5), 675–735. https://doi.org/10.1017/S0140525X05000129

Tuck, E. (2009). Suspending damage: A letter to communities. *Harvard Educational Review, 79*(3), 409–427.

Valdez, L. (1973). *Pensamiento Serpiento*. Cucaracha Publications.

Valencia, R. R. (2010). *Dismantling contemporary deficit thinking: Educational thought and practice*. Routledge.

Valenzuela, A. (1999). *Subtractive schooling: U.S.-Mexican youth and the politics of caring*. SUNY Press.

Varenne, H., & McDermott, R. P. (1998). *Successful failure: The school America builds*. Westview Press.

Vescio, T. K., Sechrist, G. B., & Paolucci, M. P. (2003). Perspective taking and prejudice reduction: The mediational role of empathy arousal and situational attributions. *European Journal of Social Psychology, 33*(4), 455–472. https://doi.org/10.1002/ejsp.163

de Vignemont, F., & Singer, T. (2006). The empathic brain: How, when, and why? *Trends in Cognitive Science, 10*(10), 435–441. https://doi.org/10.1016/j.tics.2006.08.008

Wallach, A. D., Batavia, C., Bekoff, M., Alexander, S., Baker, L., Ben-Ami, D., Boronyak, L., Cardilin, A. P. A., Carmel, Y., Celermajer, D., Coghlan, S., Dahdal, Y., Gomez, J. J., Kaplan, G., Keynan, O., Khalilieh, A., Kopnina, H., Lynn, W. S., Narayanan, Y., ... Ramp, D. (2020). Recognizing animal personhood in compassionate conservation. *Conservation Biology, 34*(5), 1097–1106. https://doi.org/10.1111/cobi.13494

Wallmark, E., Safarzadeh, K., Daukantaitė, D., & Maddux, R. E. (2013). Promoting altruism through meditation: An 8-week randomized controlled pilot study. *Mindfulness, 4*, 223–234. https://doi.org/10.1007/s12671-012-0115-4

Warm, J. S., & Parasuraman, R. (2007). Cerebral hemodynamics and vigilance. In R. Parasuraman & M. Rizzo (Eds.), *Neuroergonomics: The brain at work* (pp. 146–157). Oxford University Press.

Wilkinson, I. (2005). *Suffering: A sociological introduction*. Polity.

Wilkinson, I. (2012). Social suffering and human rights. In T. Cushman (Ed.), *Handbook of human rights* (pp. 146–154). Routledge.

Williams, A. C., & Craig, K. D. (2016). Updating the definition of pain. *Pain, 157*(11), 2420–2423. https://doi.org/10.1097/j.pain.0000000000000613

Wink, M. N., LaRusso, M. D., & Smith, R. L. (2021). Teacher empathy and students with problem behaviors: Examining teachers' perceptions, responses, relationships, and burnout. *Psychology in the Schools, 58*(8), 1575–1596. https://doi.org/10.1002/pits.22516

Worline, M. C. & Dutton, J. E. (2017). *Awakening compassion at work: The quiet power that elevates people and organizations.* Berrett-Koehler Publishers, Inc.

Wright, C., Wendell, K. B., & Paugh, P. B. (2018). "Just put it together to make no commotion:" Re-imagining urban elementary students' participation in engineering design practices. *International Journal of Education in Mathematics, Science, and Technology, 6*(3), 285–301. https://doi.org/10.18404/ijemst.428192

Wyatt, J. P., & Ampadu, G. G. (2022). Reclaiming self-care: Self-care as a social justice tool for Black wellness. *Community Mental Health Journal, 58*(2), 213–221. https://doi.org/10.1007/s10597-021-00884-9

Yang, L. (2017). *Awakening together: The spiritual practice of inclusivity and community.* Wisdom Publications.

Yarnell, L. M., & Neff, K. D. (2013). Self-compassion, interpersonal conflict resolutions, and well-being. *Self and Identity, 12*(2), 146–159. https://doi.org/10.1080/15298868.2011.649545

Yeager, D., Bryk, A., Muhich, J., Hausman, H., & Morales, L. (2013). *Practical measurement.* Retrieved from https://labs.la.utexas.edu/adrg/files/2013/12/Practical-Measurement.pdf

Young, I. M. (1990). *Justice and the politics of difference.* Princeton University Press.

Yu, H., Chen, J., Dardaine, B., & Yang, F. (2023). Moral barrier to compassion: How perceived badness of sufferers dampens observers' compassionate responses. *Cognition, 237*, 105476. https://doi.org/10.1016/j.cognition.2023.105476

Zeng, X., Chiu, C. P. K., Wang, R., Oei, T. P. S., & Leung, F. Y. K. (2015). The effect of loving kindness meditation on positive emotions: A meta-analytic review. *Frontiers in Psychology, 6*(1693), 1–14. https://doi.org/10.3389/fpsyg.2015.01693

Zessin, U., Dickhäuser, O., & Garbade, S. (2015). The relationship between self-compassion and well-being: A meta-analysis. *Applied Psychology: Health and Well-Being, 7*(3), 340–364. https://doi.org/10.1111/aphw.12051

Zhang, J. W., Chen, S., & Tomova Shakur, T. K. (2020). From me to you: Self-compassion predicts acceptance of own and others' imperfections. *Personality and Social Psychology Bulletin, 46*(2), 228–242. https://doi.org/10.1177/0146167219853846

Index